高等学校专业英语系列教材

土木工程专业

惠宽堂 曹 勇 等编著

中国建筑工业出版社

图书在版编目（CIP）数据

土木工程专业/惠宽堂等编著.—北京：中国建筑工业出版社，2006（2023.12重印）

（高等学校专业英语系列教材）

ISBN 978-7-112-08233-9

Ⅰ.土… Ⅱ.惠… Ⅲ.土木工程—英语—高等学校—教材　Ⅳ.H31

中国版本图书馆CIP数据核字（2006）第026697号

高等学校专业英语系列教材
土木工程专业
惠宽堂　曹　勇　等编著

*

中国建筑工业出版社出版、发行（北京西郊百万庄）
各地新华书店、建筑书店经销
北京天成排版公司制版
北京同文印刷有限责任公司印刷

*

开本：787×1092毫米　1/16　印张：16¾　字数：435千字
2006年6月第一版　2023年12月第十六次印刷
定价：**22.00**元
ISBN 978-7-112-08233-9
（14187）

版权所有　翻印必究
如有印装质量问题，可寄本社退换
（邮政编码　100037）

本社网址：http：//www.cabp.com.cn
网上书店：http：//www.china—building.com.cn

本书是为了配合 2004 年 8 月出版的《大学英语课程教学要求［教学大纲］》(试行)的实施编写的。本书内容选材适当，可以满足高等学校土木工程类专业英语教学的需要。

本书题材广泛，涉及工程力学、土力学与地基基础、土木工程材料、钢筋混凝土结构、钢结构、工程经济、路基路面工程、道路勘测设计、桥梁工程、土木工程施工技术和施工组织技术、结构抗震等学科。共包括 26 课(Lesson)，每一课包括课文、生词(New Words)、词组(Phrases and Expressions)、注解(Notes)、练习(Exercises)、阅读材料(Reading Material)以及科技英语阅读与写作指南。

本书可作为高等学校土木工程类专业英语教材，也可供土木工程专业技术人员和研究生作为提高专业英语阅读与写作能力的参考读物。

责任编辑：齐庆梅　王　跃
责任设计：郑秋菊
责任校对：张树梅　张　虹

前言

为了适应我国高等教育发展的新形势,深化教学改革,提高教学质量,配合2004年8月出版的《大学英语课程教学要求[教学大纲]》(试行)的实施,满足土木工程类专业英语教学的需要,编写了本书。本书的使用对象为已学完基础英语的土木工程类专业的大学生,建议在第5~7学期学习为宜。教学目的以培养读者的专业英语阅读能力为主,并适当考虑写作和翻译训练。本书可适合于90~110学时的教学安排,各校在使用时可根据自己的实际情况和专业方向灵活掌握。本书在选材上还选用了少量具有一定难度的内容,可供土木工程技术人员和研究生作为提高专业英语阅读能力的参考读物。

本书选材广泛,涉及工程力学、土力学与地基基础、土木工程材料、钢筋混凝土结构、钢结构、工程经济、路基路面工程、道路勘测设计、桥梁工程、土木工程施工技术和施工组织技术、结构抗震等课程。本书共包括26课(Lesson),每一课包括课文、生词(New Words)、词组(Phrases and Expressions)、注解(Notes)、练习(Exercises)、阅读材料(Reading Material)。在练习中配有填空、词组翻译、句子翻译、选词填空等内容,以确保基础英语和专业英语的衔接和过渡,并提高读者的学习兴趣。为了使读者尽快熟悉和掌握科技英语的特点,培养和提高读者对专业英语的阅读、翻译和写作能力,本书特别编写了科技英语阅读与写作指南。

本书由西安建筑科技大学和长安大学部分教师编写。编者有惠宽堂(1,2,5,8,17,18,19,21)、曹勇(科技英语阅读与写作指南)、冯志焱(3,7,9,13,15,20,23,24)、李红(4,6,10,11,16,25)、张倩(12,14,22,26),由惠宽堂主编。

本书部分题材选自英文原版书籍或手册(McCormac, Jack C., Nelson James K., Structural steel design:LRFD method, Upper Saddle River, N.J.:Prentice Hall:Pearson Education, Inc., c2003;Robert W. Day., Geotechnical earthquake engineering handbook. New York:McGraw-Hill, 2002;Blake L. S, Civil engineer's reference book, London:Newnes Butterworths, 2001;Wright Paul H., Highway engineering, New York:John Wiley & Sons, Inc. 1996,等),在此,编者对原作者及原出版商表示衷心的感谢!

本书审阅人为丰定国教授和陈伯顺教授，审阅中提出了许多宝贵意见和建议，在编辑审读加工过程中，中国建筑工业出版社王跃主任、齐庆梅编辑给予了多方面的具体指导和有益建议，使本书的质量得以进一步提高。对此表示衷心的感谢和敬意。

由于编者水平有限，缺点和错误在所难免，热忱欢迎使用本书的读者提出宝贵意见和建议，可发送 Email 至 jiangongshe@163.com 联系。

CONTENTS

LESSON 1　Compression Members …………………………………… 1
　Reading Material　The Principles of Virtual Work ………… 7
　科技英语阅读与写作指南　科技英语的文体特征 ………… 10
LESSON 2　Introduction to Structural Design ………… 12
　Reading Material　The LRFD Specification ………… 18
　科技英语阅读与写作指南　科技英语的语言结构特点 ………… 21
LESSON 3　Particle Size Analysis ………………………… 23
　Reading Material　Stresses in a Soil Mass
　due to Applied Loading ………………………………… 28
　科技英语阅读与写作指南　科技英语阅读——词汇的理解 ……… 30
LESSON 4　Volume Changes of Concrete ………………… 32
　Reading Material　Civil Engineering Materials ………… 38
　科技英语阅读与写作指南　科技英语阅读——句子的理解 …… 41
LESSON 5　Loads(1) ………………………………………… 43
　Reading Material　Loads(2) ………………………………… 49
　科技英语阅读与写作指南　科技英语阅读——
　文章的理解(1) ……………………………………………… 51
LESSON 6　Concepts of Structural Analysis ………… 54
　Reading Material　Cracks in Flexural Members ………… 59
　科技英语阅读与写作指南　科技英语阅读——
　文章的理解(2) ……………………………………………… 63
LESSON 7　Soil Compressibility and Settlement(1) ………… 65
　Reading Material　Soil compressibility and settlement(2) …… 71
　科技英语阅读与写作指南　科技英语阅读——
　文章的理解(3) ……………………………………………… 73
LESSON 8　Structural Steel Behaviour ………………… 75
　Reading Material　Advantages and Disadvantages
　of Structural Steel ………………………………………… 81
　科技英语阅读与写作指南　科技英语阅读——
　文章的理解(4) ……………………………………………… 83
LESSON 9　Earth Pressures ………………………………… 86

Reading Material　Piled Foundations ……… 91
科技英语阅读与写作指南　科技英语写作——文体要求 ……… 94

LESSON 10　Reinforced Concrete Beams ……… 96
Reading Material　Reinforced Concrete Columns ……… 102
科技英语阅读与写作指南　科技英语写作——
数与量的表达(1) ……… 104

LESSON 11　Prestressing Methods ……… 106
Reading Material　Types of Reinforced
Concrete Slab Construction ……… 111
科技英语阅读与写作指南　科技英语写作——
数与量的表达(2) ……… 114

LESSON 12　Prestressed Concrete Bridges(1) ……… 116
Reading Material　Prestressed Concrete Bridges(2) ……… 121
科技英语阅读与写作指南　科技英语写作——
物体形状、结构、连接 ……… 123

LESSON 13　Foundations ……… 126
Reading Material　Shear Failure and Parameters of Soil ……… 131
科技英语阅读与写作指南　科技英语写作——物体测量 ……… 134

LESSON 14　The Cable-stayed Bridge System ……… 136
Reading Material　Highway Bridges ……… 142
科技英语阅读与写作指南　科技英语写作——
定义，分类与功能用途 ……… 144

LESSON 15　Concrete placement ……… 146
Reading Material　Soil Improvement ……… 152
科技英语阅读与写作指南　科技英语写作——表格与插图 ……… 154

LESSON 16　Concrete Formwork ……… 156
Reading Material　Factory Design and Construction ……… 161
科技英语阅读与写作指南　科技英语写作——题名 ……… 163

LESSON 17　Behavior of Beam-Columns ……… 165
Reading Material　Introduction to
Second-order Analysis of Frames ……… 171
科技英语阅读与写作指南　科技英语写作——英语摘要 ……… 173

LESSON 18　Welding and Common Types of Welds ……… 175
Reading Material　Welding Inspection ……… 181
科技英语阅读与写作指南　科技英语写作——引言 ……… 183

LESSON 19　Eccentrically Loaded Bolted Connections ……… 185
Reading Material　Behaviour of Connections ……… 190
科技英语阅读与写作指南　科技英语写作——正文 ……… 192

LESSON 20　Traditional Construction Procedures ……… 194

Reading Material Movement in
Natural and Artificial Slopes ·················· 199
科技英语阅读与写作指南 科技英语写作——结论 ·············· 202
LESSON 21 Plate Girders ······················· 204
Reading Material Concrete Strength
Tests and Test Evaluation ······················· 209
LESSON 22 Alignment Design ··················· 213
Reading Material Surface Drainage ················· 218
LESSON 23 Construction Contracts(1) ············· 221
Reading Material Construction Contracts(2) ············ 227
LESSON 24 Earthquake Effects ·················· 230
Reading Material Earthquake Structural Damage ··········· 235
LESSON 25 High-Rise Buildings ·················· 240
Reading Material Structural Type of High-rise Buildings ····· 245
LESSON 26 Pavement ························ 249
Reading Material New Advancement in
Pavement Engineering in the U. S. ·················· 255

LESSON 1

Compression Members

Definition

Compression members are those structural elements that are subjected only to axial compressive forces; that is, the loads are applied along a longitudinal axis through the centroid of the member cross section, and the stress can be taken as $f_a = P/A$, where f_a is considered to be uniform over the entire cross section. This ideal state is never achieved in reality, however, and some eccentricity of the load is inevitable. This will result in bending, but it can usually be regarded as secondary and can be neglected if the theoretical loading condition is closely approximated. This cannot always be done if there is a *computed* bending moment, and situations of this type will be considered in Beam-Columns.

The most common type of compression member occurring in buildings and bridges is the *column*, a vertical member whose primary function is to support vertical loads. In many instances these members are also called upon to resist bending, and in these cases the member is a *beam-column*. Compression members can also be found in trusses and as components of bracing systems.

Column Theory

Consider the long, slender compression member shown in Fig. 1.1a. If the axial load P is slowly applied, it will ultimately reach a value large enough to cause the member to become unstable and assume the shape indicated by the dashed line. The member is said to have buckled, and the corresponding load is called the *critical buckling load*. If the member is more stocky, as the one in Fig. 1.1b, a larger load will be required to bring the member to the point of instability. For extremely stocky members, failure may be by compressive yielding rather than buckling. For these stocky members and for more slender columns before they buckle, the compressive stress P/A is uniform over the cross section at any point along the length. As we shall see, the load at which buckling occurs is a function of slenderness, and for very slender members this load could be quite small.

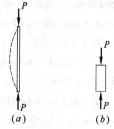

Fig. 1.1 Compression members.

If the member is so slender (a precise definition of slenderness will be given shortly) that the stress just before buckling is below the proportional limit—that is, the member is still elastic—the critical buckling load is given by

$$P_{cr}=\frac{\pi^2 EI}{L^2} \qquad (1.1)$$

where E is the modulus of elasticity of the material, I is the moment of inertia of the cross-sectional area with respect to the minor principal axis, and L is the length of the member between points of support. For Eq. 1.1 to be valid, the member must be elastic, and its ends must be free to rotate but not translate laterally. This end condition is satisfied by hinges or pins.

This remarkable relationship was first formulated by Swiss mathematician Leonhard Euler and published in 1759. The critical load is sometimes referred to as the *Euler load* or the *Euler buckling load*. The validity of Eq. 1.1 has been demonstrated convincingly by numerous tests.

It will be convenient to rewrite Eq. 1.1 as follows:

$$P_{cr}=\frac{\pi^2 EI}{L^2}=\frac{\pi^2 EAr^2}{L^2}=\frac{\pi^2 EA}{(L/r)^2} \qquad (1.1a)$$

where A is the cross-sectional area and r is the radius of gyration with respect to the axis of buckling. The ratio L/r is the slenderness ratio and is the measure of a compression member's slenderness, with large values corresponding to slender members.

If the critical load is divided by the cross-sectional area, the critical buckling stress is obtained:

$$F_{cr}=\frac{P_{cr}}{A}=\frac{\pi^2 E}{(L/r)^2} \qquad (1.2)$$

This is the compressive stress at which buckling will occur about the axis corresponding to r. Since buckling will take place as soon as the load reaches the value given by Eq. 1.1, the column will become unstable about the principal axis corresponding to the largest slenderness ratio. This usually means the axis with the smaller moment of inertia. Thus, the minimum moment of inertia and radius of gyration of the cross section should be used in Eq. 1.1 and 1.2.

Early researchers soon found that Euler's equation did not give reliable results for stocky, or less slender, compression members. This is because of the small slenderness ratio for members of this type, which results in a large buckling stress (from Eq. 1.2). If the stress at which buckling occurs is greater than the proportional limit of the material, the relation between stress and strain is not linear, and the modulus of elasticity E can no longer be used. This difficulty was initially resolved by Friedrich Engesser, who proposed in 1889 the use of a variable tangent modulus E_t in Eq. 1.1. For a material with a stress-strain curve like the one in Fig. 1.2, E is not a constant for stresses greater than the proportional limit F_{pl}. The tangent modulus E_t is defined as the slope of the tangent to the stress-strain curve for values of f between F_{pl} and F_y. If the compressive stress at buckling, P_{cr}/A, is in this region, it can be shown that

$$P_{cr}=\frac{\pi^2 E_t I}{L^2} \qquad (1.3)$$

This is identical to the Euler equation, except that E_t is substituted for E.

The stress-strain curve in Fig. 1.2 is different from the ones for ductile steel because it has a pronounced region of nonlinearity. This curve is typical of a compression test of a short length of W-shape called a *stub column*, rather than the result of testing a tensile specimen. The nonlinearity is primarily the result of the presence of residual stresses in the W-shape. When a hot-rolled shape cools after rolling, all elements of the cross section do not cool at the same rate. The tips of the flanges, for example, cool at a faster rate than the junction of the flange and the web. This uneven cooling induces stresses that remain permanently. Other factors, such as welding and cold-bending to create curvature in a beam, can contribute to the residual stress, but the cooling process is the chief source.

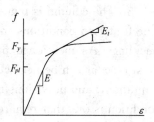

Fig. 1.2 Stress-strain curve.

Note that E_t is smaller than E, and for the same L/r corresponds to a smaller critical load P_{cr}. Because of the variability of E_t, computation of P_{cr} in the inelastic range by the use of Eq. 1.3 is difficult. In general, a trial-and-error approach must be used, and a compressive stress-strain curve such as the one in Fig. 1.2 must be used to determine E_t for trial values of P_{cr}. For this reason, most design specifications, including AISC, use empirical formulas for inelastic columns.

Engesser's tangent modulus theory had its detractors, who pointed out several inconsistencies. Engesser was convinced by their arguments, and in 1895 he refined his theory to incorporate a reduced modulus, which has a value between E and E_t. Test results, however, always agreed more closely with the tangent modulus theory. In 1947, F. R. Shanley resolved the apparent inconsistencies in the original theory, and today the tangent modulus formula, Eq. 1.3, is accepted as the correct one for inelastic buckling. Although the load predicted by this equation is actually a lower bound on the true value of the critical load, the difference is very slight.

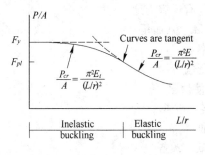

Fig. 1.3 Column strength curve.

For a given material, the critical buckling stress can be plotted as a function of slenderness ratio as in Fig. 1.3. The tangent modulus curve is tangent to the Euler curve at the point corresponding to the proportional limit of the material. The composite curve, called a *column strength curve*, completely describes the stability of any column of a given material. Other than E and E_t, which are properties of the material, the strength is a function only of the slenderness ratio.

Effective Length

Both the Euler and tangent modulus equations are based on the following assumptions:
1. The column is perfectly straight, with no initial crookedness.

2. The load is axial, with no eccentricity.
3. The column is pinned at both ends.

The first two conditions mean that there is no bending moment in the member before buckling. As mentioned previously, some accidental moment will be present, but in most cases it can be neglected. The requirement for pinned ends, however, is a serious limitation, and provisions must be made for other support conditions. [1]The pinned-end condition is one that requires that the member be restrained from lateral translation, but not rotation, at the ends. Since it is virtually impossible to construct a frictionless pin connection, even this support condition can only be closely approximated at best. Obviously, all columns must be free to deform axially. In order to account for other end conditions, the equations for critical buckling load will be written as

$$P_{cr}=\frac{\pi^2 EA}{(KL/r)^2} \quad \text{or} \quad P_{cr}=\frac{\pi^2 E_t A}{(KL/r)^2} \qquad (1.4)$$

where KL is the effective length, and K is called the effective length factor. Values of K for different cases can be determined with the aid of the Commentary to the AISC Specification.

New Words

1. achieve [əˈtʃiːv] vt. 完成，达到，实现
2. eccentricity [eksenˈtrisiti] n. 偏心，离心率
3. inevitable [inˈevitəbl] a. 不可避免的，必然的
4. truss [trʌs] n. 桁架，构架
5. bracing [ˈbreisiŋ] n. 支撑，支柱，系杆，拉条
6. slender [ˈslendə] a. 细(长)的，窄的
7. buckle [ˈbʌkl] v. 压弯，压曲，屈曲
8. stocky [ˈstɔki] a. 短而粗的，矮壮的
9. convincingly [kənˈvinsiŋli] adv. 信服地，有说服力地
10. stub [stʌb] n.(粗)短柱；a. 短(而粗)的
11. curvature [ˈkəːvətʃə] n. 弯曲，曲率
12. detractor [diˈtræktə] n. 诽谤者，贬低者
13. convince [kənˈvins] vt. 使确信，使信服
14. argument [ˈɑːgjumənt] n. 争论，辩论，论据
15. crookedness [ˈkrukidnis] n. 弯曲，挠曲
16. provision [prəˈviʒən] n. 规定，条款；预备

Phrases and Expressions

1. compression member 受压构件
2. bending moment 弯矩
3. call upon 要求，请求，需要

4. critical buckling load　临界屈曲荷载
5. cross-sectional area　横截面面积
6. radius of gyration　回转半径
7. slenderness ratio　长细比
8. tangent modulus　切线模量
9. stub column　短柱
10. trial-and-error approach　试算法，逐次逼近法
11. empirical formula　经验公式
12. residual stress　残余应力
13. hot-rolled shape　热轧型钢
14. reduced modulus　折减模量
15. lower bound　下限
16. effective length　计算长度

Notes

[1] The pinned-end condition is one that requires that the member be restrained from lateral translation, but not rotation, at the ends. require 后的从句为宾语从句，使用了虚拟语气；not rotation 为 not be restrained from rotation 的省略。全句可译为：铰支条件要求约束构件两端的横向移动，但不约束转动。

Exercises

1. Fill in the blanks with proper words.

(1) The most common type of compression member occurring in buildings and bridges is the *column*, a vertical member _____ primary function is to support vertical loads.

(2) For extremely stocky members, failure may be by compressive yielding _____ buckling.

(3) Since buckling will take place _____ the load reaches the value P_{cr}, the column will become unstable about the principal axis corresponding to the largest slenderness ratio.

(4) As we shall see, the load _____ which buckling occurs is a function of slenderness, and for very slender members this load could be quite small.

(5) Early researchers soon found that Euler's equation, _____ give reliable results for stocky, or less slender, compression members.

(6) Although the load predicted by tangent modulus theory is actually a lower bound _____ the true value of the critical load, the difference is very slight.

(7) The stress-strain curve in Fig. 1.2 is _____ a compression test of a short length of W-shape called a *stub column*, rather than the result of testing a tensile specimen.

(8) In general, a trial-and-error approach must be used, and a compressive stress-strain curve such as the one in Fig. 1.2 must be used _____ E_t for trial values of P_{cr}.

(9) In Fig. 1.3, the tangent modulus curve is _____ the Euler curve at the point corresponding to the proportional limit of the material.

(10) In Eq. 1.4, K is called the effective length factor, and values of K for different cases can be determined _____ the aid of the Commentary to the AISC Specification.

2. Translate the following phrases into Chinese/English.
   (1) compression member (6) 计算长度
   (2) critical buckling load (7) 残余应力
   (3) slenderness ratio (8) 试算法
   (4) stub column (9) 回转半径
   (5) reduced modulus (10) 切线模量

3. Translate the following sentences into Chinese.
   (1) This ideal state is never achieved in reality, however, and some eccentricity of the load is inevitable.

   (2) In many instances the members are also called upon to resist bending, and in these cases the member is a *beam-column*.

   (3) If the member is so slender that the stress just before buckling is below the proportional limit—that is, the member is still elastic—the critical buckling load is given by $P_{cr}=\dfrac{\pi^2 EI}{L^2}$.

   (4) The ratio L/r is the slenderness ratio and is the measure of a compression member's slenderness, with large values corresponding to slender members.

   (5) If the stress at which buckling occurs is greater than the proportional limit of the material, the relation between stress and strain is not linear, and the modulus of elasticity E can no longer be used.

   (6) If the member is more stocky, as the one in Fig. 1.1b, a larger load will be required to bring the member to the point of instability.

   (7) The tips of the flanges, for example, cool at a faster rate than the junction of the flange and the web. This uneven cooling induces stresses that remain permanently.

   (8) In 1947, F. R. Shanley resolved the apparent inconsistencies in the original theory, and today the tangent modulus formula, Eq. 1.3, is accepted as the correct one for inelastic buckling.

   (9) The composite curve, called a *column strength curve*, completely describes the stability of any column of a given material.

   (10) Since it is virtually impossible to construct a frictionless pin connection, even this support condition can only be closely approximated at best.

4. Fill in the blanks with the given words below.
   at, be, be, before, for, from, however, in, with

   Both the Euler and tangent modulus equations _____ based on the following assumptions: (a) the column is perfectly straight, _____ no initial crookedness, (b) the load is axial, with no eccentricity, and (c) the column is pinned _____ both ends. The first two conditions mean that there _____ no bending moment in the member _____ buckling. As mentioned previously, some accidental moment will be present, but _____ most cases it can be neglected. The requirement for pinned ends, _____, is a serious limitation, and provisions must be made _____ other support conditions. The pinned-end condition is one that requires that the member be restrained _____ lateral translation, but not rotation, at the ends.

5. Translate the following sentences into English.
   (1) 受压构件是只承受轴向压力的结构构件。
   (2) 公式1.1要成立,构件必须是弹性的并且其两端必须能自由转动但不能横向移动。
   (3) 临界荷载有时被称为欧拉荷载或欧拉屈曲荷载。
   (4) 图1.2中的应力-应变曲线不同于延性钢的应力-应变曲线,因为它有明显的非线性区域。
   (5) 其他因素,像焊接和冷弯,都能影响残余应力,但冷却过程是残余应力的主要来源。

Reading Material

The Principles of Virtual Work

Virtual work

The use of the concept of work as a basis for studying physical problems rather than directly applying Newton's laws of motion can be traced to the early philosophers of southern Europe. Leonardo da Vinci, almost 250 years before Newton was born, employed the rudiments (雏形) of these principles in his studies of the mechanics of pulleys (滑轮) and levers (杠杆); some say that the principle was used by Aristotle as early as 350 B.C. It is Jean Bernoulli, however, who is credited with the first general formulation of the principle of "virtual displacements."

Although there appears to be little consistency in the literature (文献) in regard to terminology (术语) concerning the mechanical principles evolving from the concept of work, we shall refer to them as simply the *principles of virtual work*. We have interjected the word virtual to distinguish *virtual work*—that done by true forces moving through imaginary displacements (or vice versa)—from *real work* in which true forces move through true displacements.

The principle of virtual work may be divided into two parts, the *principle of virtual displacements* and the *principle of virtual forces*. In the first of these we deal with true forces and virtual, or imaginary, displacements; in the latter we use the work done by a system of virtual or fictitious forces in moving through the true displacements of a system. We shall find that conditions of equilibrium are established through the principle of virtual displacements and that conditions of compatibility (相容性) are established through the principle of virtual forces. As before, our investigations are confined to structural systems at rest.

Virtual displacements of a particle

Consider the particle in Fig. 1.4 which is under the action of a system of n concurrent (共点的) forces $F_1, F_2, \cdots, F_i, \cdots, F_n$. Now let us imagine that the particle undergoes a completely arbitrary virtual displacement δu during which all forces remain acting in their original directions. We use the symbol δ in front of u merely to remind us that δu is a virtual displacement and, for the present, has nothing to do with any true displacement u which defines the *true motion* of the particle. We give the symbol δ a more meaningful definition later. Suppose that the direction that we have given this virtual displacement and the line of action of the force F_i differ by an angle α_i. Then, F_{iu}, the component of F_i in the direction of δu ($F_{iu} = F_i \cos\alpha_i$), performs an amount of virtual work due to δu of magnitude $\delta u F_{iu}$. For simplicity, we assume that the displacement occurs adiabatically (绝热地) and infinitesimally (无限小地) slowly so that thermal and dynamic effects can be ignored. It follows that when all n forces are considered, the *total virtual work* done by the force system during the displacement δu is

$$\delta W = F_{1u}\delta u + F_{2u}\delta u + \cdots + F_{nu}\delta u$$

or, since δu is common to all terms on the right side of this expression,

$$\delta W = \delta u \left(\sum_{i=1}^{n} F_{iu} \right) \tag{1.5}$$

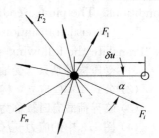

Fig. 1.4 A particle acted upon by n concurrent forces.

Again, the symbol δ is used to distinguish virtual work from the real work W.

We recognize the term in parentheses in Eq. 1.5 as the sum of components of all forces acting on the particle in the direction of the arbitrary virtual displacement δu. According to the familiar laws of statics, this sum is zero if the particle is in equilibrium. Conversely, if the particle is in equilibrium, then, for any choice of δu,

$$\delta W = 0 \tag{1.6}$$

This simple and seemingly trivial result is the mathematical statement of the principle of virtual displacements for a particle. It may be set forth as a theorem, as follows:

If a particle is in equilibrium, the total virtual work done during any arbitrary virtual displacement of the particle is zero.　(THEOREM I)

The converse of this theorem is true; but we cannot conclude that a system is in equilibrium just because the virtual work is zero due to a specific virtual displacement. This fact is amply demonstrated by the particle shown in Fig. 1.5, which, even though a displacement parallel to the x axis results in zero work, is obviously not in equilibrium. It may appear that all possible virtual

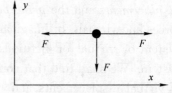

Fig. 1.5 Particle not in equilibrium.

displacements must be investigated in order to establish the equilibrium of a particle. If this were true, to use the principle to study equilibrium would be an extremely laborious and impractical task, since, even for a single particle, the number of possible virtual displacements is infinite. Fortunately, this is not the case. A quick calculation will show that *every possible displacement* of the particle in Fig. 1.5 can be expressed in terms of two *independent* virtual displacements—say one in the x direction and one in the y direction—and that when the virtual work done during these displacements is zero that we can conclude that the particle is in equilibrium. The use of two independent virtual displacements corresponds to the two degrees of freedom of a single particle in the plane. A particle in space, for example, has three degrees of freedom and, consequently, the virtual work done during three independent virtual displacements must vanish for equilibrium to exist. Similarly, two particles in a plane have four degrees of freedom and, for equilibrium, δW must vanish for any four independent virtual displacements. In view of this, we now write a useful corollary (推论) to Theorem Ⅰ:

    A system of particles is in equilibrium if the total virtual work done is zero for every independent virtual displacement.　　(THEOREM Ⅱ)

Condition 1.6 is both necessary and sufficient for equilibrium. It should come as no surprise when we recall that the principle of virtual displacements represents, in effect, an alternative to the equations of statics, though it encompasses far broader ideas than simple statics. To use statics to investigate the equilibrium of the particle shown in Fig. 1.5, for instance, we would write two independent equations, one involving the sum of forces in, say, the x direction and another the sum of forces in the y direction. In fact, we shall find it informative (有益的) from time to time to look upon the equations of virtual work as being merely the equations of statics multiplied by some arbitrary function which, in our initial studies, we have called a "virtual displacement." If δW in Eq. 1.5 is zero, for example, then that equation simply represents an equation of statics $\Sigma F_{iu} = 0$ multiplied by some irrelevant (不相干的) function δu. The quantity δu need not even be a displacement—we could have referred to it as a velocity, as did Galileo, or a pressure, a temperature, an acceleration, or just a purely mathematical function. Our choice of calling δu a displacement was solely to assign physical significance to the process that was demonstrated.

Virtual displacements of a rigid body

Since a rigid body is no more than a collection of particles constrained to remain a constant distance from one another, the extension of the principles discussed in the previous paragraphs to apply to rigid bodies is a trivial matter. We need only replace the word *particle* (or *system of particles*) with *rigid body* (or *system of rigid bodies*) in the theorems that we established. Nevertheless, certain details of the theory can be easily demonstrated by applying it to some simple examples involving rigid bodies.

    We have established that, although it is perfectly permissible to introduce every conceivable (可能的) virtual displacement in a system to arrive at the virtual work, only a number of independent virtual displacements equal to the degrees of freedom of the system is necessary to establish equilibrium. Now, two particles in the plane which are constrained to remain a constant distance apart form, in essence, a rigid body; their original four degrees of freedom have been reduced to only three because of the introduction of a *condition of constraint*. Only the virtual work due to three independent virtual displacements needs to be considered in order to establish the equilibrium of the system. This same reasoning applies to the most general mechanical system. Thus, if we find that δW is zero due to equal virtual displacements of the two particles in the x and y directions and due to a virtual rotation, in the plane, of a straight line connecting them we can conclude, without doubt, that the system is in equilibrium. We need not evaluate the virtual work done in displacing one particle relative to another (and thereby violating the condition of constraint), although such calculations may be perfectly acceptable and valid. It follows, therefore, that in order to establish equilibrium we need consider only those virtual displacements that are consistent with the constraints. With this in mind, we rewrite the principle of virtual displacements in the following form*:

> A mechanical system is in equilibrium if and only if the total virtual work done is zero for every virtual displacement consistent with the constraints. (THEOREM Ⅲ)

By "mechanical" system, we mean a collection of particles and rigid bodies as distinguished from a system whose members may deform. Again, this condition is both necessary and sufficient for equilibrium.

科技英语阅读与写作指南

科技英语的文体特征

随着现代科学技术的发展，科技英语(English for Science and Technology 简称EST)已逐渐形成了一种独立的文体形式，有关自然科学和社会科学的英语学术著作、论文、研究报告、专利产品的说明等均属于科技英语。从总体上说，科技英语涉及到的运用领域是整个科学技术界，而就语言的具体运用而言，科技英语则具体表现为某一领域的专业英语。作为一种文体，科技英语有其自身的特点，了解科技英语文体特点对科技英语的阅读与写作有很大帮助。

我们比较一下下面两段文章就可以大致了解到科技英语文章与其他文体的差别。

例1.

Della finished her cry and attended to her cheeks with the powder rag. She stood by the window and looked out dully at a gray cat walking a gray fence in a gray backyard. Tomorrow would be Christmas Day, and she had only ＄1.87 with which to buy Jim a present. She had been saving every penny she could for months, with this result. Twenty dollars a week doesn't go far. Expenses had been greater than she had calculated. They always are. Only ＄1.87 to buy a present for Jim. Her Jim. Many a happy hour she had

---

* We confine our attention to conservative systems; that is, we neglect effects of dissipative(耗散的)forces such as those due to friction. If friction were present, δW could be less than zero.

spent planning for something nice for him. Something fine and rare and sterling —— something just a little bit near to being worthy of the honor of being owned by Jim. (From O. Henry, *The Gift of the Magi*)

例2.

The presence of a pronounced yield point followed by large plastic strains is an important characteristic of mild steel that is sometimes utilized in practical design. Materials that undergo large strains before failure are classified as ductile. An advantage of ductility is that visible distortions may occur if the loads become too large, thus providing an opportunity to take remedial action before an actual fracture occurs. Also, ductile materials are capable of absorbing large amounts of energy prior to fracture. Ductile materials include mild steel, aluminum and some of its alloys, copper, magnesium, lead, molybdenum, nickel, brass, bronze, monel metal, nylon, Teflon, and many others.

第一段文章为文学作品，语言表达灵活、生动，富于很强的艺术感染力，而第二段文章语言规范，文风质朴，文理清晰，没有一丝美学修辞的痕迹，为典型的科技英语文体。

一般来说，科技英语文章有下列几点文体特征：

1. 语言规范：科技英语文章表达概念、判断一定要清楚明白，精确恰当，不含糊其词，模棱两可。这就要求语言必须规范，描述必须准确无误。

2. 语气正式：科技英语文章与其他文体的根本区别在于它的科学性，在描述科技活动时语言不随意轻率，语气上比较正式。

3. 文体质朴：科技英语文章不能像文学创作那样用含蓄或夸张手法来增强文章的"可读性"。忌用华丽的词藻修饰，忌用带感情色彩的句子，同时还忌用双关、借代等修辞手法。

4. 陈述客观：科技英语文章反映的是客观存在的自然现象及其规律，不能掺杂文章作者个人的主观意识，陈述必须客观。

5. 逻辑严密：科技英语文章的结构清晰而严谨，符合思维的一般规律，逻辑思维周密，语言简炼明确客观，格式比较固定。

6. 专业性强：科技英语文章大多是为从事该专业工作的读者写的，因此，文中会大量出现专业术语，呈现高度专业性的特征。

LESSON 2

Introduction to Structural Design

Structural Design

The structural design of buildings, whether of structural steel or reinforced concrete, requires the determination of the overall proportions and dimensions of the supporting framework and the selection of the cross sections of individual members. In most cases the functional design, including the establishment of the number of stories and the floor plan, will have been done by an architect, and the structural engineer must work within the constraints imposed by this design. Ideally, the engineer and architect will collaborate throughout the design process so that the project is completed in an efficient manner. In effect, however, the design can be summed up as follows: The architect decides how the building should look; the engineer must make sure that it doesn't fall down. Although this is an oversimplification, it affirms the first priority of the structural engineer: safety. Other important considerations include serviceability (how well the structure performs in terms of appearance and deflection) and economy. An economical structure requires an efficient use of materials and construction labor. [1] Although this can usually be accomplished by a design that requires a minimum amount of material, savings can often be realized by using slightly more material if it results in a simpler, more easily constructed project.

A good design requires the evaluation of several framing plans—that is, different arrangements of members and their connections. In other words, several alternate designs should be prepared and their costs compared. For each framing plan investigated, the individual components must be designed. This requires the structural analysis of the frame(s) of the building and the computation of forces and bending moments in the individual members. Armed with this information, the structural designer can then select the appropriate cross section. Before any analysis, however, a decision must be made on the building material to be used: it will usually be reinforced concrete, structural steel, or both. Ideally, alternate designs should be prepared with each.

Loads

The forces that act on a structure are called *loads*. They belong to one of two broad categories: *dead load and live load*. Dead loads are those that are permanent, including the weight of the structure itself, which is sometimes called the *self-weight*. Other dead loads in a building include the weight of nonstructural components such as floor coverings, suspended ceilings with light fixtures, and partitions. All of the loads

LESSON 2

mentioned thus far are forces due to gravity and are referred to as *gravity loads*. Live loads, which can also be gravity loads, are those that are not as permanent as dead loads. This type may or may not be acting on the structure at any given time, and the location may not be fixed. Examples of live load include furniture, equipment, and occupants of buildings. In general, the magnitude of a live load is not as well defined as that of a dead load, and it usually must be estimated. In many cases, a given structural member must be investigated for various positions of the live load so that a potential failure situation is not overlooked.

If the live load is applied slowly and is not removed and reapplied an excessive number of times, the structure can be analyzed as if the loads were static. If the load is applied suddenly, as would be the case when the structure supports a moving crane, we must account for the effects of impact. If the load is applied and removed many times over the life of the structure, fatigue stress becomes a problem, and we must account for its effects. Impact loading occurs in relatively few buildings, notably industrial buildings, and fatigue loading is rare, with thousands of load cycles over the life of the structure required before fatigue becomes a problem.

Wind exerts a pressure or suction on the exterior surfaces of a building; because of its transient nature, it properly belongs in the category of live loads. Because of the relative complexity of determining wind loads, however, wind is usually considered a separate category of loading. Since lateral loads are most detrimental to tall structures, wind loads are usually not as important for low buildings, but uplift on light roof systems can be critical. Although wind is present most of the time, wind loads of the magnitude considered in design are infrequent and are not considered to be fatigue loads.

[2] Earthquake actions are another special category and need to be considered only in those geographic locations where there is a reasonable probability of occurrence. A structural analysis of the effects of an earthquake requires an analysis of the structure's response to the ground motion produced by the earthquake. Simpler methods are sometimes used in which the effects of the earthquake are simulated by a system of horizontal loads, similar to those resulting from wind pressure, acting at each floor level of the building.

Snow is another live load that is treated as a separate category. Adding to the uncertainty of this load is the complication of drift, which can cause much of the load to accumulate over a relatively small area.

Other types of live load are often treated as separate categories, such as hydrostatic pressure and soil pressure, but the cases enumerated above are the ones ordinarily encountered in the design of buildings.

Building Codes

Buildings must be designed and constructed according to the provisions of a building code, which is a legal document containing requirements related to such things as structural safety, fire safety, plumbing, ventilation, and accessibility to the physically disabled. A building code has the force of law and is administered by a governmental entity such as a city, a county, or, for some large metropolitan areas, a consolidated government. Building codes do not give design procedures, but they do specify the design requirements and constraints that must be satisfied. Of particular importance to the structural engineer is the prescription of minimum live loads for buildings. Although the engineer is encouraged to investigate the actual loading conditions and attempt to determine realistic values, the structure must be able to support these specified minimum loads.

Although some large cities write their own building codes, many municipalities will adopt a "model" building code and modify it to suit their particular needs. Model codes are written by various nonprofit organizations in a form that is easily adopted by a governmental unit. Currently, there are three national model codes: the *BOCA National Building Code*, the *Uniform Building Code*, and the *Standard Building Code*. A related document, similar in form to a building code, is ASCE 7-98, *Minimum Design Loads for Buildings and Other Structures*. This standard is intended to provide load requirements in a format suitable for adoption by a building code.

Design Specifications

In contrast to building codes, design specifications give more specific guidance for the design of structural members and their connections. They present the guidelines and criteria that enable a structural engineer to achieve the objectives mandated by a building code. Design specifications represent what is considered to be good engineering practice based on their latest research. They are periodically revised and updated by supplements or by completely new editions. As with model building codes, design specifications are written in a legal format by nonprofit organizations. They have no legal standing on their own, but by presenting design criteria and limits in the form of legal mandates and prohibitions, they can easily be adopted, by reference, as part of a building code.

The specifications of most interest to the structural steel designer are those published by the following organizations:

(1) American Institute of Steel Construction (AISC): This specification provides for the design of structural steel buildings and their connections.

(2) American Association of State Highway and Transportation Officials (AASHTO): This specification covers the design of highway bridges and related structures, and it provides for all structural materials normally used in bridges, including steel, reinforced concrete, and timber.

(3) American Railway Engineering Association (AREA): This document covers the design of railway bridges and related structures.

(4) American Iron and Steel Institute (AISI): This specification deals with cold-formed steel.

LESSON 2

New Words

1. framework ['freimwə:k] n. 构架，框架，结构
2. constraint [kən'streint] n. 约束，强制
3. collaborate [kə'læbəreit] vi. 合作，通敌
4. evaluation [iˌvælju'eiʃən] n. 估价，评价，赋值
5. fixture ['fikstʃə] n. 固定设备，固定物，夹具
6. partition [pɑː'tiʃən] n. 隔断，分割，划分
7. overlook [ˌəuvə'luk] vt. 俯瞰，远眺，没注意到
8. crane [krein] n. 起重机
9. fatigue [fə'tiːg] n. 疲劳，累活；v. (使)疲劳
10. drift [drift] n. 飘移(动)，(雪)堆，漂流物
11. enumerate [i'njuːməreit] vt. 数，枚举，列举
12. plumbing ['plʌmiŋ] n. (自来水，卫生)管道
13. ventilation [ventiˈleiʃən] n. 通风，流通空气
14. accessibility [ˌækəsesi'biliti] n. 可达(及)性
15. code [kəud] n. 规范，规程，标准
16. administer [əd'ministə] v. 管理，给予，执行
17. metropolitan [metrə'pɔlɪt(ə)n] a. 大城市
18. consolidate [kən'sɔlideit] v. 联合，合并，统一
19. prescription [pri'skripʃən] n. 指示，规定，命令
20. municipality [mjuːˌnisi'pæliti] n. 市政当局
21. specification [ˌspesifi'keiʃən] n. 说明书，规程
22. mandate ['mændeit] vt. 委托，托管；n. 要求

Phrases and Expressions

1. functional design 功能设计
2. bending moment 弯矩
3. dead load 恒载
4. live load 活载
5. nonstructural components 非结构构件
6. force due to gravity 重力
7. gravity load 重力荷载
8. building code 建筑规范
9. design specifications 设计规程
10. nonprofit organization 非赢利组织(机构)
11. the National Building Code 国家建筑规范
12. the Uniform Building Code 统一建筑规范
13. the Standard Building Code 标准建筑规范

14. Building Officials and Code Administrators International(BOCA) 国际建筑公务员与法规管理人员联合会
15. AISC 美国钢结构学会
16. AASHTO 美国公路和运输工作者协会
17. AREA 美国铁道工程协会
18. AISI 美国钢铁学会

Notes

[1] Although this can usually be accomplished..., more easily constructed project. 全句可译为：虽然节省通常可以通过需求材料最少的设计来实现，但如果稍微增加材料可使工程更简单、更易施工的话，则常常采用这样的方法。

[2] Earthquake actions are... locations where there is a reasonable probability of occurrence. where 为关系副词，引导定语从句修饰 locations。全句可译为：地震作用是另一特殊种类且只需在可能发生的那些地区予以考虑。

Exercises

1. Fill in the blanks with proper words.

(1) Ideally, the engineer and architect will collaborate _____ the design process so that the project is completed in an efficient manner.

(2) Armed _____ this information, the structural designer can then select the appropriate cross section.

(3) Dead loads are _____ that are permanent, including the weight of the structure itself, _____ is sometimes called the *self-weight*.

(4) Live loads, _____ can also be gravity loads, are those that are not as permanent as dead loads.

(5) In general, the magnitude of a live load is not as well defined as _____ of a dead load, and it usually must be estimated.

(6) If the load is applied suddenly, _____ would be the case when the structure supports a moving crane, we must account for the effects of impact.

(7) Wind exerts a pressure or suction _____ the exterior surfaces of a building; because of its transient nature, it properly belongs in the category of live loads.

(8) Adding to the uncertainty of snow load is the complication of drift, _____ can cause much of the load to accumulate over a relatively small area.

(9) A building code is a legal document, _____ contains requirements related to such things as structural safety, fire safety, plumbing, ventilation, and accessibility to the physically disabled.

(10) Of particular importance _____ the structural engineer is the prescription of minimum live loads for buildings.

2. Translate the following phrases into Chinese/English.

LESSON 2

  (1) cross section   (6) 功能设计
  (2) bending moment   (7) 非结构构件
  (3) live load   (8) 非赢利组织
  (4) force due to gravity   (9) 统一建筑规范
  (5) building code   (10) 标准建筑规范

3. Translate the following sentences into Chinese.

  (1) The structural design of buildings, whether of structural steel or reinforced concrete, requires the determination of the overall proportions and dimensions of the supporting framework and the selection of the cross sections of individual members.

  (2) The architect decides how the building should look; the engineer must make sure that it doesn't fall down.

  (3) A good design requires the evaluation of several framing plans—that is, different arrangements of members and their connections.

  (4) Before any analysis, however, a decision must be made on the building material to be used: it will usually be reinforced concrete, structural steel, or both.

  (5) All of the loads mentioned thus far are forces due to gravity and are referred to as *gravity loads*.

  (6) If the load is applied and removed many times over the life of the structure, fatigue stress becomes a problem, and we must account for its effects.

  (7) Since lateral loads are most detrimental to tall structures, wind loads are usually not as important for low buildings, but uplift on light roof systems can be critical.

  (8) A structural analysis of the effects of an earthquake requires an analysis of the structure's response to the ground motion produced by the earthquake.

  (9) Other types of live load are often treated as separate categories, such as hydrostatic pressure and soil pressure.

  (10) Although some large cities write their own building codes, many municipalities will adopt a "model" building code and modify it to suit their particular needs.

4. Fill in the blanks with the given words below.

    adopt, by, enable, format, give, in, latest, to, what, with

  In contrast to building codes, design specifications _____ more specific guidance for the design of structural members and their connections. They present the guidelines and criteria that _____ a structural engineer _____ achieve the objectives mandated by a building code. Design specifications represent _____ is considered to be good engineering practice based on their _____ research. They are periodically revised and updated by supplements or by completely new editions. As _____ model building codes, design specifications are written in a legal _____ by nonprofit organizations. They have no legal standing on their own, but _____ presenting design criteria and limits _____ the form of legal mandates and prohibitions, they can easily be _____, by reference, as part of a building code.

5. Translate the following sentences into English.

  (1) 作用在结构上的力被称为荷载。

(2) 恒载就是固定不变的荷载，包括结构自身的重量。
(3) 活载不是恒载那样固定不变的荷载，活载也可以是重力荷载。
(4) 建筑规范不规定设计方法，但规定必须满足的设计要求和强制条件。
(5) 与建筑规范不同，设计规范对结构构件及其连接的设计做了更详细的指导。

Reading Material

The LRFD Specification

Reliability and the LRFD Specification

Probably fewer than 1 in 10 undergraduate engineering students take a course in statistics. Thus, these statistically untrained students are often a little dismayed when they run into a statistically based subject such as this one. In the pages which follow, these students will find that such worrying is unnecessary, as the LRFD (Load and Resistance-Factor Design) theory and calculations are usually rather simple to follow. Furthermore, they may actually gain a little statistical knowledge along the way and thereby better understand the theory behind the development of LRFD.

The word reliability, as used in this textbook, refers to the estimated percentage of times that the strength of a structure will equal or exceed the maximum loading applied to that structure during its estimated life (say 50 years).

In this section, we discuss the following:

1. how LRFD investigators developed a procedure for estimating the reliability of given designs;

2. how they set what to them were desirable reliability percentages for different situations; and

3. how they were able to adjust resistance or factors so steel designers are able to obtain the reliability percentages established in Item 2 of this list.

Before proceeding with this discussion, a few comments are presented concerning the word failure as it is used in the discussion of reliability. Let us assume that a designer states that his or her designs are 99.7 percent reliable (and this is the approximate value obtained with most LRFD designs). This means that if this person were to design 1000 different structures, three of them would probably be overloaded at some time during their estimated 50-year lives and thus would fail. The reader probably and quite reasonably thinks this to be an unacceptably high rate of failure.

A 99.7 percent reliability doesn't mean that 3 of 1000 structures are going to fall flat (倒塌，倒下) on the ground. Rather, it means that those structures at some time will be loaded into the plastic range and perhaps the strain-hardening range. As a result, deformations may be quite large during the overloading, and some slight damage may occur. It is not anticipated that any of these structures will completely collapse. (The reader who is unfamiliar with statistics might say he or she wants 100 percent reliability in design, but this is an impossible goal statistically, as we will see in the paragraphs that follow.)

For this discussion, it is assumed that we make a study of the reliability of a large number of steel structures designed at various times and with different past editions of the AISC Specification. To do this, we will compute the resistance or strength, R, of each structure as well as the maximum loading, Q, expected during the life of the structure. The structure will be deemed(认为)to be safe if $R \geqslant Q$.

The actual values of R and Q are random variables, and it is therefore impossible to say with 100 percent certainty that R is always equal to or larger than Q for a particular structure. No matter how carefully a structure is designed and constructed, there will always be some chance that Q will be greater than R or that the strength limit state will be exceeded. The goal of the preparers of the LRFD Specification was to keep this chance to a very small and consistent percentage.

Thus, the magnitudes of both resistances and loads are uncertain. If we were to plot a curve of $\ln R/Q$ values for a large number of structures, the result would be a typical bell-shaped probability curve with mean values R_m and Q_m and a standard deviation(标准差). If, at any location, $R<Q$, we will have exceeded the strength limit state.

Such a curve is plotted in Fig. 2.1. It is to be remembered that the logarithm of 1.0 is 0 and thus, if $\ln R/Q < 0$ the strength limit state has been exceeded. Such a situation is represented by the shaded area on the diagram. Another way of expressing this fact is to say that the larger the number of standard deviations from the mean values to the shaded area, the greater is the reliability. In the figure, the number of standard deviations is represented by β and is called the *reliability index*(目标可靠指标).

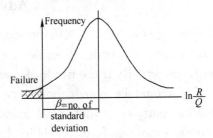

Fig. 2.1 Definition of reliability index β.

Even though the probable values of R and Q are not known very well, a formula has been developed with which values of β can be reasonably calculated. The formula follows:

$$\beta = \frac{\ln(R_m/Q_m)}{\sqrt{V_R^2 + V_Q^2}}$$

In this expression, R_m and Q_m are, respectively, the mean resistance and load effects, while V_R and V_Q are the corresponding coefficients of variation(变异系数).

As a result of the preceding work, it is now possible to design a particular element in accordance with a certain edition of the AISC Specification and with the appropriate statistical information, compute the value of β for the design. This process is called *calibration*(校准法).

The results of our study of the designs of these steel structures will show that the percentage of structures for which the design strengths equal or exceed the worst anticipated loading will vary as we examine designs made in accordance with the requirements of different editions of the AISC Specification. Furthermore, our calculations will show that this reliability will vary for the designs of different types of members (such as columns and beams) made with the same edition of the AISC Specification.

Based upon the calculations of reliability described here, the investigators decided to use consistent β values in this new specification:

1. $\beta = 3.00$ for members subject to gravity loading
2. $\beta = 4.50$ for connections. (This value reflects the usual practice that connections should be stronger than the members they connect.)
3. $\beta = 2.5$ for members subject to gravity plus wind loadings. (This value reflects an old practice that safety factors do not have to be as large for cases where lateral loads, which are of shorter duration, are involved.)
4. $\beta = 1.75$ for members subject to gravity loads plus earthquake loads.

Then the values of ϕ for the various parts of the specification were adjusted so the β values shown here would be obtained in design. In effect, this causes most LRFD designs to be almost identical with those obtained by the allowable stress method when the live to dead load ratio is three.

Advantages of LRFD

The average(普通的，一般的) person looking at this material might ask, "Will LRFD save money compared with allowable stress design (ASD)?" The answer is that it probably will, particularly if the live loads are small compared with the dead loads.

It should be noted, however, that the AISC has introduced LRFD not for the specific purpose of obtaining immediate economic advantages, but because it helps provide a more uniform reliability for all steel structures whatever the loads, and it is written in a form that facilitates the introduction of the advances in knowledge that will occur through the years in structural steel design.

Despite this stated objective of the AISC, the author would like to continue for a little while with the topic of possible steel weight savings with LRFD. In allowable stress design, the same safety factor was used for dead loads and live loads, whereas in LRFD a much smaller safety or load factor is used for dead loads (because they generally can be determined so much more accurately than can live loads). As a result of this fact, a weight of steel comparison for ASD and LRFD designs will necessarily depend on the ratio of the live loads to dead loads.

For the usual building, the live load to dead load ratio varies from approximately 0.25 to as high as 4.0 or even a little higher for some very light structures. Low-rise steel buildings generally will fall in the upper range of these ratios. In allowable stress design we use the same safety factors for dead and live loads regardless of their ratio to each other. Thus, with ASD, heavier members will result and the factor of safety will increase as the live load to dead load ratio decreases.

It can be shown that for the lower range of L to D values, that is, less than about three, there can be steel weight savings with LRFD, perhaps as much as one-sixth for tension members and columns and perhaps as much as one-tenth for beams. On the other hand, if we have very high L and D ratios there is a slight increase in steel weight with LRFD compared with ASD.

科技英语阅读与写作指南

科技英语的语言结构特点

科技英语注重科学性、逻辑性、正确性和严密性，它除具有语言规范、语气正式、文体质朴、陈述客观、逻辑严密、专业性强这些文体特征外，在词汇、语法这些语言结构方面科技英语也有其自身的特点。

1. 词汇特点

(1) 习惯使用复合词与缩略词

miniultrasonicprober＝mini＋ultra＋sonic＋prober(微型超声波金属探测仪)

pseudophotoesthesia＝pseudo＋photo＋esthesia(光幻觉)

CAD＝computer-aided＋design(计算机辅助设计)

(2) 大量使用名词化结构

If, after a body is deformed by some force, it returns to its original shape or size after *removal of the force*, the material is said to be elastic.

如果某一物体在力的作用下产生变形，去除作用力之后，又能恢复原来的形状和大小，那么这物体就称为弹性物体。

The compression of the soil under the applied stresses would force some water out of the voids.

施加压力压缩土壤会使一些水从孔隙中排出。

An important part of preliminary structural design is *the selection of the structural system* with consideration given to its relationship to construction economics.

初步结构设计的一个重要部分是选择结构体系，同时考虑它与建筑经济学的关系。

2. 语法特点

(1) 频繁使用非限定动词

Termed hydraulic cements because they react with water, the cements have the ability to harden under water.

因为这种水泥与水反应，故称为水硬性水泥，这种水泥在水下也能够硬化。

The moment-curvature relationship *chosen* is assumed to have a horizontal branch beyond yield, *with the moment remaining constant at the ultimate value*.

所选用的弯矩-曲率关系是假定超过屈服后有一个水平段，即弯矩保持在极限值不变。

(2) 广泛使用被动语态

Structural connections between steel members *are often made by* arc-welding techniques.

钢构件间的结构连接常用弧焊技术来实现。

The structural failure of the foundation may occur if the foundation itself *is not properly designed* to sustain the imposed stresses.

如果基础本身未能正确设计以承受施加的应力，基础就可能产生结构破坏。

(3) 经常使用长句

Although this method is more commonly used in the construction of silos, grain elevators, bridge piers, and other heavy structures, it lends itself at times to the construction of elevator and stair shafts usually found as part of the service core in high-rise office or apartment buildings.

这种方法通常用于筒仓、粮仓、桥墩和其他重型结构，有时也适用于高层办公楼或公寓楼中作为公共设施部分的电梯井和楼梯间的施工。

Some typical examples of buildings using the cantilever principle demonstrate that the concept is not only found on the smaller scale of overhanging eaves and cantilevered balconies, but also on the medium scale to support buildings because of unfavorable site conditions, as well as on the large scale for roofs of stadiums and hangars because of functional necessity.

一些利用悬挑原理的典型建筑例子表明悬挑概念不仅适用于小型的悬挑屋檐、悬挑阳台，而且适用于因场地条件不利而设计的用来支撑中型建筑的屋面，以及因功能需要而设计的大型体育场馆和飞机库的屋面。

LESSON 3

Particle Size Analysis

The range of particle sizes encountered in soils is very wide: from around 200mm down to the colloidal size of some clays of less than 0.001 mm. Although natural soils are mixtures of various-sized particles, it is common to find a predominance occurring within a relatively narrow band of sizes. When the width of this size band is very narrow the soil will be termed poorly-graded, if it is wide the soil is said to be well-graded. A number of engineering properties, e.g. permeability, frost susceptibility, compressibility, are related directly or indirectly to particle-size characteristics.

Fig. 3.1 shows the British Standard range of particle sizes. The particle-size analysis of a soil is carried out by determining the weight percentages falling within bands of size represented by these divisions and sub-divisions. In the case of a coarse soil, from which fine-grained particles have been removed or were absent, the usual process is a sieve analysis. A representative sample of the soil is split systematically down to a convenient sub-sample size and then oven-dried. This sample is then passed through a nest of standard test sieves arranged in descending order of mesh size. The weight of soil on retained on each sieve is determined and the cumulative percentage of the sub-sample weight passing each sieve calculated. From these figures the particle-size distribution for the soil is plotted as a semi-logarithmic curve (Fig. 3.2) known as a grading curve.

Fine				Coarse						Very coarse	
Clay	Silt			Sand			Gravel			Stone	
Colloids	fine	medium	coarse	fine	medium	coarse	fine	medium	coarse	cobbles	boulders
1	2	6	20	60	200	600	2	6	20	60	200
m μ						mm					

Fig. 3.1 British Standard range of particle sizes.

Where the soil sample contains fine-grained particles, a wet sieving procedure is first carried out to remove these and to determine the combined clay/silt fraction percentage. A suitably-sized sub-sample is first oven-dried and then sieved to separate the coarsest particles (>20mm). The sub-sample is then immersed in water containing a dispersing agent and allowed to stand before being washed through a 63μm mesh sieve. The retained fraction is again oven-dried and passed through a nest of sieves. After weighing the fractions retained on each sieve and calculating the cumulative percentages passing each sieve, the grading curve is drawn. The combined clay/silt fraction is determined from the weight difference and expressed as a percentage of the total sub-sample weight. The coarsest fraction (>20mm) can also be sieved and the results used to complete the grading curve.

A further sub-division of particle-size distribution in the fine-grained fraction is not possible by the sieving method. A process of sedimentation is normally carried out for this purpose. A small sub-sample of soil is first treated with a dispersing agent and then washed through a 63μm sieve. The soil/water suspension is then made up to 500 ml, agitated vigorously for a short while and then allowed to settle. The procedure is based on Stokes' law, which states that the velocity at which a spherical particle will sink due to gravity in a suspension is given by:

$$v = \frac{d^2(\gamma_s - \gamma_w)}{18\eta} \tag{3.1}$$

where d = diameter of particle
 γ_s = unit weight of the grain or particle
 γ_w = unit weight of the suspension fluid (usually water)
 η = velocity of the suspension fluid

The diameter of those particles that will have settled a given distance in a given time (t) may be obtained by rearranging Eq. 3.1:

$$d = \left[\frac{18\eta h}{(\gamma_s - \gamma_w)t}\right]^{1/2}$$

usually h = 100mm, giving:

$$d = \left[\frac{1800\eta}{(\gamma_s - \gamma_w)t}\right]^{1/2} \tag{3.2}$$

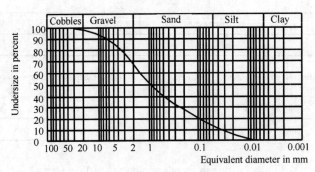

Fig. 3.2 Grading curve.

Samples taken at a depth of 100mm, at an elapsed time of t, will not, therefore, include particles of greater size than the diameter d given by Eq. 3.2; but the proportions of particles smaller than d in the suspension will remain unchanged. The procedure using a hydrometer consists of measuring the suspension density at a depth of 100mm at a series of elapsed-time intervals. The percentage-finer values corresponding to particular diameters (i.e. particle sizes) are obtained from the density readings, and thus a grading curve for the fine-grained fraction may be drawn.

The sedimentation method is not particularly accurate in an absolute sense, since errors result from a number of factors: such as the flaky nature of fine-grained particles, the near molecular size of the very fine particles, incomplete dispersion, variations in viscosity due to temperature variations. However, the equivalent spherical diameter distribution obtained in this manner provides a sufficiently useful guide for engineering purposes.

Grading Characteristics

The grading curve is a graphical representation of the particle-size distribution and is therefore useful in itself as a means of describing the soil. For this reason it is always a good idea to include copies of grading curves in laboratory and other similar reports. It should also be remembered that the primary object is to provide a descriptive term for the type of soil. This is easily done using the type of chart by estimating the range of sizes included in the most representative fraction of the soil. For example, the steep curve may be taken to represent a poorly-graded medium sand, indicating a narrow range of sizes.

A further quantitative analysis of grading curves may be carried out using certain geometric values known as grading characteristics. First of all, three points are located on the grading curve to give the following characteristic sizes:

d_{10} = Maximum size of the smallest 10 per cent of the sample

d_{30} = Maximum size of the smallest 30 per cent of the sample

d_{60} = Maximum size of the smallest 60 per cent of the sample

From these characteristic sizes, the following grading characteristics are defined:

Effective size $\qquad d_{10}$ mm $\qquad$ (3.3)

Uniformity coefficient, $\qquad C_u = \dfrac{d_{60}}{d_{10}} \qquad$ (3.4)

Coefficient of gradation, $\qquad C_g = \dfrac{(d_{30})^2}{d_{60} \times d_{10}} \qquad$ (3.5)

Both C_u and C_g will be unity for a single-sized soil, while $C_u < 3$ indicates uniform grading and $C_u > 5$ a well-graded soil.

Most well-graded soils will have grading curves that are mainly flat or slightly concave, giving values of C_g between 0.5 and 2.0. One useful application is an approximation of the coefficient of permeability, which was suggested by Hazen.

New Words

1. colloidal [kəˈlɔidl]   *a.* 胶状的，胶质的
2. sieve [siv]   *n.* 筛，滤网；*v.* 筛，过滤
3. sample [ˈsæmpl]   *n.* 标本，样品；*vt.* 取样
4. mesh [meʃ]   *n.* 网孔，网丝
5. cumulative [ˈkjuːmjulətiv]   *a.* 累积的
6. grading [ˈgreidiŋ]   *n.* 级配，等级

7. sedimentation [ˌsedimenˈteiʃən]　　　n. 沉淀，沉降
8. suspension [səsˈpenʃən]　　　n. 悬浮，悬浮液
9. agitate [ˈædʒiteit]　　　v. 搅动，混合
10. hydrometer [haiˈdrɔmitə]　　　n. (液体)比重计
11. viscosity [visˈkɔsiti]　　　n. 黏性[度，力]，黏滞性
12. flaky [ˈfleiki]　　　a. 薄片的，片状的
13. pipette [piˈpet]　　　n. 吸液管
14. irrecoverable [ˌiriˈkʌvərəbl]　　　a. 不能恢复的
15. concave [ˈkɔnˈkeiv]　　　a. 凹的，向外弯曲的
16. permeability [ˌpəːmiəˈbiliti]　　　n. 渗透性

Phrases and Expressions

1. frost susceptibility　霜冻敏感性
2. sieving method　筛分法
3. semi-logarithmic curve　半对数曲线
4. grading curve　级配曲线
5. wet sieving　湿法筛分
6. dispersing agent　分散剂
7. Stokes'law　斯托克定律
8. unit weight　重度
9. coefficient of grading　曲率系数
10. sedimentation method　沉降法
11. particle-size distribution　粒径分布

Exercises

1. Fill in the blanks with proper words.

(1) When the width of this size band is very narrow the soil will be termed poorly-graded, if it is wide the soil is said to be _____.

(2) The _____ of a soil is carried out by determining the weight percentages falling within bands of size represented by these divisions and sub-divisions.

(3) A suitably-sized sub-sample is first oven-dried and then _____ to separate the coarsest particles (>20mm).

(4) After weighing the fractions retained on each sieve and calculating the cumulative percentages passing each sieve, the _____ curve is drawn.

(5) Samples taken at a depth of 100mm, at an _____ time of t, will not, therefore, include particles of greater size than the diameter d given by Eq. 3.2.

(6) For example, the _____ curve may be taken to represent a poorly-graded medium sand, indicating a narrow range of sizes.

(7) A further quantitative analysis of grading curves may be carried out using certain

geometric values known as _____ characteristics.

(8) Where the soil sample contains fine-grained particles, a _____ procedure is first carried out to remove these and to determine the combined clay/silt fraction percentage.

(9) The consistency of a soil is its physical state characteristic at a given water _____. Four consistency states may be defined for cohesive soils: solid, semi-plastic solid, plastic and liquid.

2. Translate the following phrases into Chinese /English

(1) well-graded soils　　　　　　　(5) 级配不良的
(2) uniformity coefficient　　　　　(6) 筛分法
(3) coefficient of gradation　　　　(7) 级配曲线
(4) irrecoverable deformation　　　(8) 半对数曲线

3. Translate the following sentences into Chinese

(1) Although natural soils are mixtures of various-sized particles, it is common to find a predominance occurring within a relatively narrow band of sizes.

(2) Where the soil sample contains fine-grained particles, a wet sieving procedure is first carried out to remove these and to determine the combined clay/silt fraction percentage.

(3) A further sub-division of particle-size distribution in the fine-grained fraction is not possible by the sieving method.

(4) For example, the steep curve may be taken to represent a poorly-graded medium sand, indicating a narrow range of sizes.

(5) Also, soils with flaky particles behave as plastic material: an increase in applied stress usually brings about an irrecoverable deformation.

(6) The two most important of these are the liquid and plastic limits, which represent respectively the upper and lower bounds of the plastic state; the range of the plastic state is given by their difference, and is termed the plasticity index.

(7) The combined clay/silt fraction is determined from the weight difference and expressed as a percentage of the total sub-sample weight.

(8) The coarsest fraction (>20mm) can also be sieved and the results used to complete the grading curve.

(9) The distribution of contact pressure depends on both the rigidity of the footing and on the stiffness of the foundation soil.

4. Fill in the blanks with the given words below.

　　　　　also, by, for, in, means, other, therefore, to

The grading curve is a graphical representation of the particle-size distribution and is _____ useful _____ itself as a _____ of describing the soil. _____ this reason it is always a good idea _____ include copies of grading curves in laboratory and _____ similar reports. It should _____ be remembered that the primary object is to provide a descriptive term for the type of soil. This is easily done using the type of chart _____ estimating the range of sizes included in the most

representative fraction of the soil.
5. Translate the following sentences into English.
   (1) 如果土颗粒大小范围很小，则称之为级配不良，若颗粒范围较大，则称为级配良好。
   (2) 土的颗粒尺寸范围非常大：从大约 200mm 到一些黏土胶体颗粒不足 0.001mm。
   (3) 土的许多工程性质，如渗透性、霜冻敏感性、压缩性，都直接或间接与其颗粒级配特性有关。
   (4) 土的颗粒大小分布绘成的半对数曲线称为级配曲线。
   (5) 然而，这种方法所得到的等效球直径分布可为实际工程提供十分有用的指导。

Reading Material

Stresses in a Soil Mass due to Applied Loading

Contact Pressure

Contact pressure is the intensity of loading transmitted from the underside of a foundation to the soil. The distribution of contact pressure depends on both the rigidity of the footing and on the stiffness of the foundation soil.

Consider a footing carrying concentrated column loads. When supported on hard soil or rock, which has a high displacement modulus, the load is transmitted to a relatively small area, since a high intensity of stress can develop. On a less stiff foundation medium the loading is distributed laterally, producing lower values of contact pressure, until in a soft soil it may be almost uniform.

When there is a relatively thick layer of compressible soil beneath a footing the settlement profile tends to become dish-shaped. A uniformly loaded footing of perfect flexibility will theoretically transmit a uniform contact pressure in order to produce this dish shape. A perfectly rigid footing will settle uniformly across its breadth. Thus, in a compressible soil a rigid footing, in settling uniformly, will transmit a higher contact pressure near the edges.

In sands, the contact pressure near the edge will be lower (tending to zero under shallow footings) and that under the centre will be higher because of the higher confining pressure. Under deeper footings the confining pressure and therefore the contact pressure is more uniform.

Most footings are neither perfectly flexible, nor perfectly rigid, so that actual distributions are somewhere between these extremes. In designing wide reinforced concrete foundations a sensible distribution of contact pressure should be sought, bearing in mind the stiffness of both the footing and the foundation soil. It should also be remembered that the contact pressure distribution will also affect the bending moments in the footing. For the purpose of calculating stresses and displacements within the soil mass sufficient accuracy may be obtained by assuming a uniform distribution of contact pressure.

LESSON 3

Stresses in a Soil Mass due to Applied Loading

Soil masses in practical situations mostly have a horizontal surface from which the depth (z) is measured downwards, with x and y being lateral dimensions. The magnitudes of x, y and z are usually large compared with the size of the structure. The conceptual model of the soil mass is therefore a semi-infinite elastic half-space, the boundaries of which are sufficiently remote not to affect the analysis. The soil is assumed to be homogeneous(均质的) and isotropically(各向相等的) elastic, thus a straightforward application of elastic theory is the normal approach. Of course soils do not comply with such ideal conditions, but providing the stresses stay well below the yield point, the magnitude of errors will be small, and well within natural variations of other properties.

In 1885 Boussinesq(布辛奈斯克)published solutions for the stresses and displacements beneath a point load applied at the surface of such a soil mass. The force acting on the surface represents the load of structure; this load changes the state of stress which had existed in the soil before the structure was built, and is the cause of displacement. Subsequently, many other solutions have been developed for both stresses and displacements relating to different types of loading, layers of finite thickness, multi-layered masses and internally loaded masses.

Boussinesq assumed a homogeneous and isotropic mass defined by two elastic constants E and ν. The concept of homogeneity implies the equality of the constants at all points, and that of isotropy of the constants in all directions. On these assumptions, the vertical normal stress on a horizontal plane at a point caused by a concentrated load P acting at and normal to the surface is

$$\sigma_z = \frac{P}{z^2} \frac{3}{2\pi} \frac{1}{[1+(r/z)^2]^{5/2}} = \frac{P}{z^2} K \tag{3.6}$$

where z denotes the depth below the surface, and r the horizontal component of the distance of the calculating point from the point of P, $K = \frac{3}{2\pi} \frac{1}{[1+(r/z)^2]^{5/2}}$ is the coefficient as a function of r/z. Eq. 3.6 can also be used with sufficient approximation for loads applied by a footing to a large area, if the depth z is greater than twice the footing width B.

If the load is applied to a large area and the depth z is smaller than $2B$ practical calculation may be made by one of the following methods: the summation of corner stresses, the influence chart and the summation of elementary loads.

Stresses due to a Uniformly-loaded Rectangular Area

This application is perhaps the most widely used in soil engineering design. Expressions for the component stresses can be obtained by integrating the Boussinesq expressions. Several types of solution have been proposed involving formulae, tables and charts. The principle expression is for the increase in vertical stress beneath one corner of a flexible rectangular area carrying a uniform load

$$\Delta\sigma_z = qI_R$$

where I_R is an influence factor dependent on the length (L) and breadth (B) of the loaded area. And the depth (z) of the point at which the stress is required. It is usual to express I_R in terms of the parameters $m=B/z$ and $n=L/z$.

Any foundation which has a rectilinear plan may be considered as a series of rectangles, each with a corner coincident with the point beneath which the increase in stress is required; the value of stress increase at the point is then found using the principle of superposition.

Distribution of Stress-Pressure Bulbs

From the foregoing section in this chapter, it will be seen that the intensity of stress below a foundation induced by the foundation loading decreases both vertically and laterally. It follows, therefore, that at some depth and/or lateral distance away from the foundation the intensity of stress will become relatively insignificant with respect to a particular practical problem.

If equal values of vertical stress are plotted on a cross-section a diagram known as a pressure bulb is obtained. Figures showing the pressure bulbs can drawn for different foundation types, in which the stress, given as a fraction of the applied loading intensity, is plotted against the breadth of the foundation. The extent of a pressure bulb of a given value can provide a useful guide when considering which parts of the soil mass below a foundation will be significantly affected by the applied loading.

科技英语阅读与写作指南

科技英语阅读——词汇的理解

准确地把握词义是理解科技英语文章的前提和基础。我们知道,科技英语最大的特点就是大量使用科技词汇。具体地说,一是常用词汇的专业化。很多词在公共英语中是一个意思,在专业英语中又有了特殊的含义。二是同一词语词义的多专业化。换句话说,同一个常用词在不同的专业中代表不同的概念,甚至在同一专业中也有不同的意思。此外,科技英语还利用传统构词法的各种手段来丰富自己的词汇。

1. 常用词汇专业化

angle	角度→角钢
channel	海峡,渠道→槽钢
cap	帽子→柱头,棚架顶梁
mouth	嘴→开度
foot	脚→底部,底座
throat	喉咙→(火箭)(喷管的)临界截面;焊喉
horse	马→支架
web	网→工字梁腹板

2. 同一词汇词义多专业化

  power   乘方、幂(数学),功率(物理),放大率(光学),动力(机械),委任

状(法律)

phase　　　　　　　相(物理)，周相、盈亏(天文)，型、期(动物)，相位(电工)
base　　　　　　　　底座(机械)，碱(化学)，基极(电子)，底边(数学)

3. 构词法

(1) 派生(derivation)：利用词的前缀与后缀作为词素构成新词。

anti＋seismic　　　　　　antiseismic　抗震的
sub＋soil　　　　　　　　subsoil　地基下层土；天然地基
semi＋diameter　　　　　semidiameter　半径
multi＋layer　　　　　　 multiplayer　多层
micro＋meter　　　　　　micrometer　测微计

(2) 复合(compounding)：将两个或两个以上的词按照一定的次序排列构成新词，可以构成复合名词、复合动词、复合形容词等。

dust＋tight　　　　　　　dust-tight　防尘的
earth＋fill　　　　　　　 earth-fill　填土
dumb＋board　　　　　　dumboard　隔声板
pipe＋line　　　　　　　 pipeline　管线，管道
wall＋mounted　　　　　wall-mounted　嵌墙的

(3) 拼缀(blending)：将两个单词的前部拼接、前后拼接或将一个单词前部与另一词拼接构成新词。

smoke＋fog　　　　　　　smog　烟雾
escalator＋lift　　　　　　escalift　自动电梯
stagnation＋inflation　　　stagflation　经济滞胀
helicopter＋pad　　　　　helipad　直升飞机升降场
communication ＋ satellite　comsat　通信卫星

(4) 缩略(shortening)：将较长的单词取其首部或主干构成与原词同义的短单词，或将某一词语组合中所有主要词的第一个字母拼接成一个大写字母的字符。

hydrostatics　　　　　　　hyd.　流体静力学
key-word-in-context　　　 KWIC　关键词在文内
freezing point　　　　　　 fp　冰点，凝固点
automatic data processing　ADP　自动数据处理
tensile strength　　　　　　TS　抗拉强度，拉力强度

LESSON 4

Volume Changes of Concrete

Concrete undergoes volume changes during hardening. If it loses moisture by evaporation, it shrinks, but if the concrete hardens in water, it expands. The causes of the volume changes in concrete can be attributed to changes in moisture content, chemical reaction of the cement with water, variation in temperature, and applied loads.

Shrinkage

The change in the volume of drying concrete is not equal to the volume of water removed. The evaporation of free water causes little or no shrinkage. As concrete continues to dry, water evaporates and the volume of the restrained cement paste changes, causing concrete to shrink, probably due to the capillary tension that develops in the water remaining in concrete. Emptying of the capillaries causes a loss of water without shrinkage. But once the absorbed water is removed, shrinkage occurs.

[1] Many factors influence the shrinkage of concrete caused by the variations in moisture conditions.

1. Cement and water content. The more cement or water content in the concrete mix, the greater the shrinkage.

2. Composition and fineness of cement. High-early-strength and low-heat cements show more shrinkage than normal Portland cement. The finer the cement, the greater is the expansion under moist conditions.

3. Type, amount, and gradation of aggregate. The smaller the size of aggregate particles, the greater is the shrinkage. The greater the aggregate content, the smaller is the shrinkage.

4. Ambient conditions, moisture, and temperature. Concrete specimens subjected to moist conditions undergo an expansion of 200 to 300×10^{-6}, but if they are left to dry in air, they shrink. High temperature speeds the evaporation of water and, consequently, increases shrinkage.

5. Admixtures. Admixtures that increase the water requirement of concrete increase the shrinkage value.

6. Size and shape of specimen. As shrinkage takes place in a reinforced concrete member, tension stresses develop in the concrete, and equal compressive stresses develop in the steel. These stresses are added to those developed by the loading action. Therefore, cracks may develop in concrete when a high percentage of steel is used. Proper distribution of reinforcement, by producing better distribution of tensile stresses in concrete, can reduce differential internal stresses.

The values of final shrinkage for ordinary concrete vary between 200 and 700×10^{-6}. For normal-weight concrete, a value of 300×10^{-6} may be used. The British Code CP110 gives a value of 500×10^{-6}, which represents an unrestrained shrinkage of 1.5mm in 3m length in thin, plain concrete sections. If the member is restrained, a tensile stress of about $10N/mm^2$ (1400psi) arises. If concrete is kept moist for a certain period after setting, shrinkage is reduced; therefore, it is important to cure the concrete for a period of no fewer than 7 days.

Exposure of concrete to wind increases the shrinkage rate on the upwind side. Shrinkage causes an increase in the deflection of structural members, which in turn increases with time. Symmetrical reinforcement in the concrete section may prevent curvature and deflection due to shrinkage.

Generally, concrete shrinks at a high rate during the initial period of hardening, but at later stages the rate diminishes gradually. It can be said that 15% to 30% of the shrinkage value occurs in 2 weeks, 40% to 80% occurs in 1 month, and 70% to 85% occurs in 1 year.

Expansion due to Rise in Temperature

Concrete expands with increasing temperature and contracts with decreasing temperature. The coefficient of thermal expansion of concrete varies between 4 and 7×10^{-6} per degree Fahrenheit. An average value of 5.5×10^{-6} per degree Fahrenheit (12×10^{-6} per degree Celsius) can be used for ordinary concrete. The B. S. Code suggests a value of 10^{-5} per degree Celsius. This value represents a change of length of 10mm in a 30m member subjected to a change in temperature of 33℃. If the member is restrained and unreinforced, a stress of about $7N/mm^2$ (1000 psi) may develop.

In long reinforced concrete structures, expansion joints must be provided at lengths of 100 to 200 ft (30 to 60m). The width of the expansion joint is about 1 in. (25mm). Concrete is not a good conductor of heat, whereas steel is a good one. The ability of concrete to carry load is not much affected by temperature.

Creep

Concrete is an elastoplastic material, and beginning with small stresses, plastic strains develop in addition to elastic ones. Under sustained load, plastic deformation continues to develop over a period that may last for years. Such deformation increases at a high rate during the first 4 months after application of the load. This slow plastic deformation under constant stress is called creep.

Fig. 4.1 shows a concrete cylinder that is loaded. The instantaneous deformation is ε_1, which is equal to the stress divided by the modulus of elasticity. If the same stress is kept for a period of time, an additional strain ε_2, due to creep effect, can be recorded. If load is then released, the elastic strain, ε_1, will be recovered, in addition to some creep strain. The final permanent plastic strain, ε_3, will be left, as shown in Fig. 4.1. In this case $\varepsilon_3 = (1-\alpha)\varepsilon_2$, where α is the ratio of the recovered creep strain to the total creep strain. The ratio α ranges between 0.1 and 0.2. The magnitude of creep recovery varies with the previous creep and depends appreciably upon the period of the sustained load. Creep recovery rate will be less if the loading period is increased, probably due to the hardening of concrete while in a deformed condition.

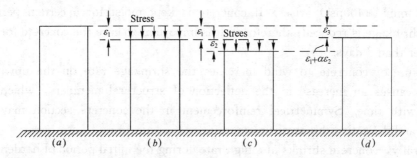

Fig. 4.1 Deformation in a loaded concrete cylinder.
(a) specimen unloaded; (b) elastic deformation; (c) elastic plus creep deformation;
(d) permanent deformation after release of load.

The ultimate magnitude of creep varies between 0.2×10^{-6} and 2×10^{-6} per unit stress (1b/in.^{2}) per unit length. A value of 1×10^{-6} can be used in practice. The ratio of creep strain to elastic strain may be as high as 4.

Creep takes place in the hardened cement matrix around the strong aggregate. It may be attributed to slippage along planes within the crystal lattice, internal stresses caused by changes in the crystal lattice, and gradual loss of water from the cement gel in the concrete.

The different factors that affect the creep of concrete can be summarized as follows.

1. The level of stress. [2] Creep increases with an increase of stress in specimens made from concrete of the same strength and with the same duration of load.

2. Duration of loading. Creep increases with the loading period. About 80% of the creep occurs within the first 4 months; 90% occurs after about 2 years.

3. Strength and age of concrete. Creep tends to be smaller if concrete is loaded at a late age. Also, creep of 2000 psi-(14N/mm^2-) strength concrete is about 1.41×10^{-6} whereas that of 4000 psi-(28N/mm^2-) strength concrete is about 0.8×10^{-6} per unit stress and length of time.

4. Ambient conditions. Creep is reduced with an increase in the humidity of the ambient air.

5. Rate of loading. Creep increases with an increase in the rate of loading when followed by prolonged loading.

6. Percentage and distribution of steel reinforcement in a reinforced concrete member. Creep tends to be smaller for higher proportion or better distribution of steel.

7. Size of the concrete mass. Creep decreases with an increase in the size of the tested specimen.

8. Type, fineness, and content of cement. The amount of cement greatly affects the final creep of concrete, as cement creeps about 15 times as much as concrete.

9. Water-cement ratio. Creep increases with an increase in the water-cement ratio.

10. Type and grading of aggregate. Well-graded aggregate will produce dense concrete and consequently a reduction in creep.

11. Type of curing. High-temperature steam curing of concrete as well as the proper use of a plasticizer will reduce the amount of creep.

Creep develops not only in compression, but also in tension, bending, and torsion.

The ratio of the rate of creep in tension to that in compression will be greater than 1 in the first 2 weeks, but this ratio decreases over longer periods.

Creep in concrete under compression has been tested by many investigators. Troxell, Davis, and Raphael measured creep strains periodically for up to 20 years and estimated that of the total creep after 20 years, 18% to 35% occurred in 2 weeks, 30% to 70% occurred in 3 months, and 64% to 83% occurred in 1 year.

For normal concrete loaded after 28 days, $C_r = 0.13\sqrt[3]{t}$, where C_r = creep strain per unit stress per unit length. Creep augments the deflection of reinforced concrete beams appreciably with time. In the design of reinforced concrete members, long-term deflection may be critical and has to be considered in proper design. Extensive deformation may influence the stability of the structure.

Sustained loads affect the strength as well as the deformation of concrete. A reduction of up to 30% of the strength of unreinforced concrete may be expected when concrete is subjected to a concentric sustained load for 1 year.

The fatigue strength of concrete is much smaller than its static strength. Repeated loading and unloading cycles in compression lead to a gradual accumulation of plastic deformations. If concrete in compression is subjected to about 2 million cycles, its fatigue limit is about 50% to 60% of the static compression strength. In beams, the fatigue limit of concrete is about 55% of its static strength.

New Words

1. undergo [ˌʌndəˈgəu]　　　　　　vt. 经历，遭受，忍受
2. evaporation [iˌvæpəˈreiʃən]　　n. 蒸发(作用)
3. shrinkage [ˈʃrinkidʒ]　　　　　n. 收缩
4. capillary [kəˈpiləri]　　　　　　a. 毛细作用的
5. evaporate [iˈvæpəreit]　　　　v. (使)蒸发，消失
6. paste [peist]　　　　　　　　　n. 糊，黏土团
7. ambient [ˈæmbiənt]　　　　　　a. 周围的；n. 周围环境
8. specimen [ˈspesimin]　　　　　n. 样品，样本，试样
9. plasticizer [ˈplæstisaizə]　　　n. 塑化剂，增塑剂
10. upwind [ˈʌpˈwind]　　　　　　a. 迎风的，顶风的；ad. 迎风地，顶风地
11. diminish [diˈminiʃ]　　　　　v. (使)减少，(使)变小
12. creep [kri:p]　　　　　　　　n. 徐变
13. slippage [ˈslipidʒ]　　　　　　n. 滑动，滑移，滑程

14. humidity [hju:ˈmiditi] 　　　　　　　*n.* 湿气，潮湿，湿度
15. augment [ɔ:gˈment] 　　　　　　　　*v.* 增加，增大；*n.* 增加
16. sustained [səsˈteind] 　　　　　　　*a.* 持续不变的，相同的

Phrases and Expressions

1. moisture content   含水量，含湿度
2. cement paste   水泥浆
3. the capillary tension   毛细管张力，微张力
4. gradation of aggregate   骨料级配
5. The British Code   CP110 英国混凝土规范 CP110
6. The coefficient of thermal expansion of concrete   混凝土热膨胀系数
7. The B. S Code   英国标准规范
8. sustained load   永久荷载，长期荷载
9. permanent plastic strain   永久的塑性应变
10. crystal lattice   晶体点阵，晶格
11. cement gel   水泥凝胶体
12. water-cement ratio   水灰比
13. the expansion joint   伸缩缝
14. the stability of the structure   结构的稳定性
15. the fatigue strength of concrete   混凝土的疲劳强度

Notes

[1] Many factors influence the shrinkage of concrete caused by the variations in moisture conditions. 全句可译为：许多因素都对潮湿环境变化造成的混凝土收缩有影响。

[2] Creep...specimens made from...with the same duration of load. made from... 和 with...作后置定语，修饰句中的 specimens。全句可译为：对于相同混凝土强度、相同荷载持续时间的试件来说，徐变随着应力的增大而增大。

Exercises

1. Fill in the blanks with proper words.

(1) Concrete undergoes volume changes _____ hardening. If it loses moisture by evaporation, it shrinks, but _____ the concrete hardens in water, it expands.

(2) The change in the volume of drying concrete is not equal _____ the volume of water removed. The evaporation of free water causes little _____ no shrinkage.

(3) Emptying of the capillaries causes a loss _____ water without shrinkage, _____ once the absorbed water is removed shrinkage occurs.

(4) Concrete specimens subjected _____ moist conditions undergo an expansion of 200 to 300×10^{-6}, but _____ they are left to dry in air, they shrink.

LESSON 4

(5) _____ shrinkage takes place in a reinforced concrete member, tension stresses develop in the concrete, _____ equal compressive stresses develop in the steel.

(6) The values of final shrinkage for ordinary concrete vary _____ 200 and 700×10^{-6}.

(7) Concrete is not a good conductor of heat, _____ steel is a good one.

(8) In this case $\varepsilon_3 = (1-\alpha)\varepsilon_2$, _____ α is the ratio of the recovered creep strain to the total creep strain.

(9) The different factors _____ affect the creep of concrete can be summarized _____ follows.

(10) Creep tends to be smaller _____ concrete is loaded at a late age.

2. Translate the following phrases into Chinese/English.

(1) sustained load
(2) cement gel
(3) water-cement ratio
(4) the stability of the structure
(5) the expansion joint
(6) 含水量
(7) 水泥浆
(8) 混凝土热膨胀系数
(9) 永久的塑性应变
(10) 混凝土的疲劳强度

3. Translate the following sentences into Chinese.

(1) The causes of the volume changes in concrete can be attributed to changes in moisture content, chemical reaction of the cement with water, variation in temperature, and applied loads.

(2) High-early-strength and low-heat cements show more shrinkage than normal Portland cement.

(3) The greater the aggregate content, the smaller is the shrinkage.

(4) Therefore, cracks may develop in concrete when a high percentage of steel is used.

(5) Generally, concrete shrinks at a high rate during the initial period of hardening, but at later stages the rate diminishes gradually.

(6) Under sustained load, plastic deformation continues to develop over a period that may last for years.

(7) Creep increases with an increase of stress in specimens made from concrete of the same strength and with the same duration of load.

(8) Creep is reduced with an increase in the humidity of the ambient air.

(9) Creep decreases with an increase in the size of the tested specimen.

(10) High-temperature steam curing of concrete as well as the proper use of a plasticizer will reduce the amount of creep.

4. Fill in the blanks with the given words below.

after, also, and, been, in, in, of, than, to

Creep develops not only in compression, but _____ in tension, bending, _____ torsion.

The ratio of the rate of creep _____ tension to that in compression will be greeter _____ 1in the first 2 weeks, but this ratio decreases over longer periods.

Creep in concrete under compression has _____ tested by many investigators. Troxell, Davis, and Raphael measured creep strains periodically for up _____ 20 years and estimated that of the total creep after 20 years, 18% to 35% occurred _____ 2 weeks, 30% to 70% occurred in 3 months, and 64% to 83% occurred in 1 year.

For normal concrete loaded _____ 28 days, $C_r = 0.13 \sqrt[3]{t}$, where C_r = creep strain per unit stress per unit length. Creep augments the deflection of reinforced concrete beams appreciably with time. In the design of reinforced concrete members, long-term deflection may be critical and has to be considered in proper design. Extensive deformation may influence the stability _____ the structure.

5. Translate the following sentences into English.
   (1) 如果通过蒸发失去水分，混凝土就会收缩，但在水中硬化则会膨胀。
   (2) 影响混凝土收缩的因素很多，如水泥和水的含量、骨料的级配以及环境条件等。
   (3) 混凝土拌和物中的水泥含量越多或含水量越多，收缩量则越大。
   (4) 混凝土不是热的良导体，而钢筋是。
   (5) 在荷载作用期间，大约80%的徐变产生在前4个月内，大约2年后完成90%的徐变。

Reading Material

Civil Engineering Materials

The basic materials used in civil engineering applications or in construction are: wood, concrete, bitumen(沥青), structural clay and concrete units, reinforcing and structural steel.

These materials are sometimes called structural materials. Added to these materials are plastics, soils, and aluminum. All these materials are used in a number of civil engineering structures, such as dams, bridges, roads, foundations, liquid-retaining structures, waterfront structures, buildings, and retaining walls. The most important highway materials are soils, aggregates, bituminous binder, lime, and cement.

Wood is derived from trees and can be used directly as pieces of lumber obtained from the log(原木)or as a raw material in the manufacture of various wood products. Plywood, glulaminated timber, and oriented strandboard are some of the wood products used most commonly in construction.

Concrete is a basic construction material made with Portland cement as a primary ingredient. Portland cement (and other types of cement) are also used in the manufacture of many other construction materials. Concrete is used in combination with other distinctly different materials, such as steel reinforcing bar, polypropylene fibers, and high-strength wires to produce different types of concrete.

Bitumen, which comes in variety of forms, is combined with other raw materials in

LESSON 4

the construction of pavements, roof shingles, waterproofing compounds, and many others. Structural clay and concrete units, commonly called bricks and blocks, are the principal elements in the construction of masonry walls. Structural steel is used in many forms and shapes for the construction of railroad ties, high-rise buildings, roof trusses, and many more. These basic materials are selected for their properties, performance, availability, aesthetics, and cost. Knowledge of all these aspects is essential in selecting a suitable material for a particular situation.

In addition to the basic materials described above, there are a significant number of secondary materials of construction. Sealants(密封剂), adhesives, floor and wall coverings, fasteners, and doors and windows come under this category. Most of these materials, also called nonstructural materials, are selected based on quality guidelines and aesthetic considerations.

Properties of Engineering Materials

Materials for engineering applications are selected so that perform satisfactorily during service. The material for use in a highway bridge should have adequate strength, rough surface, and sufficient rigidity. A water-retaining structure can be built using materials that are impermeable, crack-free, strong, and do not react with water. A road surface can be built using materials that show little movement under load, are water resistant, and are easy to repair. The performance requirements are not the same for all structures. To evaluate the performance characteristics of engineering materials and to assist in the process of selection of the best material for a particular application, we need to study the properties of materials. In general, most properties of engineering materials are grouped under three major headings: Physical properties; Mechanical properties; Chemical properties.

Physical properties are those derived from proportion of matter or physical structure. They include density, porosity or voids, moisture content, specific gravity, permeability, and structure (micro or macro). In addition, properties such as texture, color, and shape come under this classification. The physical properties are helpful in evaluating a material in terms of appearance, weight, permeability, and water retention(保水性).

Mechanical properties measure the resistance of a material to applied loads or forces. Some of them reflect the strength of the material, whereas others measure the deformation capacity or stiffness. Strength is a measure of the maximum load per unit area, and can be in tension, compression, shear, flexure, torsion, or impact. When we compare the physical strength of one person with the emotional strength of a second person we know that the two "strengths" are not the same and the comparison is not appropriate. The same reasoning can be applied to describing the strength of a material: it is important to know the type of strength being dealt with.

But it should be noted that a material can be subjected to a combination of loads which will result in more than one type of stress acting on it. For example, a floor joist may be subjected to loads that cause bending moment and shear as well as torsion. In these situations, measurement of the inherent strength becomes analytically and experimentally complex, and in many situations cannot be done. As in the maintenance of good health in a human body, for which both emotional and physical strength is critical, so is the performance of a construction material, which requires adequate strength of all types.

The deformation capacity or stiffness is measured in terms of elastic modulus, which will be explained later. It is important to note that a knowledge of both the strength (or various types of strength) and deformation capacity of materials is absolutely essential in the selection of a construction material. A high-strength material need not possess a high deformation capacity or stiffness, and vice versa.

In addition to strength and deformation capacity, mechanical properties include other properties, such as brittleness, plasticity, and ductility. Note that all these three properties reflect deformation characteristics of the material.

Chemical properties are those pertaining to the composition and potential reaction of a material. The compounds of composition, such as oxides and carbonates, describe the chemical nature of the material. They explain the way a material behaves in a certain environment. For example, by knowing the principal compounds of cement we are able to choose the type of cement for a particular application. A knowledge of chemical composition of clays is indispensable(不可缺少的)in evaluating the characteristics that can be expected in burned-brick. Other chemical properties that are noteworthy are acidity, alkalinity, and resistance to corrosion.

In addition to physical, mechanical, and chemical properties, thermal, electrical, magnetic, acoustical, and optical properties are also important in civil engineering. For example, the coefficient of thermal expansion of concrete, which is a thermal property, is fundamental to calculate the expansion potential of a concrete slab. Thermal properties, customarily, represent the behavior of a material under heat or temperature. Acoustical properties such as sound transmission and sound reflection are important in selecting materials that should provide sound resistance and act as sound barriers. Optical properties such as color, light transmission, and light reflection are essential in determining the energy consumption capacity of a material. Properties such as electrical conductivity and magnetic permeability(导磁性)are needed in materials used in electrical works.

In civil engineering construction, some materials are selected based primarily on their physical properties or physical characteristics, whereas most others are chosen because of their mechanical properties. For example, lightweight aggregates such as pumice(浮岩) and shale are used in the manufacture of lightweight concrete floor slabs, due primarily to their low density. In an area of high seismic activity, structural steel is chosen for columns in a multistory building for its high tensile strength and ductility.

Thus a proper understanding of the environment and constraints in which a particular construction is to be developed is important in the material selection process. The goal of engineering design should be to select the best material for a particular job. An understanding of all relevant properties of various materials available and an appreciation of their performance characteristics are of fundamental important in achieving this goal.

科技英语阅读与写作指南

科技英语阅读——句子的理解

　　科技英语是一种重要的英语文体，与其他文体的英语在语言结构方面并无本质的区别。由于科技英语特别讲究以严谨的推理和准确的叙述来表达多重密切相关的概念，这样就会增加一些修饰性、限制性的成分，使得句子结构变得十分复杂。因此，要正确地理解英语科技文章的长句，必须首先分析理解原文的句法结构。一般可以按照下面三个步骤来进行分析。

　　1. 拨开枝杈，找出句子主干，明确句子结构，抓住中心内容；
　　2. 变长为短，区分主从句及修饰成分，理清句子各层次的意思；
　　3. 分析理解各层意思之间的逻辑关系。

　　The bending moments, shear and axial forces, and deflections of reinforced concrete frames at any stage of loading from zero to ultimate load can be determined analytically using the conditions of static equilibrium and geometric compatibility, if the moment-curvature relationships of the sections are known.

　　分析：这是一个主从复合句。句子主干为 The bending ... to ultimate can be determined ...，if 引导条件从句，主句较长，主句的主语为 the bending moments ... from zero to ultimate load，在主句中 using ... geometric compatibility 为状语，修饰主句动词 can be determined。

　　理解：如果截面的弯矩——曲率关系已知，钢筋混凝土框架从零到极限荷载间任一加载阶段的弯矩、剪力、轴力和变位，均可以通过静力平衡与几何相容两个条件应用解析方法来确定。

　　During the work of boring, all the excavated material must be brought out through the narrow confines of the bore itself, and in preserving the line of his bore, which he must do with the most minute accuracy, the engineer is deprived of any means of checking his position by reference to external objects, as he can do with any surface line.

　　分析：该句为并列复合句。句子主干为 all the excavated material must be brought out ... and ... the engineer is deprived of ...。and 并列的后一个句子带有两个定语从句，which 引导的从句修饰前面的 preserving the line of his bore；as 引导的从句修饰前面的 checking his position by reference to external objects。

　　理解：在掘进工作中，所有掘出的土石都必须通过洞身的狭窄通道运出来。工程师必须以最高的精密度来保证洞的走向。在这一方面，与地面线路施工不同，工程师是无法参照外部物体来检验他的位置的。

　　Untold numbers of organisms in past geological periods were buried beneath silt and sand, and, in the absence of oxygen, were transformed by heat, pressure, and time into the deposits of fossil-fuels——coal, petroleum and natural gas——that now yield their bound energies to man.

　　分析：该句是一个主从复合句。主句的谓语是由 and 连接的两个并列结构：were buried ... sand 和 were transformed ... fossil-fuels；that now yield their bound energies to man 是定语从句修饰 the deposits of fossil-fuels。

理解：在过去的地质时期，无数的生物体埋藏在淤泥和沙粒之下。在缺氧的环境下，由于长时期温度和压力的影响而转化成为矿物燃料：煤、石油和天然气。这些燃料现在为人类产生各种各样的结合能。

The structural design itself includes two different tasks, the design of the structure, in which the sizes and locations of the main members are settled, and the analysis of this structure by mathematical or graphical methods or both, to work out how the loads pass through the structure with the particular members chosen.

分析：该句的主干为 the structural design itself includes...tasks。the design of the structure 和 the analysis of this structure 为 tasks 的两个同位语，前一个同位语后有一个定语从句 in which...settled，后一个同位语由介词短语 by mathematical or graphical methods or both 和不定式短语 to work out how...来修饰。

理解：结构设计本身包含着两个不同的任务：(1)设计结构，即确定主要构件的尺寸和位置；(2)分析结构，用数学法或图解法或二者兼用来进行，以便在构件选定后计算出各荷载通过结构的情况。

LESSON 5

Loads(1)

Introduction

Normally, a design specification does not prescribe the magnitudes of the loads that are to be used as the basic input to the structural analysis, with the exception of special cases such as crane design specifications. [1] It is the role of the specification to detail the methods and criteria to be used in arriving at satisfactory member and connection sizes for the structural material in question, given the magnitudes of the loads and their effects. The specification therefore reflects the requirements that must be satisfied by the structure in order that it will have a response that allows it to achieve the performance that is needed. Loads, on the other hand, are governed by the type of occupancy of the building, which in turn is dictated by the applicable local, regional, and national laws that are more commonly known as building codes.

The building code loads have traditionally been given as nominal values, determined on the basis of material properties (e.g., dead load) or load surveys (e.g., live load and snow load). To be reasonably certain that the loads are not exceeded in a given structure, the code values have tended to be higher than the loads on a random structure at an arbitrary point in time. This may, in fact, be one of the reasons why excessive gravity loads are rarely the obvious cause of structural failures. [2] Be that as it may, the fact of the matter is that all of the various types of structural loads exhibit random variations that are functions of time, and the manner of variation also depends on the type of load. Rather than dealing with nominal loads that appear to be deterministic in nature, a realistic design procedure should take load variability into account along with that of the strength, in order that adequate structural safety can be achieved through rational means.

Since the random variation of the loads is a function of time as well as a number of other factors, the modeling, strictly speaking, should take this into account by using stochastic analyses to reflect the time and space interdependence. Many studies have dealt with this highly complex phenomenon, especially as it pertains to live load in buildings. In practice, however, the use of time-dependent loads is cumbersome at best, although the relationship must be accounted for in certain cases (i.e., seismic action). For most design situations the code will specify the magnitude of the loads as if they were static. Their time and space variation are covered through the use of the maximum load occurring over a certain reference (return) period, and its statistics. For example, American live load criteria are based on a reference period of 50 years, while Canadian criteria use a 30-

year interval.

The geographical location of the structure plays an important role for certain loads. It is particularly applicable to snow, wind, and seismic action, the first being of special importance in north-central and north-eastern areas of the United States, the second in high wind coastal and mountain areas, and the last in areas having earthquake fault lines.

Design for wind effects is complicated by a number of phenomena. Like snow loads and earthquake action, wind loads are given more attention in certain parts of the country. At the same time wind loads are neither static nor uniformly varying, and are heavily influenced by the geometry of the structure as well as the surrounding structures and the landscape. To a certain degree this also applies to the magnitude of the snow load. Building codes treat these effects as static phenomena and relate them to the actual conditions through semiempirical equations. This gives the designer a better handle on a difficult problem, but can lead to difficulties when the real structure departs significantly from the bases of the code. For that reason wind loads, and sometimes earthquake and snow loads, are determined on the basis of model tests. In particular, wind tunnel testing has become a useful and practical tool in these endeavors.

The loads on the structure are normally assumed to be independent of the type of structure and structural material, with the exception of dead loads. The response of a building, however, will be different for different materials, depending on the type of load. For example, the behavior of a moment-resistant steel frame will be quite unlike that of a braced frame, when subjected to lateral loads, especially those due to an earthquake. On the other hand, the response of these two frames to gravity loads will not be all that different.

The size of a structure (height, floor area) has a significant impact on the magnitudes of most loads. All loads are influenced by the increasing height of a multistory building, for example. Similarly, the greater the floor area that is to be supported by a single member, the smaller will be the probability that the code live load will appear with its full intensity over the entire area. In such cases a live load reduction method is used to arrive at more realistic design data.

Loads on Building Structures

There are many types of loads that may act on a building structure at one time or other, and this section provides a general description of the characteristics of the most important ones.

The following loads are of primary concern to a building designer:

Gravity loads: Dead load; Live load; Snow load;

Lateral loads: Wind load; Seismic action; Special loads and load effects

Special loads and load effects include the influence of temperature variations, structural foundation settlements, impact, and blast. They are given only a brief description here; the reader interested in the details is advised to seek out the specialized publications that deal with this type of loading.

Each of the primary types of loads can be divided into several subtypes.

1 Dead Load

In theory, at least, the dead load on a structure is supposed to remain constant. In reality, the word constant is a relative measure, because the dead load includes not only the self-weight of the structure, but also the weight of permanent construction materials, partitions, floor and ceiling materials, machinery and other equipment, and so on. Also included in this category are the load effects of prestressing forces.

The weight of all of these elements can be determined exactly only by actually weighing and/or measuring the pieces. This is almost always an impractical solution, and the designer will therefore rely on published material data to arrive at the dead loads. Some variation consequently will occur in the real structure, accounting for some of the deviation from constancy. Similarly, there are bound to be differences between otherwise identical structures, representing the major source of dead load variability. However, compared to the other structural loads, the dead load variations are relatively small, and the actual mean values are quite close to the code-prescribed data.

2 Live Load

Live load, or more accurately the gravity live load, is the name that is commonly used for the loads on the structure that are not part of the permanent installations. [3] To that end it includes the weight of the occupants of the building, furniture and movable equipment, and so on. The fluctuations in this load are bound to be substantial. From being essentially zero immediately before the tenants take possession to a maximum value that may be several times as high as the dead load, the magnitude of the live load at any given time may be quite different from that specified by the building code. This is one of the reasons why numerous attempts have been made to model the live load and its variations, and why live load measurements in actual buildings continue to be made.

The live load on the structure at any given time is also called the arbitrary point-in-time live load. As shown by Fig. 5.1, this is the load that is determined in a live load survey. Part of the total load may now be directly attributable to the occupants of the structure: As soon as the room is emptied, the transient live load (TLL) is reduced to zero or near zero.

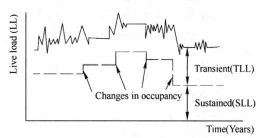

Fig. 5.1 Variation of live load with time.

The load that remains, say, due to furniture and the like, is a sustained live load (SLL) that changes very little as long as the same tenant occupies the premises. Significant variations in the SLL may come about when the occupancy changes: As one company moves out, the SLL may drop to near zero. It will remain at this level until the next tenant moves in, at which time it will increase to a level that may be quite different from the SLL of the earlier occupant.

As demonstrated later, live loads in general are a function of the size of the floor area under consideration. The larger the area, the smaller is the chance that the full code load will appear over the entire area. This affects the magnitude of the arbitrary point-in-time loads as well as the maximum lifetime live load, which represents the maximum live load that the structure may experience in its lifetime. In American practice the life of a structure is expected to be 50 years; hence, a 50-year reference period forms the basis for many of the live load models that have been developed.

The live load on the structure at any time is normally well below the code value; the maximum lifetime (50-year) live load may be a certain amount larger. Current load statistics and code recommendations take these phenomena into account.

New Words

1. prescribe [pris'kraib]   v. 指示，规定
2. criterion [krai'tiəriən]   n. 标准，规范，准则
3. dictate [dik'teit]   v. 规定，指示，命令
4. survey [sə'vei]   n. 调查，测量；vt. 调查
5. variation [ˌvɛəri'eiʃən]   n. 变更，变化，变异
6. deterministic [diˌtə:mi'nistik] a. 确定性的
7. rational ['ræʃənl]   a. 合理的，理性的
8. stochastic [stəu'kæstik]   a. 随机的
9. pertain [pə(:)'tein]   v. 适合，属于
10. cumbersome ['kʌmbəsəm]   a. 讨厌的，麻烦的
11. landscape ['lændskeip]   n. 地形，风景，前景
12. endeavor [in'devə]   n. ；vi. 尽力，努力
13. deviation [ˌdi:vi'eiʃən]   n. 背离
14. constancy ['kɔnstənsi]   n. 恒定性，不变性
15. occupant ['ɔkju:pənt]   n. 居住者，占有者
16. fluctuation [ˌflʌktju'eiʃən] n. 波动，起伏
17. tenant ['tenənt]   n. 房客，承租人 v. 出租
18. transient ['trænziənt]   a. 瞬时的；n. 瞬时现象
19. sustain [səs'tein]   vt. 撑住，维持，持续
20. premise ['premis]   n. 前提；vt. 假定

Phrases and Expressions

1. nominal value   标准值，名义值
2. in practice   实际上，在实践上
3. at best   充其量，最好也只不过
4. building code   建筑规范

5. seismic action   地震作用
6. reference (return) period   重现期
7. semiempirical equation   半经验公式
8. wind tunnel testing   风洞试验
9. mean value   均值
10. code-prescribed data   规范规定的数值
11. transient live load   瞬时活荷载
12. sustained live load   持续活荷载

Notes

[1] It is the role of the specification to detail ..., given the magnitudes of the loads and their effects. It 为形式主语，to detail... 为真正的主语。全句可译为：设计规范的作用是，在已知荷载大小及其效应的情况下，详述对拟采用的结构材料得出满意构件和连接尺寸的方法和准则。

[2] Be that as it may, the fact of the matter is that..., and the manner of variation also depends on the type of load. Be that as it may 为让步状语从句。全句可译为：尽管如此，事实上各种类型的结构荷载都表现为时间函数的随机变量，并且变化的方式视荷载类型而定。

[3] To that end it includes the weight of the occupants of the building, furniture and movable equipment, and so on. 全句可译为：所以，活荷载包括建筑物中居住者、家具和可移动设备的重量，等等。

Exercises

1. Fill in the blanks with proper words.

(1) It is the role of the specification to detail the methods and criteria to be used in arriving at satisfactory member and connection sizes _____ the structural material in question, given the magnitudes of the loads and their effects.

(2) Rather than dealing with nominal loads _____ appear to be deterministic in nature, a realistic design procedure should take load variability into account along with _____ of the strength, in order that adequate structural safety can be achieved through rational means.

(3) In practice, however, the use of time-dependent loads is cumbersome _____ best, although the relationship must be accounted for in certain cases (i.e., seismic action).

(4) The loads on the structure are normally assumed to be independent _____ the type of structure and structural material, with the exception of dead loads.

(5) However, compared _____ the other structural loads, the dead load variations are relatively small, and the actual mean values are quite close to the code-prescribed data.

(6) This is one of the reasons _____ numerous attempts have been made to model the live load and its variations, and _____ live load measurements in actual buildings continue to be made.

(7) It is almost always impractical _____ exactly determine the weight of all of the elements by actually weighing and/or measuring the pieces, and the designer will therefore rely on published material data _____ arrive at the dead loads.

(8) Similarly, the greater the floor area that is to be supported by a single member, the smaller will be the probability that the code live load will appear _____ its full intensity over the entire area.

2. Translate the following phrases into Chinese/English.
  (1) building code
  (2) stochastic analyse
  (3) multistory building
  (4) code-prescribed data
  (5) transient live load
  (6) 随机变量
  (7) 半经验公式
  (8) 风洞试验
  (9) 持续活荷载
  (10) 名义值

3. Translate the following sentences into Chinese.

(1) The building code loads have traditionally been given as nominal values, determined on the basis of material properties (e. g., dead load) or load surveys (e. g., live load and snow load).

(2) Since the random variation of the loads is a function of time as well as a number of other factors, the modeling, strictly speaking, should take this into account by using stochastic analyses to reflect the time and space interdependence.

(3) For example, American live load criteria are based on a reference period of 50 years, while Canadian criteria use a 30-year interval.

(4) Building codes treat these effects as static phenomena and relate them to the actual conditions through semiempirical equations.

(5) The response of a building, however, will be different for different materials, depending on the type of load.

(6) There are many types of loads that may act on a building structure at one time or other, and this section provides a general description of the characteristics of the most important ones.

(7) The dead load includes not only the self-weight of the structure, but also the weight of permanent construction materials, partitions, floor and ceiling materials, machinery and other equipment, and so on.

(8) Live load, or more accurately the gravity live load, is the name that is commonly used for the loads on the structure that are not part of the permanent installations.

(9) The live load on the structure at any given time is also called the arbitrary point-in-time live load.

(10) The live load on the structure at any time is normally well below the code value; the maximum lifetime (50-year) live load may be a certain amount larger.

4. Fill in the blanks with the given words below.
   function, hence, in, lifetime, period, that, that, the, under, which
   As demonstrated later, live loads in general are a _____ of the size of the floor area _____ consideration. The larger the area, _____ smaller is the chance _____ the full code load will appear over the entire area. This affects the magnitude of the arbitrary point-in-time loads as well as the maximum _____ live load, _____ represents the maximum live load that the structure may experience _____ its lifetime. In American practice the life of a structure is expected to be 50 years; _____, a 50-year reference _____ forms the basis for many of the live load models _____ have been developed.

5. Translate the following sentences into English.
   (1) 对某些荷载来说，结构的地理位置起重要作用。
   (2) 风荷载既不是静荷载也不是均匀变化的荷载，并且除了受周围结构和地形影响外还受结构几何形状的严重影响。
   (3) 风荷载和雪荷载可根据模型试验来确定。
   (4) 特殊荷载及荷载效应包括温度变化、结构地基沉降、冲击和爆炸的影响。
   (5) 至少在理论上，结构上的恒载被认为是保持不变的。

Reading Material

Loads(2)

3 Snow Load

Although snow is a form of live load, unique conditions govern its magnitude and distribution. It is the primary roof load in many geographical areas, and it is heavily dependent on structural geometry, exposure(方位), and local climate.

Snow load data are normally based on surveys that have produced isoline(等值线) maps, showing areas of equal depth of ground snowfall (actually, the maps show the water-equivalent of the amount of snow). On this basis annual extreme snowfalls have been determined for a period of several years, and further analyzed through statistical models to find the lifetime maximum snow loads. The reference period is again the 50-year anticipated life of a structure.

A major difficulty is encountered in the method of translating the ground snow load into roof snow load. This is effected(实现)through a semiempirical relationship, whereby the ground snow load is multiplied by a factor that takes factors such as roof geometry into account. Much work continues to be done to improve the method of snow load computation.

4 Wind Load

By its very nature, wind is a highly dynamic natural phenomenon. For this reason, it is also a complex problem from a structural point of view. Not only do the wind forces fluctuate significantly, they also are influenced by the geometry of the structure (height, width, depth, plan, and elevation shape), as well as the surrounding landscape(地形). It has already been observed that in some of the more difficult cases a designer must resort to(诉诸于，采取) wind tunnel tests to determine the loads and behavior of the building under high winds, and even that may not be sufficient in some cases. Nevertheless, the basic approach to wind load analysis is to treat the phenomenon as a static load problem, using the Bernoulli equation to translate wind speed into wind pressure. In a treatment akin to(类似于) what is used for snow loads, a semiempirical equation then gives the wind load at a certain level as a function of a number of constants, each representing effects such as wind gusts(阵风), landscape, and structural geometry.

The data that have been provided for wind loads are all based on measured wind speeds, since these are relatively easy to determine. Meteorological data(气象资料) from many locations throughout the country yield the local wind speed data for daily and annual maxima; these are then used to model long-term characteristics. In particular, the maximum wind speed is needed for the 50-year reference period. In some cases this number is available; in other cases it must be extrapolated using a statistical model.

Wind loads are highly dependent on local conditions, in the same way that snow loads are. The designer must consult local requirements; there are no general, national specifications, other than a compilation of meteorological data.

5 Seismic Action

The treatment of seismic action effects is extremely complicated, because of the stochastic(随机的) character of this natural phenomenon and the many factors that influence the impact of an earthquake on a structure. In addition, since the ground rather than the building moves, the inertia effects cannot be overlooked.

For most buildings it is sufficient to deal with the seismic effects as if they represent a static load, provided the magnitude of this equivalent load reflects the dynamic background. Thus, the magnitude of the peak ground acceleration is needed, as is knowledge of the type of structure (frequency and damping properties). The structural material is also important, especially in view of the need for structural ductility. After all, the load effects produced by a major earthquake are expected to be well in excess of normal service loads, producing significant permanent deformations.

The primary load that is developed under seismic conditions is the base shear, and building codes contain detailed provisions for its computation.

6 Special Loads and Load Effects

Impact. Most building loads are static or essentially so, meaning that their rate of application is so slow that the kinetic energy associated with their motion is insignificant. For example, a person entering a room is actually exerting a dynamic load on the structure by virtue of his motion. However, because of the small mass and slow movement of the individual, his kinetic energy is essentially zero.

When loads are large and/or their rate of application is very high, the influence of the energy that is brought to bear on the structure as the movement of the loads suddenly is restrained must be taken into account. This is the phenomenon of impact. The kinetic energy of the moving mass is translated into a load on the structure. Depending on the rate of application, the effect of the impact is that the structure "feels" a load that may be as large as two times its static value.

Impact is of particular importance for structures where machinery and the like are operating. For example, elevators, cranes, and equipment such as printing presses and weaving looms(纺织机) all produce impact effects. The LRFD specification has detailed rules for the computation of these influences.

Blast. Blast effects, whether due to gas or other explosions, have influences similar to impact. They do not occur as often as impact in normal structures, but under certain circumstances they must be considered. This is particularly true for certain industrial installations, where the product that is manufactured may be of a volatile(爆炸性的) nature. Analysis and design data for blast effects are limited; certain defense specifications will have rules.

Thermal Effects. Steel expands or contracts under changing temperatures, and in doing so may exert considerable forces if the members are restrained from moving. The use of expansion joints, properly located throughout a structure, can be important. However, for most building structures the thermal effects are less significant than others for structural strength and behavior. The movement (or restraint effect) results from the total temperature differential, and is directly proportional to the length of the structural member. Naturally, an uneven temperature distribution will cause some of the movement to be translated into a bending effect; this may have to be combined with bending from other sources in certain cases.

Foundation Settlements. For a statically determinate structure a foundation settlement will do nothing but make the structure unsightly and possibly create some cracked partitions and the like. The structural effects are minimal, unless, of course, the settlement is very large. For a statically indeterminate structure(超静定结构), however, any such movement will produce additional loads on members and connections which must be taken into account. Of course, a settlement rarely occurs until after the structure has been completed; the designer should reanalyze the building to ascertain that the added stress resultants can be carried by all of the affected components.

科技英语阅读与写作指南

科技英语阅读——文章的理解(1)

科技英语阅读的主要目的是从专业科技英语书刊中获取所需要的信息和知识,但科技英语资料浩如烟海,只有有效地利用不同的阅读方法和技巧,提高阅读速度,提高理解的准确性,才能满足需要。因此,掌握快速阅读方法十分必要。用于快速阅读的常见方法有意群阅读（reading by sense group）、略读（skimming）和查读（scanning）。

1. 意群阅读

意群是指一组在意义上和语法结构上有关联的词。以意群为单位进行阅读是一个比较容易且有效地培养和提高阅读速度的方法。在阅读时，用眼睛的视野将每句按意群为单位分割成"块状"，眼睛只须注视每个"块状意群"，这样就避免了逐词阅读，阅读和理解的速度就会大大提高。

//Footings generally // can be classified as // wall and column footings. //The horizontal outlines // of the most common types // are given in Fig. 8. //A wall footing // is simply a strip of reinforced concrete, // wider than the wall, // which distributes its pressure. //Single-column footings // are usually square, sometimes rectangular, // and represent the simplest and most economical type. //Their use // under exterior columns // meets with difficulties // if property rights // prevent the use of // footings projecting beyond the exterior walls. //In this case // combined footings or strap footings // are used // which will not project // beyond the wall column. //

按照意群阅读的方法读这段文章时，大脑中出现的理解模式应为：基础→分为→墙基、柱基→平面图→见图 8→墙基→钢筋混凝土条带→比墙宽→分散墙的压力→单柱基础→正方形、长方形→代表最简单、最经济的类型→使用（基础）→在外柱下→遇到困难→如果地产权→不允许使用→突出外墙的地基→这种情况下→复合式基础、条形基础→被使用→不突出→墙外

2. 略读

略读是指快速浏览一篇文章，跳过文章的细节，跳过不重要的描述，仅注意文章的主题思想。通过略读，可以快速了解所读材料的体裁、结构和逻辑关系，了解文章的大意和主旨。略读时要充分利用文章章节的标题、文章中的重点词、斜体词。还应特别注意文章的开始段和结束段以及每一段的段首句和结尾句，从这些地方往往可以把握住文章的主题。

The requirement of tolerable settlements is concerned with total and differential settlements of all foundations under the planned structure. The differential settlements must be limited in order not to cause structural distress or excessive tilting of the superstructure and they are also often limited by the serviceability requirements of the superstructure. The total settlements must be limited because they invariably induce differential settlements, even in apparently homogeneous soil conditions. They are also often limited by considerations of such factors as access to adjacent buildings, water and sewage connections, etc.

采用略读的方法可迅速了解本文的主题即段首句：The requirement of tolerable settlements is concerned with total and differential settlements...，接着，文章分别叙述控制 the differential settlements（不均匀沉降）和 the total settlements（总沉降）的目的和原因 The differential settlements must be limited in order not to cause... / they are also limited by...；The total settlements must be limited because... / They are also often limited by considerations of...

3. 查读

查读就是带着目的去读，是阅读者根据自己的需要，以最快的速度扫视所读材料，在文章中寻找某一个或某几个具体内容和细节，如人物、事件、时间、地点、数字等。进行查读时要注意：首先确定自己要寻找什么信息，然后确定所查寻的信息范围；注意所查寻信息的

LESSON 5

特点；运用扫视来扩大视觉范围，从而快而准确地捕捉到所要查找的信息。

下面我们通过查读的方法从下面文章中查阅有关霍金的出生日期，地点，读书的学校等，不必通读全文。

Like with any story, we must begin at the beginning. Stephen William Hawking was born on January 8, 1942, exactly 300 years after the death of Galileo. He came from a relatively modest background. His family did have a rather strong academic tradition though. Both of his parents had attended and graduated from Oxford, and his father, Frank, was appointed Head of the Division of Parasitology at the National Institute of Medical Research after the end of World War II. His family lived in the small town of St. Albans. When Stephen was 10 he was sent to St. Albans School, a private school with an excellent academic reputation. Stephen was naturally gifted and remained near the top of his class. He ran with a small group of friends who were all good students and they spent a great deal of time discussing intellectual matters. Hawking graduated from St Albans and was admitted to Oxford on a scholarship.

通过查读可以了解到霍金出生于 1942 年 1 月 8 日，住在 St. Albans，在 St. Albans School 上学，毕业后进 Oxford 大学学习。

LESSON 6

Concepts of Structural Analysis

Structures can be classified in a variety of ways. The casual observer might first consider classifying structures according to their respective functions: buildings, bridges, ships, aircraft, towers, and so on. This basis for structural classification is in fact fundamental; all structures have some functional reasons for existence. It is the need to fulfill some function that prompts the designer to give life to a structure. Furthermore, it is the need for a safe, serviceable, feasible, and aesthetically pleasing fulfillment of a function that dictates the form, material, and manner of loading of a structure.

Once the form and material have been determined, a structure may be further classified according to either its form (e. g. , an arch, truss, or suspension structure) or the material out of which it is constructed(e. g. , steel, concrete, or timber). The form and material of a structure in turn dictate its behavior, which in turn dictates the character of the analytical model. Fig. 6.1 illustrates schematically the relationships among the function a structure is to fulfill, the form and material and loading on the

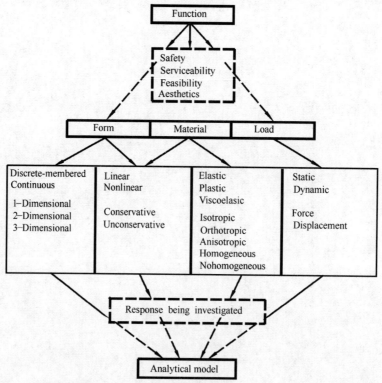

Fig. 6.1 Relationship between the function of a structure and its analytical model.

structure, the behavior of the structure, and the analytical model of the structure. At this point we need to discuss some of the aspects of structural behavior indicated in Fig. 6.1 and to explain their respective relationships to the form and material of the structure. A structure is linear if its response to loading, say displacement at a point, is directly proportional to the magnitude of the applied load. If this proportionality does not exist, the structure is said to be nonlinear. Structural nonlinearities are of two types: (1) material nonlinearities that arise when stress is not proportional to strain, and (2) geometric nonlinearities that arise when the configuration of the structure under load is markedly changed from the unloaded configuration. (The presence of cables in a structure often leads to geometric nonlinearity because displacements can occur owing to a change in cable sag, which can be shown to be nonlinearly related to the force in the cable.) Materials, and therefore structures built from them, may be classified as elastic, plastic, or viscoelastic. Elastic materials rebound to their initial configuration when the load is removed, whereas plastic materials retain a permanent set. The deformations of viscoelastic materials depend on time and therefore load history, whereas the deformations of elastic and plastic materials do not. A structural system is unconservative or conservative depending on whether or not energy is lost from the system during a cycle of loading and unloading. Energy is generally lost if a system does not recover its initial shape after unloading owing either to plastic behavior of the material or to friction forces within or between parts of the structure.

All these behavioral aspects of the structure will have a significant influence on the nature of the analysis used in studying the structure. In addition, in developing the analytical model it will be necessary to consider whether the structural material is homogeneous or nonhomogeneous and whether it is isotropic, orthotropic, or anisotropic. (The physical properties of homogeneous materials are the same at each point; those of nonhomogeneous material are not. The physical properties of isotropic materials are the same in all directions at a point; those of anisotropic materials are not. An orthotropic material is a special anisotropic material whose properties are different in three principal directions but whose properties in all other directions are dependent on those in the principal directions.) [1]Other aspects of the structure, although important design considerations, will not usually have a significant impact on the analysis technique. These include brittleness, ductility, flammability, texture, color, hardness, and machinability.

Finally, the nature of the loading, which is dependent on the function of the structure, will also influence the analysis. The only truly static loading on a structure is the dead, or gravity, loading. However, if other loadings are applied gradually enough, they are called quasi-static loadings and may be considered static for analysis purposes. Whether or not the rate of loading is gradual enough depends on whether or not the time it takes to apply the load is longer than the fundamental period of vibration of the structure being analyzed. Loads usually need be treated as dynamic only if they are periodic in nature or if they are applied very suddenly. Even then, sometimes an "impact factor" is applied to an analysis with a static-loading result to account for the effect of a suddenly applied load. Loads can also be categorized as either external applied forces or internal initial distortions. Thermal loading is an example of an internal initial distortion (or initial strain) loading.

Unfortunately, the picture of structural behavior is generally not so clear as that just painted. [2] That is, materials are not either "linear" or "nonlinear" and "elastic" or "plastic"; instead, their behavior depends on circumstances such as environment and rate of loading. [3] The picture is further clouded in that the type of behavior that must be considered in an analysis may depend on the type of response being investigated. For example, a simpler analytical model may suffice to obtain static displacement and stress results than that which would be required for vibration or buckling results.

To clarify this picture for purposes of a rational presentation of matrix analysis of structures, we will make simplifying assumptions as to the nature of the behavior of structures. Thus we will consider only the displacement and stress response due to static loading of linear, elastic, conservative structures. We will further restrict our attention to discrete-membered structures (rigid—and pin-jointed frameworks) as opposed to continuous structures. However, it is important to recognize at the outset that the concepts that will be presented can be extended to the solution of many other classes of structural problems, including those involving dynamic response, material and geometric nonlinearities, inelasticity, instability, and continuous systems. Furthermore, the same concepts can be applied to problems from other areas of engineering, such as geotechnics, hydraulics, and heat transfer, as well as to problems outside of engineering altogether. Finally, to conserve space and time, most of our studies will deal with planar structures subjected to planar loadings in the plane of the structure. This approach will retain enough generality that the resulting analysis methods can be readily extended to three-dimensional applications.

New Words

1. prompt [prɔmpt]　　　　　　　　*vt.* 促使，敦促，提示，鼓动
2. serviceable ['səːvisəbl]　　　　　*a.* 适用的，耐用的
3. aesthetically [iːs'θetikəli]　　　　*ad.* 审美地，美学观点上地
4. truss [trʌs]　　　　　　　　　　*n.* 桁架，构架
5. suspension [səs'penʃən]　　　　　*n.* 悬吊物，悬，吊
6. sag [sæg]　　　　　　　　　　　*v.* 下垂，松弛；*n.* 下垂
7. viscoelastic [ˌviskəui'læstik]　　　*a.* 粘弹性的
8. rebound [ri'baund]　　　　　　　*v.* 回弹，跳回；*n.* 回弹
9. homogenous [hə'mɔdʒinəs]　　　*a.* 均匀的，同质的
10. isotropic [aisəu'trɔpik]　　　　　*a.* 各向同性的
11. orthotropic [ˌɔːθəu'trɔpik]　　　　*a.* 正交各向异性的
12. anisotropic [əˌnaisəu'trɔpik]　　　*a.* 各向异性的

LESSON 6

13. flammability [ˌflæməˈbiləti] n. 易燃，可燃性
14. machinability [məʃiːnəˈbiliti] n. 可加工性
15. quasi-static [ˈkweisaiˈstætik] a. 拟静力
16. texture [ˈtekstʃə] n. 结构组织，质地
17. distortion [disˈtɔːʃən] n. 变形，扭曲
18. geotechnics [ˌdʒi(ː)əuˈtekniks] n. 土力学，岩土工程学
19. hydraulics [ˈhaiˈdrɔːliks] n. 水力学

Phrases and Expressions

1. suspension structure   悬挂结构
2. elastic material   弹性材料
3. plastic material   塑性材料
4. quasi-static loadings   拟静力荷载
5. thermal loading   热负荷
6. analytical model   分析模型
7. planar structure   平面结构
8. planar load   面荷载

Notes

[1] Other aspects of the structure, although important design considerations,... impact on the analysis technique. 全句可译为：结构的其他方面，尽管也是设计中考虑的重要因素，常常不会对分析方法产生重要影响。

[2] That is, materials are not either "linear" or "nonlinear" and "elastic" or "plastic"; instead,... loading. and 后省略了 materials are not。全句可译为：这就是说，材料既不是"线性的"或"非线性的"，也不是"弹性的"或"塑性的"；实际上它们的性能取决于环境和加荷速率这样的条件。

[3] The picture is further clouded in that the type of behavior ... may depend on the type of response being investigated. in that 意为"因为"，引导原因状语从句。全句可译为：这种情况更为复杂，因为分析中要考虑的性能类型可能取决于被考察的反应类型。

Exercises

1. Fill in the blanks with proper words.

(1) This basis for structural classification is _____ fact fundamental; all structures have some functional reasons _____ existence.

(2) It is the need _____ fulfill some function _____ prompts the designer to give life to a structure.

(3) _____ the form and material have been determined, a structure may be further classified according _____ either its form (e.g., an arch, truss, or

suspension structure) or the material out of which it is constructed (e.g., steel, concrete, or timber).

(4) The form and material of a structure _____ turn dictate its behavior, _____ in turn dictates the character of the analytical model.

(5) A structure is linear _____ its response to loading, say displacement at a point, is directly proportional _____ the magnitude of the applied load.

(6) The presence of cables in a structure often leads _____ geometric nonlinearity because displacements can occur owing to a change in cable sag, _____ can be shown to be nonlinearly related to the force in the cable.

(7) Elastic materials rebound to their initial configuration _____ the load is removed, _____ plastic materials retain a permanent set.

(8) A structural system is unconservative _____ conservative depending on _____ or not energy is lost from the system during a cycle of loading and unloading.

(9) _____ clarify this picture for purposes of a rational presentation of matrix analysis of structures, we will make simplifying assumptions _____ to the nature of the behavior of structures.

(10) Furthermore, the same concepts can be applied to problems from other areas of engineering, _____ as geotechnics, hydraulics, and heat transfer, _____ well as to problems outside of engineering altogether.

2. Translate the following phrases into Chinese/English.

(1) the magnitude of the applied load   (6) 悬挂结构
(2) quasi-static loading   (7) 应力应变成正比
(3) planar structure   (8) 结构的变形
(4) planar loading   (9) 分析模型
(5) plastic material   (10) 弹性材料

3. Translate the following sentences into Chinese.

(1) Furthermore, it is the need for a safe, serviceable, feasible, and aesthetically pleasing fulfillment of a function that dictates the form, material, and manner of loading of a structure.

(2) Fig. 6.1 illustrates schematically the relationships among the function a structure is to fulfill, the form and material and loading on the structure, the behavior of the structure, and the analytical model of the structure.

(3) At this point we need to discuss some of the aspects of structural behavior indicated in Fig. 6.1 and to explain their respective relationships to the form and material of the structure.

(4) Materials may be classified as elastic, plastic, or viscoelastic.

(5) The deformations of viscoelastic materials depend on time and therefore load history, whereas the deformations of elastic and plastic materials do not.

(6) Energy is generally lost if a system does not recover its initial shape after unloading owing either to plastic behavior of the material or to friction forces within or between parts of the structure.

(7) All these behavioral aspects of the structure will have a significant influence on the nature of the analysis used in studying the structure.

(8) In addition, in developing the analytical model it will be necessary to consider whether the structural material is homogeneous or nonhomogeneous and whether it is isotropic, orthotropic, or anisotropic.

(9) It is important to recognize at the outset that the concepts that will be presented can be extended to the solution of many other classes of structural problems, including those involving dynamic response, material and geometric nonlinearities, inelasticity, instability, and continuous systems.

(10) Loads usually need be treated as dynamic only if they are periodic in nature or if they are applied very suddenly.

4. Translate the following sentences into English.

(1) 结构的分类有多种方法，普通观察者会首先根据它们各自的功能把结构分为房屋、桥梁、船舶、塔架等等。

(2) 结构设计中，需要考虑的是结构的安全性、适用性和可行性。

(3) 如果结构对荷载的反应，比如一点的位移，与施加的荷载大小成正比，则结构为线性的。

(4) 各向同性材料的物理性能在任一点的所有方向是相同的。

(5) 结构的性能通常是很难清楚描述的，因为结构的材料既不是线性或非线性的，也不是弹性或塑性的。

5. Fill in the blanks with the given words below.

as, for, for, if, on, on, or, whether, which

Finally, the nature of the loading, _____ is dependent on the function of the structure, will also influence the analysis. The only truly static loading _____ a structure is the dead, or gravity, loading. However, _____ other loadings are applied gradually enough, they are called quasi-static loadings and may be considered static _____ analysis purposes. _____ or not the rate of loading is gradual enough depends _____ whether or not the time it takes to apply the load is longer than the fundamental period of vibration of the structure being analyzed. Loads usually need be treated _____ dynamic only if they are periodic in nature _____ if they are applied very suddenly. Even then, sometimes an "impact factor" is applied to an analysis with a static-loading result to account _____ the effect of a suddenly applied load. Loads can also be categorized as either external applied forces or internal initial distortions. Thermal loading is an example of an internal initial distortion (or initial strain) loading.

Reading Material

Cracks in Flexural Members

The study of crack formation, behavior of cracks under increasing load, and control of cracking is necessary for proper designer of reinforced concrete structure. In flexural members, cracks develop under working loads, and because concrete is weak in tension, reinforcement is placed in the cracked tension zone to resist the tension force produced by the external loads.

Flexural cracks develop when the stress at the extreme tension fibers exceeds the modulus of rupture of concrete. With the use of high-strength reinforced bars, excessive cracking may develop in reinforced concrete member. The use of high-tensile steel has many advantages, yet the development of undesirable cracks seems to be inevitable. Wide cracks may allow corrosion of the reinforcement or leakage of water structures and may spoil the appearance of the structure.

A crack is formed in concrete when a narrow opening of indefinite dimension has developed in the concrete beam as the result of internal tensile stresses. These internal stresses may be due to one or more of the following:
- external forces such as direct axial tension, flexure, or torsion
- shrinkage
- creep
- internal expansion resulting from a change of properties of the concrete constituents

In general, cracks may be divided into two main types, secondary cracks and main cracks.

Secondary Cracks

Secondary cracks, very small cracks that develop in the first stage of cracking, are produced by the internal expansion and contraction of the concrete constituents and by low flexural tension stresses due to the self-weight of the member and any other dead loads. There are three types of secondary cracks.

Shrinkage cracks Shrinkage cracks are important cracks, because they affect the pattern of cracking that is produced by loads in flexural members. When they develop, they form a weak path in the concrete. When load is applied, cracks start to appear at the weakest sections, such as along the reinforcing bars. The number of cracks formed is limited by the amount of shrinkage in concrete and the presence of restraints. Shrinkage cracks are difficult to control.

Secondary flexural cracks Usually secondary flexural cracks are widely spaced, and one cracks does not influence the formation of others. They are expected to occur under low loads, such as dead loads. When a load is applied gradually on a simple beam, tensile stress develops at the bottom fibers, and when it exceeds the flexural tensile stress of concrete, cracks start to develop. They widen gradually and extend toward the neutral axis. It is difficult to predict the sections at which secondary cracks start because concrete is not a homogeneous, isotropic material.

Salinger and Billing estimated the steel stress just before cracking to be from about 6000 to 7000psi (42 to 49 MPa). An initial crack width of the order of 0.001 in. (0.025mm) is expected at the extreme concrete tensile fibers. Once cracks are formed, the tensile stress of concrete at the cracked section decreases to zero, and the steel bars take all the tensile force. At this moment, some slip occurs between the steel bars and the concrete due to the differential elongation of concrete and steel and extends to a section where the concrete and steel strains are equal.

Corrosion secondary cracks Corrosion secondary cracks form when moisture containing deleterious(有害的) agents such as sodium chloride, carbon dioxide, and dissolved oxygen penetrates the concrete surface, corroding the steel reinforcement. The oxide compounds formed by deterioration(变质) of steel bars occupy a larger volume than the steel and exert mechanical pressure that perpetuates extensive cracking. This type of cracking may be severe enough to result in eventual failure of the structure. Corrosion cracking may be forestalled(阻止) by using proper construction methods and high-quality concrete.

Main Cracks

Main cracks develop at a later stage than secondary cracks. They are caused by the difference in strains in steel and concrete at the section considered. The behavior of main cracks changes at two different stages. At low tensile stresses in steel bars, the number of cracks increases, whereas the widths of cracks remain small; as tensile stresses are increased, an equilibrium stage is reached. When stresses are further increased, the second stage of cracking develops, and crack widths increase without any significant increase in the number of cracks. Usually one or two cracks start to widen more than the others, forming critical cracks.

Main cracks in beams and axially tensioned members have been studied by many investigators. Prediction of the width of cracks and crack control were among the problems studied. These are discussed here, along with the requirement of the ACI Code.

Crack width Crack width and crack spacing, according to existing crack theories, depend on many factors, which include steel percentage, its distribution in the concrete section, steel flexural stress at service load, concrete cover, and properties of the concrete constituents. Different equations for predicting the width and spacing of cracks in reinforced concrete members were presented at the Symposium on Bond and Crack Formation in Reinforced Concrete in Stockholm, Sweden, in 1957. Chi and Kirstein presented equations for the crack width and spacing as a function of an effective area of concrete around the steel bars: A concrete circular area of diameter equal to four times the diameter of the bars was used to calculate crack width. Other equations were presented over the next decade.

An empirical formula to estimate the maximum crack width w at the steel level is

$$w_{max} = 0.115 f_s \sqrt[4]{A} \times 10^{-6} \quad (\text{in.})$$

where A—area of concrete surrounding each bar, equal to the effective tension area of concrete having the same centroid as of the reinforcing bars divided by the number of bars, in square inches;

f_s—the stress in the steel bars, psi;

At the tension concrete face, the following formula was suggested:

$$w_{max}=0.115\beta f_s \sqrt[4]{A}\times 10^{-6} \quad \text{(in.)}$$

where β is the ratio of distances from the neutral axis to the tension face and to the steel centroid and A and f_s are as defined previously.

Gergely and Lutz presented the following formula for the limiting crack width:

$$w=0.076\beta f_s \sqrt[3]{Ad_c}\times 10^{-6} \quad \text{(in.)}$$

where β, A, and f_s are as defined previously and d_c—thickness of concrete cover measured from the extreme tension fiber to the center of the closest bar. The value of β can be taken approximately equal to 1.2 for beams and 1.35 for slabs. Note that f_s is in psi and ω is in inches.

The mean ratio of maximum crack width to average crack width was found to vary between 1.5 to 2.0, as reported by many investigators. An average value of 1.75 may be used.

In SI units (mm and MPa), equation is

$$w=11.0\beta f_s \sqrt[3]{Ad_c}\times 10^{-6} \quad \text{(mm)}$$

Tolerable crack width The formation of cracks in reinforced concrete members is unavoidable. Hairline cracks occur even in carefully designed and constructed structures. Cracks are usually measured at the face of the concrete, but actually they are related to crack width at the steel level, where corrosion is expected. The permissible crack width is also influenced by aesthetic and appearance requirements. The naked eye can detect a crack about 0.006 in. (0.15mm) wide, depending on the surface texture of concrete. Different values for permissible crack width at the steel level have been suggested by many investigators, ranging from 0.010 to 0.016 in. (0.25~0.40mm) for interior members and from 0.006 to 0.010 in. (0.15~0.25mm) for exterior exposed members. A limiting crack width of 0.016 in. (0.4mm) for interior members and 0.013 in. (0.32mm) for exterior members under dry condition can be tolerated.

Crack control Control grows in importance with the use of high-strength steel in reinforced concrete members, as large cracks develop under working loads because of the high allowable stresses. Control of cracking depends on the permissible crack width. It is always preferable to have a large number of fine cracks rather than a small number of large cracks. Secondary cracks are minimized by controlling the total amount of cement paste, water-cement ratio, permeability of aggregate and concrete, rate of curing, shrinkage, and end-restraint conditions.

The factors involved in controlling main cracks are the reinforcement stress, the bond characteristics of reinforcement, the distribution of reinforcement, the diameter of the steel bars used, the steel percentage, the concrete cover, and the properties of concrete constituents. Any improvement in these factors will help in reducing the width of cracks.

LESSON 6

科技英语阅读与写作指南

科技英语阅读——文章的理解(2)

  科技英语文章往往是根据主题思想的各个方面、各个层次进行说明、阐述和论证的,总是按照所叙述的内容的各个方面、各个层次分成若干段落,每一个段落侧重于一个方面,而且就这一方面的内容进行展开。英语科技文章的段落都是通过主题句(topic sentence)来表达主题思想的,主题句常常位于段首或段尾处,间或出现在段落中间。科技英语文章通常有比较明显的主题思想,其结构也比较清楚。因此,在阅读科技英语文章时,掌握段落的主题句,对于了解段落和文章的主题思想,获取主要信息,是十分重要的。

1. **段首主题句**:主题句位于段落的第一句,一开始就明确主题,然后展开说明、阐述或论证,即采用演绎法,由一般到个体,由概述到详解。

  <u>The larger scale may require unique building configurations quite different from traditional forms as well as other materials and nonconventional detailing techniques.</u> It requires a more precise evaluation of loading conditions than just provided by codes, this includes the placement of expansion joints as well as the inclusion of secondary stresses due to the deformations of the members and their interaction, which cannot be ignored any more as for small-scale buildings or structures of high redundancy. Further, it requires a much more comprehensive field inspection to control the quality during the erection phase; post-construction building maintenance and periodic inspection is necessary to monitor the effects of loading and weather on member behavior in addition to the potential deterioration of the materials.

  本段第一句引出主题 "The larger scale may require... detailing techniques."。随后通过 "It requires a more precise... Further, it requires a much more comprehensive..." 的句子加以具体说明。

2. **段尾主题句**:主题句位于段落末尾,以加强说服力。段落先提供具体的事实,然后再作出结论,即采用归纳法,先阐述、后概括。

  Imagine a world in which children would be the rulers and could decide not only the outcome of each and every occurrence, but also dictate the very structure and form of the environment. In this world, a child's wildest thoughts would become reality limited only by the extent of his or her imagination. While such a world might sound both fantastic and frightening, at least from a logical, adult perspective, it does exist. What's more, it has been in existence for some time and is populated by hundreds of thousands of children who spend hours within its boundaries experimenting and learning. This world is not real, at least not in the traditional sense, but exists within a computer and is generated by an educational programming language called LOGO. Unlike other computer languages and programs that are designed to test children and provide applications that formally dispense information, LOGO allows children, even preschool children to be in total control. <u>Children teach the computer to think and as a result develop and sharpen their own reasoning ability.</u>

  本段先设想一个由儿童统治的世界 "Imagine a world......"。接着叙述这个世界 "exists within a computer and is generated by an educational programming language called LOGO.",在介绍完 LOGO 之后,引出主题 "Children teach the computer to think and as a result develop and sharpen their own reasoning ability."

3. 段中主题句：段落开始一两句都是铺叙以引出主题，主题句后有一些句子进一步论证或说明这一主题。即先阐述、后概括、再详解。

  That the plates are moving is now beyond dispute. Africa and South America, for example, are moving away from each other as new material is injected into the seafloor between them. The complementary coastlines and certain geological features that seem to span the ocean are reminders of where the two continents were once joined. The relative motion of the plates carrying these continents has been constructed in detail, but the motion of one plate with respect to another cannot readily be translated into motion with respect to the earth's interior. It is not possible to determine whether both continents are moving in opposite directions or whether one continent is stationary and the other is drifting away from it. <u>Hot spots, anchored in the deeper layers of the earth, provide the measuring instruments needed to resolve the question</u>. From an analysis of the hot-spot population it appears that the African plate is stationary and that it has not moved during the past 30 million years.

  本段先以"That the plates are moving is now beyond dispute."引出话题，接着谈板块漂移的理论及遇到的问题"It is not possible to determine……drifting away from it."然后引出主题"Hot spots, anchored in the deeper layers of the earth, provide the measuring instruments needed to resolve the question."最后一句作为例证以进一步说明主题。

Lesson 7

Soil Compressibility and Settlement(1)

Types of Ground Movements and Causes of Settlement

The relationship between ground movement and the stability of related structures is a complex one. First of all, there are several mechanisms which may produce ground movement, and furthermore there are many types of structure, each with a varying potential to withstand or to be distressed by movement. Some buildings, such as those of brick and masonry construction, are exceedingly brittle and may sustain cracks and even structural damage following very small foundation displacements. Others may be constructed to sustain movements of considerable magnitude without suffering real damage.

[1] It is important to realize that soil conditions are apt to change, sometimes considerably, from before, to during, and also after construction. It is the prediction of these changes that presents the most difficult task to the designer. Most building damage that occurs because of foundation movement occurs when unforeseen soil conditions arise; inadequate site investigations and a lack of understanding of soil behavior are largely the root causes. As will be shown in this chapter, there are methods available by which the amount and rate of foundation settlement due to certain mechanisms can be estimate. These estimates will remain reasonably reliable providing that the soil conditions assumed for the calculation are: (a) a fair representation of the actual conditions, and (b) likely to persist throughout the life of the building.

It is useful to start a study of settlement by considering briefly a number of ground movement mechanisms which are potential causes of settlement.

Compaction

Compaction is a process whereby the soil particles are forced into a closer state of packing with a corresponding reduction in volume and the expulsion of air. An input of mechanical energy is required and this is usually the result of self-weight loading or a surface surcharge. Vibrations due to traffic movement, heavy machinery and certain construction operations, such as pile-driving, have also been known to cause compaction settlement. In earthquake zones, seismic shock waves may have a similar effect. The most susceptible soils are loosely-packed sands or gravel-sands and fill material, particularly that which has been placed without adequate rolling or tamping.

Consolidation

In saturated cohesive soils the effect of increasing the load is to squeeze out some of the porewater, this process is called consolidation. A gradual reduction in volume takes place until internal pore pressure equilibrium is reached; a reduction in loading may cause swelling providing that the soil can remain saturated. A large part of the remainder of this chapter is devoted to a detailed study of the consolidation process and to methods of assessing resulting settlements. It is essential to understand that a change in loading is required to start the process and that it may take several years for the final settlement to be achieved.

The most susceptible soils are normally-consolidated clays and silts, and certain types of saturated fill. Peat and peaty soils can be highly compressible, resulting in changes in stratum thickness of as much as 20 per cent under quite modest loading.

Elastic Volumetric Settlement

In overconsolidated clays increases in effective stress which do not exceed the yield point (σ_y') cause elastic (approximately) compression. As the stress increases beyond the yield point, non-linear (consolidation) settlement occurs. In heavily overconsolidated clays, therefore, since the yield point will be very high, settlement calculations can be based on elastic theory, using parameters referred to effective stresses (E', E'_0, ν', etc.). Alternatively, estimates may be based on the slope of the swelling-recompression curve (C_s or κ). The elastic behavior of clays is probably attributable to the flexing of thin and flakey clay particles.

Immediate or Undrained Settlement

[2] Immediate or undrained settlement is that amount that takes place during the application of loading, but before any significant volume change has occurred. Although it theoretically occurs in all loading situations, with slowly applied loading, it is masked by consolidation settlement as volume changes occur. The calculation of amounts of immediate settlement are therefore normally related to quickly applied loading e.g. beneath building structure. The undrained stiffness (E_u) can be assumed as an elastic constant for a given depth and so estimates can be obtained using elastic theory.

Moisture Movement

Some types of clay show a marked increase or decrease in volume as the water content is respectively increased or decreased. Clays exhibiting these characteristics are alternatively called shrinkable clays or expansive clays and are found in certain areas of the southern and eastern countries.

In this country, it has been found that the effects of seasonal variations in water content can extend down to about 0.8m below the ground surface. Annual surface movements in the south-east of England as high as 50mm may be expected. These clays characteristically possess high liquid limits and plasticity indices.

Effects of Vegetation

Another factor associated with highly plastic clays that may bring about settlement is the effect of the roots of trees. The radial extent of some tree root systems is greater than the height of the tree; they may also reach depths of several meters. A movement of 100mm was recorded in house foundations 25m away from a row of poplars. The removal of such trees means that more moisture is held in the soil and so swelling occurs. Where well-established trees and shrubs have to be removed from a site, a period of one or two winters should be allowed so that equilibrium may be achieved.

The planting of seedlings adjacent to buildings should be carefully controlled where shrinkable clays exist. A useful rule is always to site new plantings at a distance away from the building of at least 1.5 times the mature height of the tree. Pruning and pollarding can also affect the ground moisture loss and thus bring about swelling. [3] The degree of desiccation (and therefore swelling potential) can be estimated by comparing moisture content and liquid limit readings taken near to existing (or recently removed) trees with readings taken in similar soil in open ground.

Effects of Groundwater Lowering

As water is pumped from an excavation, the water table in the surrounding ground may be lowered. Settlement can result from this reduction in hydrostatic conditions due to two processes. Firstly, in some clays, as discussed above, a decrease in moisture content will result in a decrease in volume. The soil above the reduced groundwater level may therefore shrink. Secondly, a reduction in hydrostatic pore pressure results in an increase of the effective overburden stress on the layers below. Accordingly, the soil (especially in soft clays or peat) beneath the reduced groundwater level may be consolidated by the increase in effective stress.

Effects of Temperature Changes

Quite severe shrinkage can occur in clay soils as they dry out beneath foundations to furnaces, kilns, ovens and boilers. In one case, a boiler building on the London Clay settled 150mm at the centre and 75mm at the sides in less than two years. It is usual to provide an open or rubble-filled air gap between such heat sources and the foundation soil.

In some soils, such as silts, fine sands and chalky soils, and in the chalk itself, there is a possibility of frost heave at sustained low temperatures. Water expands by approximately 9 per cent upon freezing and thus a 1m layer of saturated soil having a porosity of 45 per cent would expand by $0.09 \times 0.45 \times 10^3 = 40$mm. In this country the depth of frozen ground due to winter frost rarely exceeds 400mm. Nevertheless, frost expansions of 30 per cent of the surface layer thickness have been observed. Severe expansion can also take place in soils under cold storage buildings unless insulation is provided.

Effects of Seepage and Scouring

In certain sandy soils, such as fine dry sands and loess, the movement of water can move some of the fine particles. Scouring is the removal of material by surface water and streams, but this can also occur where sewers or water mains have been fractured. Where excavations are taken well below groundwater level within coffer dams and the like, the upward flow of water may cause a form of instability called piping. In arid areas the same soils are liable to surface erosion due to wind action.

In certain rocks and soils the mineral cement in the matrix may be dissolved due to groundwater movement. The formation of caverns and swallets is a feature of limestone and chalk areas, subsidence following the collapse of these is not uncommon.

Loss of Lateral Support

[4] A common form of foundation movement, often leading to serious, even catastrophic, building failure is associated with the excavation of deep holes alongside the foundation. Many cases have been recorded in which adjacent excavation has resulted in a failure. The bearing capacity of the soil directly beneath a footing is dependent on the lateral support afforded it by the soil alongside; in calculating the ultimate bearing capacity of the soil this is taken into account. If this lateral support is removed, as may occur in an untimbered excavation, the likely outcome is a shear slip in the soil beneath the footing, taking the footing into excavation. Similarly, settlement might occur as a result of movement of natural earth slopes or cuttings, due to sliding or flowing.

New Words

1. tamping ['tæmpiŋ]　　　　　　　　n. 夯实　捣紧
2. fill [fil]　　　　　　　　　　　　vt., n. 填方, 填土
3. peat [piːt]　　　　　　　　　　　n. 泥煤, 泥炭块
4. flexing ['fleksiŋ]　　　　　　　　n. 挠曲
5. vegetation [ˌvedʒi'teiʃən]　　　　n. 植被, 植物生长
6. poplar ['pɔplə]　　　　　　　　　n. 白杨, 白杨木
7. shrub [ʃrʌb]　　　　　　　　　　n. 灌木, 灌木丛
8. seedling ['siːdliŋ]　　　　　　　　n. 秧苗, 树苗
9. pruning ['pruːniŋ]　　　　　　　　n. 修枝, 剪枝
10. pollard ['pɔləd]　　　　　　　　vt. 修剪树枝
11. desiccation [desi'keiʃən]　　　　n. 干燥
12. loess ['ləuis]　　　　　　　　　　n. 黄土
13. sewer ['sjuə]　　　　　　　　　　n. 下水道, 污水管
14. coffer ['kɔfə]　　　　　　　　　　n. 围堰; vt. 筑围堰
15. piping ['paipiŋ]　　　　　　　　n. 管涌
16. matrix ['meitriks]　　　　　　　　n. 胶结材料, 填充料
17. swallet ['swɔlit]　　　　　　　　n. 地下川, 小溪流入地下的进口
18. subsidence ['sʌbsidəns]　　　　n. 沉降, 下陷
19. excavation [ˌekskə'veiʃən]　　　n. 开挖, 挖掘
20. seepage ['siːpidʒ]　　　　　　　n. 渗流, 渗透

21. rolling ['rəuliŋ]　　　　　　　　　n. 碾压，轧
22. untimbered [ʌn'timbəd]　　　　　　a. 无支撑的

Phrases and Expressions

1. brick and masonry construction　　砖石建筑
2. site investigations　　场地调查，场地勘察
3. self-weight loading　　自重荷载
4. surface surcharge　　表面超载
5. immediate or undrained settlement　　瞬时沉降或不排水沉降
6. water content　　含水量
7. liquid limit　　液限
8. plasticity index　　塑性指数
9. water table　　地下水位
10. hydrostatic pore pressure　　静止孔隙压力

Notes

[1] It is important to realize that … after construction. be apt to do 意为"有…倾向，易于做…"。全句可译为：重要的是要认识到土性条件在施工前、施工期间、施工后往往都会变化，有时变化还很大。

[2] Immediate or undrained settlement is that amount that…, but before any significant volume change has occurred. 全句可译为：瞬时沉降或不排水沉降是加荷期间、体积发生重大变化之前产生的沉降量。

[3] The degree of desiccation(and therefore swelling potential)can be estimated… in open ground. 全句可译为：通过比较树旁（或刚移走的树旁）场地和空旷场地相似土中的含水量与液限来估算土的干燥程度（因此也可估算膨胀的程度）。

[4] A common form of foundation movement, often leading to serious, even catastrophic,… the foundation. 全句可译为：经常引起建筑物严重、甚至是灾难性破坏的常见地基位移常与基础旁边的深孔开挖有关。

Exercises

1. Fill in the blanks with proper words.

(1) Some buildings, such as those of brick and masonry construction, are exceedingly _____ and may sustain cracks and even structural damage following very small foundation displacements.

(2) It is important to realize that soil conditions are apt to change, sometimes considerably, from before, to during, and also after _____.

(3) Compaction is a process whereby the soil particles are forced into a closer state of packing with a corresponding _____ in volume and the expulsion of air.

(4) In saturated cohesive soils the effect of increasing the load is to squeeze out some of the porewater, this process is called _____.

(5) In overconsolidated clays increases in effective stress which do not exceed the yield point (σ_y') cause _____ (approximately) compression. As the stress increases beyond the yield point, non-linear (consolidation) settlement occurs.

(6) Immediate or undrained settlement is that amount that takes place during the application of loading, but before any significant _____ change has occurred.

(7) A useful rule is always to site new plantings at a distance _____ from the building of at least 1.5 times the mature height of the tree.

(8) As water is pumped from an excavation, the water table in the surrounding ground may be _____.

(9) Accordingly, the soil (especially in soft clays or peat) beneath the reduced groundwater level may be consolidated by the _____ in effective stress.

(10) Where excavations are taken well below groundwater level within coffer dams and the like, the upward flow of water may cause a form of instability called _____.

2. Translate the following phrases into Chinese/English

(1) undrained settlement
(2) bearing capacity
(3) site investigations
(4) brick and masonry construction
(5) lateral support
(6) 极限承载力
(7) 瞬时沉降
(8) 表面超载
(9) 静水压力
(10) 饱和黏性土

3. Translate the following sentences into Chinese

(1) Most building damage that occurs because of foundation movement occurs when unforeseen soil conditions arise; inadequate site investigations and a lack of understanding of soil behavior are largely the root causes.

(2) In heavily overconsolidated clays, therefore, since the yield point will be very high, settlement calculations can be based on elastic theory, using parameters referred to effective stresses (E', E_0', ν', etc.).

(3) A large part of the remainder of this chapter is devoted to a detailed study of the consolidation process and to methods of assessing resulting settlements.

(4) The radial extent of some tree root systems is greater than the height of the tree; they may also reach depths of several meters.

(5) One of the most important soil properties in the context of foundation engineering is its compressibility.

(6) Terzaghi assumed that both the solid particles and the pore water are incompressible. Therefore, the magnitude of the settlement is related directly to the change in volume of the voids, and the rate of settlement in a saturated soil is governed by the rate pore water escapes from the voids.

(7) Soil is a particulate material, so its stress-strain properties are much more complex than those of other more familiar materials such as steel.

(8) The process of consolidation is intimately tied with the buildup and dissipation of

excess pore water pressures and the corresponding changes in effective stress.

(9) The test procedure and methods of correcting the test results to compensate for sample disturbance are described in Chapter 4.

4. Fill in the blanks with the given words below.

     as, by, even, in, in, into, into, on, to, with

A common form of foundation movement, often leading to serious, _____ catastrophic, building failure is associated _____ the excavation of deep holes alongside the foundation. Many cases have been recorded _____ which adjacent excavation has resulted _____ a failure. The bearing capacity of the soil directly beneath a footing is dependent _____ the lateral support afforded it _____ the soil alongside; in calculating the ultimate bearing capacity of the soil this is taken _____ account. If this lateral support is removed, _____ may occur in an untimbered excavation, the likely outcome is a shear slip in the soil beneath the footing, taking the footing _____ excavation. Similarly, settlement might occur as a result of movement of natural earth slopes or cuttings, due _____ sliding or flowing.

5. Translate the following sentences into English

(1) 不排水模量(E_u)在某一深度处可假设为弹性常量，因而可用弹性理论进行沉降估算。

(2) 本章的其余大部分都用来详细研究固结过程和估计其所引起的沉降的方法。

(3) 在有些岩石和土体中，地下水的运动可以溶解岩土体填充物中的胶结矿物。

(4) 经常导致严重的、甚至是灾难性建筑破坏的常见基础位移与基础旁的深孔开挖有关。

(5) 如上所述，有些黏土含水量的降低将引起体积的减小，因此降低后的地下水位以上的土体会收缩。

Reading Material

Soil compressibility and settlement(2)

One of the most important soil properties in the context of foundation engineering is its compressibility. This refers to the soil's response to changes in normal stress. For example, if a foundation is built and loaded, the normal stress in the soil below will increase and a corresponding normal strain will occur. This strain will, in turn, produce a corresponding settlement.

Stress-Strain Properties of Soil

Soil is a particulate material, so its stress-strain properties are much more complex than those of other more familiar materials such as steel. These properties depend on the arrangement of these particles, their interaction with each other, their physical and chemical properties, and many other factors. Therefore, the foundation engineer must consider this complex behavior when conducting settlement computations.

Nonlinear and Inelastic Stress-Strain Behavior

Another complication enters when we consider that the stress-strain curve for soil is nonlinear and inelastic, as shown in Fig. 7.1. Nonlinear means that stress is not proportional to strain (as compared to the curve for steel, which is nearly straight throughout the normal range of working stress). Inelastic means some or all of the deformation is plastic (or permanent). Therefore, if soil is unloaded, it will not rebound to its original volume.

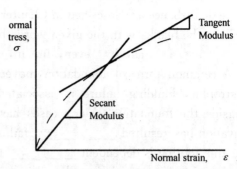

Fig. 7.1 Typical stress-strain curve for a soil. Note that this curve is both nonlinear and inelastic

Because of this behavior, there is no unique value for the modulus of elasticity, even if we consider only one of the lateral constraint conditions described earlier. Sometimes engineers use the tangent modulus, which is the slope of the stress-strain curve at a given point. Other times, we use the secant modulus, which is the slope of a line that connects the origin within point on the curve. Both of these modulus values decrease as the normal stress increases. This is part of the reason for the wide ranges in the typical modulus values.

One-Dimensional Consolidation Settlement

For most soils, the rate and magnitude of settlement are primarily governed by the ability of the soil particles to rearrange into a tighter packing in response to applied normal loads. Karl Terzaghi(太沙基) was the first to address this consolidation process. He developed a theory of consolidation in the 1920s while teaching in Istanbul and it has become the basis for nearly all consolidation analyses.

Terzaghi assumed that both the solid particles and the pore water are incompressible. Therefore, the magnitude of the settlement is related directly to the change in volume of the voids, and the rate of settlement in a saturated soil is governed by the rate pore water escapes from the voids.

The process of consolidation is intimately tied with the buildup and dissipation of excess pore water pressures and the corresponding changes in effective stress. When a vertical external load is applied, the total stress immediately rises by an amount $\Delta\sigma_v$. However, if the soil is saturated, its volume will initially remain constant because both the solid particles and the water are incompressible, and the pore water pressure will rise by an amount equal to $\Delta\sigma_v$ (i.e., $\Delta u = \Delta\sigma_v$). This temporary increase in pore water pressure, Δu, is known as the excess pore water pressure, u_e.

This increased pore water pressure generates a hydraulic gradient and some of the water gradually moves out of the voids. As the water escapes, consolidation occurs and the volume of the soil decreases. Simultaneously, the excess pore water pressure dissipate and the effective stress increases until u_e eventually becomes equal to zero and $\Delta\sigma_v'$ increases by an amount equal to $\Delta\sigma_v$.

In clayey soils, this process occurs very slowly because their low hydraulic conductivity (coefficient of permeability) impedes the flow of water. However, in sandy soils, the hydraulic conductivity is much higher, the water flows more easily, and consolidation occurs much more rapidly.

Engineers have traditionally described the consolidation process using the relationship between the void ratio, e, and the effective stress, σ_v', as shown in the semi-logarithmic plot in Fig. 7.2. Each soil has a unique plot. With it, we can determine the change in void ratio, e, that will occur as a result of a certain change in effective stress, $\Delta\sigma_v'$. This information then produces a prediction of the settlement that will occur in the field.

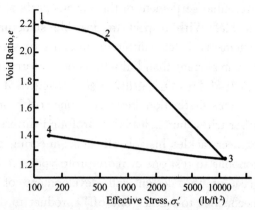

Fig. 7.2 Typical void ratio vs. effective stress plot. The soil is gradually loaded from point 1 to point 3, then unloaded back to point 4.

An alternate method of expressing the consolidation characteristics of a soil is a strain vs. effective stress plot. It has the same shape as Fig. 7.2, but is simpler to produce from the laboratory test data and it simplifies the settlement computations. Many also find it easier to visualize the consolidation process by thinking in terms of strain instead of changes in void ratio.

Note how the use of a semi-log plot produces a stress-strain curve that can be idealized as a series of straight lines.

Engineers develop the e-log$\Delta\sigma_v'$ or ε_v-log$\Delta\sigma_v'$ curve for a particular soil by conducting a laboratory consolidation test.

科技英语阅读与写作指南

科技英语阅读——文章的理解（3）

段落主题句因推理方式的不同可出现在段首、段尾和段中，用以扩展主题的段落细节句（引导句、扩展句）的组织方式也会因推理方式的不同而灵活多变。就科技英语文章而言，大多以举例与归纳(Illustration and Induction)、定义说明(Definition)、类比与对比(Analogy and Contrast)、原因与结果(Cause and Effect)、分类(Classification)等方式扩展主题。

1. 举例与归纳：通过例证展开段落可以使主题句的抽象意义具体化。

The idea of using the bridge not only for traffic but also for buildings is not new. <u>The Old London Bridge and the Ponte Veddhio in Florence are famous examples, where shops, housing, etc. were / are an integral part of the bridge.</u> Present technology makes it possible that a bridge need not support the building, but, instead, that one beam building constitutes the bridge.

2. 定义说明：通过下定义解释某些抽象、含混或有争议的概念

The substructure, or foundation, is that part of a structure which is usually placed below the surface of the ground and which transmits the load to the underlying soil or rock. All soils compress noticeably when loaded and cause the supported structure to settle. The two essential requirements in the design of foundations are that the total settlement of the structure shall be limited to a tolerably small amount and that differential settlement of the various parts of the structure shall be eliminated as nearly as possible. With respect to possible structural damage, the elimination of differential settlement, i. e., different amounts of settlement within the same structure, is even more important than limitations on uniform overall settlement.

3. 类比与对比：通过指出两事物的异同来阐明具体问题

This distinction between "one-off" production and mass production may sound rather trite, but it leads to profound differences in attitude and in the way the design engineer tackles his job. If an engineering product is to be mass-produced, then it is economic to test one or more prototypes; in fact, prototype testing becomes an essential phase of the design and development of the product. By contrast, it is clearly uneconomic to test a "one-off" product to destruction although its performance may be examined by proof tests.

4. 原因与结果：用于说明事物之间内在的因果关系，以探究事物的原因与结果。

The idea of using cables to support bridge spans is by no means new, and a number of examples of this type of construction were recorded a long time ago. Unfortunately, the system in general met with little success, due to the fact that the statics were not fully understood and that unsuitable materials such as bars and chains were used to form the inclined supports or stays. Stays made in this manner could not be fully tensioned and in a slack condition allowed large deformations of the deck before they could participate in taking the tensile loads for which they were intended.

5. 分类：将被说明对象按照某种标准分成若干个部分，分别加以说明。

The requirement of tolerable settlements is concerned with total and differential settlements of all foundations under the planned structure. The differential settlements must be limited in order not to cause structural distress or excessive tilting of the superstructure and they are also often limited by the serviceability requirements of the superstructure; for example, crane tracks and many machines have limits of tolerable tilt. The total settlements must be limited because they invariably induce differential settlements, even in apparently homogeneous soil conditions. They are also often limited by considerations of such factors as access to adjacent buildings, water and sewage connections, etc.

LESSON 8

Structural Steel Behaviour

Mechanical Properties under Static Load

The important mechanical properties of most structural steels under static load are indicated in the idealized tensile stress-strain diagram shown in Fig. 8.1. Initially the steel has a linear stress-strain curve whose slope is the Young's modulus of elasticity. The values of E vary in the range 200000~210000MPa, and the approximate value of 200000MPa is often assumed. The steel remains elastic while in this linear range, and recovers perfectly on unloading. The limit of the linear elastic behaviour is often closely approximated by the yield stress F_y, and the corresponding yield strain $\varepsilon_y = F_y/E$. Beyond this limit the steel flows plastically without any increase in stress until the strain-hardening strain ε_{st} is reached. This plastic range is usually considerable, and accounts for the ductility of the steel. The stress increases above the yield stress F_y when the strain-hardening strain ε_{st} is exceeded, and this continues until the ultimate tensile stress F_u is reached. After this, large local reductions in the cross-section occur, and the load capacity decreases until tensile fracture takes place.

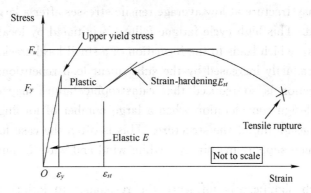

Fig. 8.1 Idealized Stress-strain relation for structural steel.

The yield stress F_y is perhaps the most important strength characteristic of a structural steel. This varies significantly with the chemical constituents of the steel, the most important of which are carbon and manganese, both of which increase the yield stress. The yield stress varies with the heat treatment used and with the amount of working which occurs during the rolling process. Thus thinner plates which are more worked have higher yield stresses than thicker plates of the same constituency. The yield stress is also increased by cold working. The rate of straining affects the yield stress, and high rates of strain increase the upper or first yield stress, as well as the lower yield stress F_y. The strain rates used in tests to determine the yield stress of a particular steel type are significantly higher than the nearly static rate often encountered in actual structures.

For design purposes, a 'minimum' yield stress is identified for each different steel classification. In Australia and England, these classifications are made on the basis of the chemical composition and the heat treatment, and so the yield stresses in each classification decrease as the greatest thickness of the rolled section or plate increases. On the other hand, American practice is to vary the composition and heat treatment within each classification, and the quoted yield stress do not vary with thickness. The 'minimum' yield stress of a particular steel is determined from the results of a number of standard tension tests. There is a significant scatter in these results because of small variations in the local composition, heat treatment, amount of working, thickness and rate of testing, and this scatter closely follows a normal distribution curve. [1]Because of this, the 'minimum' yield stress F_y quoted for a particular steel and used in design is usually a characteristic value which has a particular chance (often 95%) of being exceeded in any standard tension test. Consequently, it is likely that an isolated test result will be significantly higher than the quoted yield stress. [2] This difference will, of course, be accentuated if the test is made for any but the thickest portion of the cross-section.

The yield stress F_y determined for uniaxial tension is usually accepted as being valid for uniaxial compression.

Fatigue Failure under Repeated Loads

Structural steel may fracture at low average tensile stresses after a large number of cycles of fluctuating load. This high-cycle fatigue failure is initiated by local damage caused by the repeated loads, which leads to the formation of a small local crack. The extent of the fatigue crack is gradually increased by the subsequent load repetitions, until finally the effective cross-section is so reduced that catastrophic failure may occur. High-cycle fatigue is only a design consideration when a large number of loading cycles is likely to occur during the design life of the structure. This is often the case for bridges, cranes, and structures which support machinery, while wind and wave loading may also lead to fatigue problems.

Factors which significantly influence the resistance to fatigue failure include the number of load cycles, the range of stress during a load cycle, and the magnitudes of local stress concentrations.

It is generally accepted for design purposes that the fatigue life N varies with the stress range

$$f_r = f_{max} - f_{min}$$

according to equations of the type

$$N = K f_r^{-m}$$

in which the constant K depends on the details of the fatigue site, and the constant m may increase with the number of cycles N.

Fatigue failure under variable amplitude stress cycles is assessed using Miner's rule

$$\Sigma N_i/N_{im} \leqslant 1$$

in which N_i is the number of cycles of a particular stress range f'_{ri} and N_{im} is the constant amplitude fatigue life for that stress range.

Designing against fatigue involves a consideration of joint arrangement as well as of permissible stress. [3] Joints should generally be arranged so as to minimize stress concentrations and to produce as smooth a 'stress flow' through the joint as is practicable. Weld details should also be determined with this in mind, and unnecessary 'stress-raisers' should be avoided. It will also be advantageous to restrict, where practicable, the locations of joints to low stress regions such as at points of contraflexure or near the neutral axis.

Brittle Fracture under Impact Load

Structural steel does not always exhibit a ductile behaviour, and under some circumstances sudden and catastrophic fracture may occur, even though the nominal tensile stresses are low. Brittle fracture is initiated by the existence or formation of a small crack in a region of high local stress. Once initiated, the crack may propagate in a ductile (or stable) fashion for which the external forces must supply the energy required to tear the steel. More serious are cracks which propagate at high speed in a brittle (or unstable) fashion, for which some of the internal elastic strain energy stored in steel is released and used to fracture the steel. [4] Such a crack is self-propagating while there is sufficient internal strain energy, and will continue until arrested by ductile elements in its path which have sufficient deformation capacity to absorb the internal energy released.

The resistance of a structure to brittle fracture depends on the magnitude of local stress concentrations, on the ductility of the steel, and on the three-dimensional geometrical constraints. High local stresses facilitate crack initiation, and so stress concentrations due to poor geometry and loading arrangements (including impact loading) are dangerous. Also of great importance are flaws and defects in the material, which not only increase the local stresses, but also provide potential sites for crack initiation.

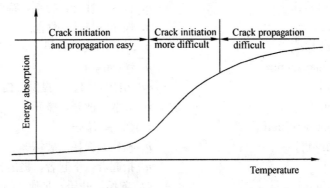

Fig. 8.2　Fffect of temperature on resistance to brittle fracture.

The ductility of a structural steel depends on its composition, heat treatment, and thickness, and varies with temperature and strain rate. Fig. 8.2 shows the increase with temperature of the capacity of the steel to absorb energy during impact. At low temperatures the energy absorption is low and initiation and propagation of brittle fractures are comparatively easy, while at high temperatures the energy absorption is high because of ductile yielding, and propagating cracks can be arrested. Between these two extremes is a transitional range in which crack initiation becomes increasingly difficult. The likelihood of brittle fracture is also increased by high strain rates due to dynamic loading, since the consequent increase in the yield stress reduces the possibility of energy absorption by ductile yielding. The chemical composition of a steel has a marked influence on its ductility: brittleness is increased by the presence of excessive amounts of most non-metallic elements, while ductility is increased by the presence of some metallic elements. A steel with large grain size tends to be more brittle, and this is significantly influenced by heat treatment of steel, and by its thickness (the grain size tends to be larger in thicker sections).

Three-dimensional geometrical constraints, such as those occurring in thicker or more massive elements, also encourage brittleness, because of the higher local stresses, and because of the greater release of energy during cracking and consequent increase in the ease of propagation of the crack.

The risk of brittle fracture can be reduced by selecting steel types which have ductilities appropriate to the service temperatures, and by designing joints with a view to minimizing stress concentrations and geometrical constraints. Fabrication techniques should be such as will avoid introducing potentially dangerous flaws or defects. Critical details in important structures may be subjected to inspection procedures aimed at detecting significant flaws. Of course, the designer must give proper consideration to the extra cost of special steels, fabrication techniques, and inspection and correction procedures.

New Words

1. behaviour [biˈheivjə]　　　　　　 n. 行为，性能，特点，特性
2. property [ˈprɔpəti]　　　　　　　 n. 性质，特性，性能
3. fracture [ˈfræktʃə]　　　　　　　 n.；v. 断裂，破裂
4. manganese [ˈmæŋɡəˈniːz]　　　　 n. 锰(元素)
5. quote [kwəut]　　　　　　　　　 vt. 引用，引证，提供，提出
6. scatter [ˈskætə]　　　　　　　　 v. 分散，散开，撒开
7. accentuate [ækˈsentjueit]　　　　 v. 强调，增强
8. damage [ˈdæmidʒ]　　　　　　　 n. 损伤，损耗，破坏
9. raiser [ˈreizə]　　　　　　　　　 n. 抬起者，举起者，提出者
10. initiate [iˈniʃieit]　　　　　　　 vt. 起始，开始，足使
11. arrest [əˈrest]　　　　　　　　　vt. 阻止，抑制，中断
12. flaw [flɔː]　　　　　　　　　　 n. 缺陷，裂纹，瑕疵

LESSON 8

13. defect [diˈfekt]　　　　　　　　　　　　*n.* 缺点，缺陷，毛病
14. transitional [trænˈsiʒənəl]　　　　　　　*a.* 过渡的，不稳定的

Phrases and Expressions

1. mechanical property　　力学性能，机械性能
2. Young's modulus of elasticity　　杨氏弹性模量
3. account for　　是(造成…的)原因，说明(原因，用途)
4. heat treatment　　热处理
5. cold working　　冷作，冷加工
6. standard tension test　　标准拉伸试验
7. normal distribution curve　　正态分布曲线
8. fluctuating load　　交变荷载，脉动荷载
9. high-cycle fatigue　　高周疲劳
10. stress range　　应力幅(范围)
11. fatigue life　　疲劳寿命

Notes

[1] Because of this, the 'minimum' yield stress F_y quoted for a particular steel and used in design is usually a characteristic value which … test. quoted for a particular steel 和 used in design 修饰 yield stress F_y. 全句可译为：因此，对某一种钢材引用的、设计中使用的最小屈服应力 F_y 通常是一个在任一标准拉伸试验中有一定超越机率(常为 95%)的标准值。

[2] This difference will, of course,… but the thickest portion of the cross-section. but 为介词，意为"除了…以外"。全句可译为：当然，如果对横截面除最厚部分以外的任意部分做试验，这种差异会增大。

[3] Joints should generally be arranged so as to minimize… as is practicable. so as to… and to… 为目的状语；as is practicable 省略了主语 a 'stress flow' through the joint。全句可译为：节点应当布置得使应力集中减少到最小，以使通过节点的'应力流'尽可能平滑。

[4] Such a crack is self-propagating…, and will continue until arrested by ductile elements in its path which… to absorb the internal energy released. until 引导时间状语从句，省去了 the crack is；which 引导定语从句修饰 ductile elements。全句可译为：只要有足够的内应变能，这种裂纹是自扩展的并且将延伸至被扩展路径中的延性元件止裂。这种延性元件具有足够的变形能力吸收释放的内能。

Exercises

1. Fill in the blanks with proper words.

　　(1) Initially the steel has a linear stress-strain curve whose _____ is the Young's

79

modulus of elasticity.

(2) The plastic range is usually considerable, and accounts _____ the ductility of the steel.

(3) The 'minimum' yield stress of a particular steel is _____ the results of a number of standard tension tests.

(4) The high-cycle fatigue failure is initiated by _____ by the repeated loads, which leads to the formation of a small local crack.

(5) It is generally accepted for design purposes _____ the fatigue life N varies with the stress range f_r according to equation $N = K f_r^{-m}$.

(6) Between these two extremes is a transitional range _____ crack initiation becomes increasingly difficult.

(7) A steel with large grain size tends to be more brittle, and this is significantly influenced _____ heat treatment of steel, and _____ its thickness.

(8) Three-dimensional geometrical constraints also encourage brittleness, _____ the higher local stresses, and _____ the greater release of energy during cracking and consequent increase in the ease of propagation of the crack.

(9) Critical details in important structures may be subjected to inspection procedures _____ detecting significant flaws.

(10) The ductility of a structural steel _____ its composition, heat treatment, and thickness, and _____ temperature and strain rate.

2. Translate the following phrases into English/Chinese.

(1) chemical composition (6) 应力—应变曲线
(2) cold working (7) 拉伸断裂
(3) normal distribution curve (8) 热处理
(4) local damage (9) 反复荷载
(5) brittle fracture (10) 变幅应力循环

3. Translate the following sentences into Chinese.

(1) The important mechanical properties of most structural steels under static load are indicated in the idealized tensile stress-strain diagram shown in Fig. 8.1.

(2) The values of E vary in the range 200000~210000MPa, and the approximate value of 200000MPa is often assumed.

(3) Beyond this limit the steel flows plastically without any increase in stress until the strain-hardening strain ε_{st} is reached.

(4) The rate of straining affects the yield stress, and high rates of strain increase the upper or first yield stress, as well as the lower yield stress F_y.

(5) For design purposes, a 'minimum' yield stress is identified for each different steel classification.

(6) Consequently, it is likely that an isolated test result will be significantly higher than the quoted yield stress.

(7) Perhaps the most generally accepted theory of two-dimensional yielding under biaxial stresses is the maximum distortion energy theory.

(8) Joints should generally be arranged so as to minimize stress concentrations and to produce as smooth a 'stress flow' through the joint as is practicable.

(9) Brittle fracture is initiated by the existence or formation of a small crack in a region of high local stress.

(10) High local stresses facilitate crack initiation, and so stress concentrations due to poor geometry and loading arrangements (including impact loading) are dangerous.

4. Fill in the blanks with the given words below.

by, for, in, in, in, in, though, under, until, which

Structural steel does not always exhibit a ductile behaviour, and _____ some circumstances sudden and catastrophic fracture may occur, even _____ the nominal tensile stresses are low. Brittle fracture is initiated _____ the existence or formation of a small crack _____ a region of high local stress. Once initiated, the crack may propagate _____ a ductile (or stable) fashion _____ which the external forces must supply the energy required to tear the steel. More serious are cracks _____ propagate at hight speed _____ a brittle (or unstable) fashion, for which some of the internal elastic strain energy stored _____ steel is released and used to fracture the steel. Such a crack is self-propagating while there is sufficient internal strain energy, and will continue _____ arrested by ductile elements in its path.

5. Translate the following sentences into English.

(1) 通常认为单向拉伸确定的屈服应力 F_y 对单向压缩也正确。

(2) 显著影响疲劳强度的因素有荷载循环次数、荷载循环中的应力幅以及局部应力集中的大小。

(3) 疲劳设计除考虑容许应力外还应考虑节点的布置。

(4) 结构钢不总是表现出延性特性，在有些情况下，即使名义拉应力很低，突然的、灾难性的断裂也会发生。

(5) 结构钢的延性取决于钢材的组成、热处理方法和钢材的厚度，并且随温度和应变率的变化而变化。

Reading Material

Advantages and Disadvantages of Structural Steel

Advantages of Steel as a Structural Material

A person traveling in the United States might quite understandably decide that steel was the perfect structural material. He or she would see an endless number of steel bridges, buildings, towers, and other structures. After seeing these numerous steel structures, this traveler might be surprised to learn that steel was not economically made in the United States until late in the nineteenth century, and the first wide-flange（宽翼缘）

beams were not rolled until 1908.

The assumption of the perfection of this metal, perhaps the most versatile of structural materials, would appear to be even more reasonable when its great strength, light weight, ease of fabrication, and many other desirable properties are considered. These and other advantages of structural steel are discussed in detail in the paragraphs that follow.

High Strength. Steel has high strength per unit weight. The weight of the steel constitutes a small part of the load that can be supported by a steel structure. It permits more volume or space in the structure because the structural members are relatively slender(细长的). This property is important in the design of structures such as tall buildings, long-span bridges, and airplane hangars(飞机库).

Uniformity(材质均匀). Because of the control exercised by the steel manufacturers, both the properties of steel and uniformity of structural shapes can be assured. This eliminates the need to overdesign a member because of uncertainty about the steel.

Elasticity. Steel behaves closer to design assumptions than most materials because it follows Hooke's law up to fairly high stresses. The moments of inertia of a steel structure can be accurately calculated, while the values obtained for a reinforced-concrete structure are rather indefinite.

Permanence(耐久性). Steel frames that are properly maintained will last indefinitely. Research on some of the newer steels indicates that under certain conditions no painting maintenance whatsoever will be required.

Ductility(延性). The property of a material by which it can withstand extensive deformation without failure under high tensile stresses is said to be its ductility. When a mild or low-carbon structural steel member is being tested in tension, a considerable reduction in cross section and a large amount of elongation will occur at the point of failure before the actual fracture occurs. A material that does not have this property is generally unacceptable and is probably hard and brittle, and it might break if subjected to a sudden shock.

In structural members under normal loads, high stress concentrations develop at various points. The ductile nature of the usual structural steels enables them to yield locally at those points, thus preventing premature failures. A further advantage of ductile structures is that when overloaded their large deflections give visible evidence of impending(即将发生的)failure.

Toughness(韧性). Structural steels are tough—that is, they have both strength and ductility. A steel member loaded until it has large deformations will still be able to withstand large forces. This is a very important characteristic because it means that steel members can be subjected to large deformations during fabrication and erection without fracture—thus allowing them to be bent, hammered, sheared, and have holes punched(冲孔) in them without visible damage. The ability of a material to absorb energy in large amounts is called toughness.

Additions to Existing Structures. Steel structures are quite well suited to having additions made to them. New bays or even entire new wings can be added to existing steel frame buildings, and steel bridges may, often be widened.

Miscellaneous(其他)　Several other important advantages of structural steel are as follows: (a) ability to be fastened together by several simple connection devices including welds and bolts, (b) adaptation to prefabrication, (c) speed of erection, (d) ability to be rolled into a wide variety of sizes and shapes as described before, (e) fatigue strength, (f) possible reuse after a structure is disassembled, and (g) scrap value, even though not reusable in its existing form. Steel is the ultimate recyclable material.

Disadvantages of Steel as a Structural Material

In general, steel has the following disadvantages:

Maintenance Costs.　Most steels are susceptible to corrosion when freely exposed to air and water and therefore must be painted periodically. The use of weathering steels, however, in suitable applications tends to eliminate this cost.

Fireproofing Costs.　Although structural members are incombustible(不燃烧的), their strength is tremendously reduced at temperatures commonly reached in fires when the other materials in a building burn. Many disastrous fires have occurred in empty buildings where the only fuel for the fires was the buildings themselves. Furthermore, steel is an excellent heat conductor—nonfireproofed steel members may transmit enough heat from a burning section or compartment of a building to ignite(点燃)materials with which they are in contact in adjoining sections of the building. As a result, the steel frame of a building may have to be protected by materials with certain insulating characteristics, and the building may have to include a sprinkler(喷水装置)system if it is to meet the building code requirements of the locality in question.

Susceptibility to Buckling.　As the length and slenderness of a compression member is increased, its danger of buckling increases. For most structures the use of steel columns is very economical because of their high strength-to-weight ratios. Occasionally, however, some additional steel is needed to stiffen them so they will not buckle. This tends to reduce their economy.

Fatigue.　Another undesirable property of steel is that its strength may be reduced if it is subjected to a large number of stress reversals or even to a large number of variations of tensile stress. (Fatigue problems occur only when tension is involved.) The present practice is to reduce the estimated strengths of such members if it is anticipated that they will have more than a prescribed number of cycles of stress variation.

Brittle Fracture.　Under certain conditions steel may lose its ductility, and brittle fracture may occur at places of stress concentration. Fatigue type loadings and very low temperatures aggravate the situation.

科技英语阅读与写作指南

科技英语阅读——文章的理解(4)

任何文章都应是一些意义相关的句子通过一定连接手段合乎逻辑地组织起来的语义整体,

也就是说,要通过一些作为连接手段的逻辑、词汇、语法等纽带使整个文章在意义上具有连贯性。这些连句成篇的手段就是逻辑纽带、语法纽带和词汇纽带。了解这方面的知识对于科技英语文章的理解和表达会起着十分重要的作用。

1. 逻辑纽带:用表示各种逻辑意义的连接词说明文章前后是如何系统地连接。常见的连接词有表示时间关系的(first, then, next, soon, meanwhile 等)、表示因果关系的(so, thus, hence, consequently, so that, otherwise 等)、表示转折关系的(yet, but, however, nevertheless, in fact, on the contrary, rather 等)、表示递进关系的(and, and also, besides, furthermore, in addition, moreover, in other words, likewise, similarly 等)。

The inspection process is only as good as the quality of the inspectors. Employment of competent inspectors is only one aspect of assuring weld quality. **In addition**, good welding procedures and the use of qualified and certified welders contribute to an acceptable weld. The weld testing methods generally used for structures may be categorized as nondestructive and include visual, magnetic particle, radiographic, liquid penetrant, and ultrasonic methods.

In addition 在这里表示递进。

Once the beam span of reinforced concrete exceeds 70 to 90 feet, the dead weight of the beam becomes excessive, resulting in heavier members and, consequently, greater long-term deflection and cracking. **Thus**, for larger spans, prestressed concrete becomes mandatory since arches are expensive to construct and do not perform as well due to the severe long-term shrinkage and creep they undergo.

Thus 在这里表示上下文的因果关系。

2. 语法纽带:运用动词的时、体形式和照应手段实现上下文的连贯。动词的时、体形式标志时间概念、暗示作者论证思路的转变;照应标志词语与它所指对象之间的关系。照应分为人称照应(I, me, you, we, us, he, mine, your, ours, its 等)、指示照应(this, these, that, those, here, there, now, then 等)、比较照应(形容词、副词的比较级、比较事物异同的词语等)

In the first year or so of Web business, most of the action has revolved around efforts to tap the consumer market. More recently, as the Web proved to be more than a fashion, companies have started to buy and sell products and services with one another. Such business-to-business sales make sense because business people typically know what product they're looking for.

More recently 表示文章前后的时间照应。

Flexible structures must be prestressed so that <u>they</u> are stable. <u>This</u> can be done by air pressure as for pneumatic structures or by directly tensioning double curvature anticlastic surfaces as for tent structures.

本段 they 指代 flexible structures,而 this 指代 flexible structures must be prestressed so that they are stable。这样通过指示代词实现了上下文的连贯。

3. 词汇纽带:通过文章关键词的重复、同义词或近义词实现上下文的联系。

Structural steel may **fracture** at low average tensile stresses after a large number of cycles of **fluctuating load**. This high-cycle **fatigue failure** is initiated by local damage caused by the **repeated loads**, which leads to the formation of a small local **crack**. The extent of the **fatigue crack** is gradually increased by the subsequent **load repetitions**; until finally the effective cross-section is so reduced that *catastrophic failure* may occur. High-cycle *fatigue* is only a design consideration when **a large number of loading cycles** is likely to occur during the design life of the structure. This is often the case for bridges, cranes, and structures which support machinery, while wind and wave loading may also lead to *fatigue* problems.

上文通过重复关键词、近义词的相互参照实现了上下文语义的联系。

Earth Pressures

Stability Conditions of Gravity Walls

[1] In the design of retaining walls a number of possible modes of failure must be considered that are either ultimate or serviceability limit states; calculations must show that adequate provision is made against the occurrence of adverse limit states pertaining to a particular type of wall. For the purpose of checking external stability, a gravity wall is treated as a rigid monolith (i.e. no internal yielding or distortion). In some types of construction checks are also required on internal stability, e.g. reinforced concrete walls, reinforced earth walls. Gravity walls depend essentially upon their own weight for external stability and the following limit states should be examined:

(a) Overturning　　　　　　　　　　　[recommended factor safety=2.0]
(b) Forward sliding　　　　　　　　　　[recommended factor safety=2.0]
(c) Bearing pressure failure under base　[recommended factor safety=3.0]
(d) Occurrence of tension in lateral joints, e.g. masonry/brickwork walls
(e) Overall slip failure, e.g. under sloping ground surface

The use of a factor of safety as indicated above is the traditional approach to design. The limit state approach recommended in BS 8002: 1994 requires the application of a *mobilization factor* (M) to the representative strength value in order to obtain a design value, e.g. design c_u = representative c_u/M. The value for M used against undrained strength should not be less than 1.5 if the wall displacements are required to be less than 0.5 per cent of the wall height, for bearing capacity calculations M should be in the range 2.0~3.0; for effective stress parameters M should not be less than 1.2. Structural forces and moments should be determined using design earth pressures and water pressures.

For convenience, the forces acting on a retaining wall are calculated in terms of vertical and horizontal components. Vertical forces include the weight of the wall and any vertical loads it may have to carry, together with the weight of soil over the heel of L-shaped and T-shaped walls. There may also be a vertical component of the earth pressure resultant when the support face is not vertical, the ground surface is sloping or where wall friction is included. Horizontal forces will include the resultants of earth pressure distributions and any horizontal loads. Earth pressure resultants must include (where appropriate) the effects of surface surcharge loads, compaction pressures and any horizontal loads.

LESSON 9

Earth Pressure of Walls

In foundation construction, three types of earth pressure are commonly encountered:

Active earth pressure. This exerts horizontal and vertical load components against any structure that impedes the tendency of the earth to fall, slide, or creep into its natural state of equilibrium but yields slightly under the pressure.

Passive earth pressure. This pressure is mobilized when a structure tends to compress the earth.

At-rest pressure. This is a horizontal pressure exerted by soil against a non-yielding vertical surface.

Each of these pressures is dependent on many of the physical properties of the soil, as well as the relative rigidity of the soil and structure. The most important properties of the soil appear to be density, angle of internal friction in sands, and cohesion and over consolidation ratio in clays.

Active Earth Pressure. [2] The horizontal component of active earth pressure for any material acting against an ordinary wall is closely given by the general wedge theory for the case of a vertical and fill with a substantially horizontal top surface. This wall is assumed to be backfilled by usual construction methods and capable of a small rotational movement (of the magnitude of 0.001 its height), to mobilize the internal friction of the backfill. This rotation is equivalent to an outward movement of 1/4 in at the top of a 20-ft wall under earth pressure.

The horizontal component of lateral pressure, p_a, kPa, at depth h is given for vertical walls and horizontal fills by

$$p_a = \gamma h K_a - 2c\sqrt{K_a} \tag{9.1}$$

where γ = average unit weight, kN/m³, of the soil
h = depth, m
c = cohesion of the soil, kPa
$K_a = \tan^2(45° - \phi/2)$
ϕ = angle of internal friction, deg.

The general wedge-theory formulas (taking into account friction along the surface of a wall) may also be used for evaluation of the horizontal component for all other conditions of wall and sloping fills. However, comparison with experimental results indicates that the results are somewhat too small for negative surcharges and somewhat too large for positive surcharges, but the differences are no greater than 10%. It is quite accurate enough, taking into account the uncertainties of conditions as to actual slope, referred to as the simplified case of vertical wall and horizontal fill.

The vertical component of lateral pressure, in all cases, is such that the resultant pressure forms an angle with the normal to the back of the wall equal to the angle of wall friction. However, under no condition can this angle exceed the angle of internal friction of the fill.

The pressure of soils that, because of lack of drainage and because of their nature, may become fluid at any time—whether such fluid material is widespread or only a narrow layer against the wall—is the same as hydrostatic pressure of a liquid having the same density as that soil.

The pressure of submerged soils is given by Eq. 9.1 with the weight of material reduced by buoyancy and the coefficient of internal friction evaluated for the submerged condition; in addition, full hydrostatic pressure of water must be included. For granular materials, submergence affects the coefficients of internal and wall friction very little.

The pressure of fills during saturation and prior to complete submergence and the pressure during drainage periods are affected by the rapidity of water movement. Drainage produces a slight temporary decrease in pressure from normal. Submergence produces an expansion of the fill with consequent increase in pressure. Such variations will not occur if adequate provision is made for drainage; if such provision is not made, the soil may become submerged and the pressure should be computed as for a submerged soil.

Surface loading increases the lateral pressure on the wall. For a uniform surcharge, the lateral pressure on the wall is increased by the surcharge pressure multiplied by the appropriate earth-pressure coefficient.

Passive Earth Pressure. The horizontal component p_p, kPa, of passive pressure at depth h may be computed from

$$p_p = \gamma h K_p + 2c\sqrt{K_p} \tag{9.2}$$

where γ = average unit weight, kN/m³, of the soil

h = depth, m

$K_p = \tan^2(45° + \phi/2)$

c = cohesion of the soil, kPa

ϕ = angle of internal friction, deg

At-Rest Pressure. Such pressures represent an intermediate case between the limiting cases of active and passive pressures. Pressures at rest are calculated as for active or passive conditions from Eq. 9.1 or 9.2, except that the coefficient K_0 is employed.

$$K_0 = 1 - \sin\phi \tag{9.3}$$

for cohesionless soils and

$$K_0 = 0.95 - \sin\phi \tag{9.4}$$

For clays, K_0 will increase with overconsolidation ration (OCR), the ratio of preconsolidation pressure to overburden pressure, and may approach a value of 3 for very high values of OCR.

New Words

1. surcharge [səːˈtʃɑːdʒ]　　　　　　　　n. 超载，附加载荷
2. monolith [ˈmɔnəuliθ]　　　　　　　　n. 独块巨石，单成岩
3. overturn [ˌəuvəˈtəːn]　　　　　　　　n. 倾覆；vt. 推翻
4. backfill [ˈbækfil]　　　　　　　　　vt. n. 装填，回填
5. buoyancy [ˈbɔiənsi]　　　　　　　　n. 浮力

6. granular ['grænjulə]　　　　　　　　　*a.* 粒状的
7. provision [prə'viʒən]　　　　　　　　*n.* 预备，供应，规定
8. joint [dʒɔint]　　　　　　　　　　　　*n.* 接缝；*a.* 连接的；*vt.* 连接，
9. impede [im'pi:d]　　　　　　　　　　*v.* 阻止
10. submerged [səb'mə:dʒd]　　　　　　*a.* 在水中的，淹没的

Phrases and Expressions

1. retaining wall　挡土墙
2. ultimate limit state　极限状态
3. serviceability limit state　正常使用极限状态
4. active earth pressures　主动土压力
5. at-rest earth pressures　静止土压力
6. passive earth pressure　被动土压力
7. gravity wall　重力式挡墙
8. surcharge load　超载
9. over consolidation ratio(OCR)　超固结比(OCR)
10. wedge theory　土压力楔体理论

Notes

[1] In the design... a number of possible modes of failure must be considered that are... limit states;... show that adequate provision is made... a particular type of wall. that 引导的定语从句修饰 a number of possible modes of failure。全句可译为：设计挡土墙时，必须考虑极限状态或正常使用极限状态的许多可能的破坏模式，计算应表明有足够的储备防范某一类挡土墙不利极限状态的出现。

[2] The horizontal component of active earth pressure... is closely given by the general wedge theory... surface. 全句可译为：就任意土体材料来说，作用在常见挡土墙上的主动土压力水平分量可由针对墙背竖直、填土面基本水平的一般楔体理论很好地给出。

Excises

1. Fill in the blanks with proper words.

(1) If a wall structure is caused to move _____ the soil being supported，the horizontal pressures in the soil will increase；these are then referred to as passive pressures.

(2) If the wall moves _____ from the supported soil, the horizontal soil pressures decrease and are referred to then as active pressures.

(3) Gravity walls depend largely upon their own _____ for stability，have wide bases and usually a rigid construction.

(4) In-situ walls differ from gravity walls in that they rely primarily on their

_____ strength, not their mass.

(5) In the design of retaining walls a number of possible modes of failure must be considered that are either ultimate or _____ limit states.

(6) Each of these pressures is dependent on many of the physical properties of the soil, as well as the relative rigidity of the _____ and structure.

(7) In the analysis and design of earth-retaining structures of all types it is necessary first to establish the distribution of vertical and horizontal _____ pressures acting on the structure.

(8) Externally stabilized systems are those that resist the applied earth loads by virtue of their weight and _____.

(9) Surface loading _____ the lateral pressure on the wall.

(10) For a uniform surcharge, the lateral pressure on the wall is increased by the surcharge pressure multiplied by the appropriate earth-pressure _____.

2. Translate the following phrases into Chinese/English

(1) gravity wall
(2) uniform surcharge
(3) reinforced concrete cantilever walls
(4) temporary structures
(5) 破坏模式
(6) 静止土压力
(7) 挡土结构
(8) 土压力楔体理论

3. Translate the following sentences into Chinese

(1) If the wall structure is rigid and does not yield, the horizontal soil pressures are said to be at-rest pressures.

(2) In stability analyses, both the nature of the wall structure and that of supported material are important, as too is the way the wall may move or yield after construction.

(3) In the design of retaining walls a number of possible modes of failure must be considered that are either ultimate or serviceability limit states; calculations must show that adequate provision is made against the occurrence of adverse limit states pertaining to a particular type of wall.

(4) O'Rourke and Jones classified earth retaining structures into broad categories: externally stabilized systems and internally stabilized systems.

(5) Active earth pressure exerts horizontal and vertical load components against any structure that impedes the tendency of the earth to fall, slide, or creep into its natural state of equilibrium but yields slightly under the pressure.

(6) Anchored or tied-back walls are used for a wide range of applications in different soils, for heights up to 20m.

(7) Each of these pressures is dependent on many of the physical properties of the soil, the relative rigidity of the soil and structure.

(8) For a uniform surcharge, the lateral pressure on the wall is increased by the surcharge pressure multiplied by the appropriate earth-pressure coefficient.

4. Fill in the blanks with the given words below.

also, any, for, of, of, on, over, together, where

_____ convenience, the forces acting _____ a retaining wall are calculated in terms _____ vertical and horizontal components. Vertical forces include the weight of the wall and any vertical loads it may have to carry, _____ with the weight of soil _____ the heel of L-shaped and T-shaped walls. There may _____ be a vertical component of the earth pressure resultant when the support face is not vertical, the ground surface is sloping or _____ wall friction is included. Horizontal forces will include the resultants of earth pressure distributions and _____ horizontal loads. Earth pressure resultants must include (where appropriate) the effects _____ surface surcharge loads, compaction pressures and any horizontal loads.

5. Translate the following sentences into English
   (1) 当挡土结构挤压墙后土体时，产生被动土压力。
   (2) 土最重要的性质有密度、砂土的内摩擦角、黏性土的黏聚力和超固结比。
   (3) 静止土压力表示介于主动和被动两种极限状态之间的情况。
   (4) 上述应用安全系数的方法是一种传统的设计方法。
   (5) 土压力合力必须包括地表超载、夯实压力和水平荷载的作用。

Reading Material

Piled Foundations

There is a large variety of types of pile used for foundation work. The choice depends on the environmental and ground conditions, the presence or absence of groundwater, the function of the pile, i.e. whether compression, uplift or lateral loads are to be carried, the desired speed of construction and consideration of relative cost. The ability of the pile to resist aggressive substances or organisms in the ground or in surrounding water must also be considered.

In BS(British Standard 英国标准)8004, piles are grouped into three categories:

(1) *Large displacement piles*(大量排土桩): these include all solid piles, including timber and precast concrete and steel or concrete tubes closed at the lower end by a shoe or plug, which may be either left in place or extruded to form an enlarged foot.

(2) *Small displacement piles*(少量排土桩): these include rolled-steel sections, open-ended tubes and hollow sections if the ground enters freely during driving.

(3) *Replacement piles*(钻孔灌注桩): these are formed by boring or other methods of excavation; the borehole may be lined with a casing or tube that is either left in place or extracted as the hole is filled.

Large or small displacement piles. In preformed sections these are suitable for open sites where large numbers of piles are required. They can be precast or fabricated by mass-production methods and driven at a fast rate by mobile rigs. They are suitable for soft and aggressive soil conditions when the whole material of the pile can be checked for soundness before being driven. Preformed piles(预制桩)are not damaged by the driving of adjacent piles, nor is their installation affected by groundwater.

They are normally selected for river and marine works where they can be driven through water and in sections suitable for resisting lateral and uplift loads. They can also be driven in very long lengths.

Displacement piles in preformed sections cannot be varied readily in length to suit the varying level of the bearing stratum(持力层), but certain types of precast concrete piles can be assembled from short sections jointed to form assemblies of variable length. In hard driving conditions preformed piles may break causing delays when the broken units are withdrawn or replacement piles driven. A worse feature is unseen damage particularly when driving slender units in long lengths which may be deflected from the correct alignment to the extent that the bending stresses cause fracture of the pile.

When solid pile sections are driven in large groups the resulting displacement of the ground may lift piles already driven from their seating on the bearing stratum, or may damage existing underground structures or services. Problems of ground heave can be overcome or partially overcome in some circumstances by redriving risen piles, or by inserting the piles in prebored holes. Small-displacement piles are advantageous for soil conditions giving rise to ground heave.

Displacement piles suffer a major disadvantage when used in urban areas where the noise and vibration caused by driving them can cause a nuisance to the public and damage to existing structures. Other disadvantages are the inability to drive them in very large diameters, and they cannot be used where the available headroom is insufficient to accommodate the driving rig.

Driven and cast-in-place piles. These are widely used in the displacement pile group. A tube closed at its lower end by a detachable shoe(活动垫座) or by a plug of gravel or dry concrete is driven to the desired penetration. Steel reinforcement is lowered down the tube and the latter is then withdrawn during or after placing injected at intervals into the space between the back of the tube and the latter is then withdrawn during or after placing the concrete. These types have the advantages that: (1) the length can be varied readily to suit variation in the level of the bearing stratum; (2) the closed end excludes groundwater; (3) an enlarged base(扩底) can be formed by hammering out the concrete placed at the toe; (4) the reinforcement is required only for the function of the pile as a foundation element, i.e. not from considerations of lifting and driving as for the precast concrete pile; and (5) the noise and vibration are not severe when the piles are driven by a drop hammer operating within the drive tube.

Driven and cast-in-place piles may not be suitable for very soft soil conditions where the newly placed concrete can be squeezed inwards as the drive tube is withdrawn causing 'necking'(颈缩现象) of the pile shaft(桩身), nor is the uncased shaft suitable for ground where water is encountered under artesian head which washes out the cement from the unset concrete(未凝结混凝土). These problems can be overcome by providing a permanent casing. Ground heave can damage adjacent piles before the concrete has hardened, and heaved piles cannot easily be redriven. However, this problem can be overcome either by preboring or by driving a number of tubes in a group in advance of placing the concrete.

The latter is delayed until pile driving has proceeded to a distance of at least 6.5 pile diameters from the one being concreted if small (up to 3mm) uplift is permitted, or 8 diameters away if negligible (less than 3mm) uplift must be achieved. The lengths of driven and cast-in-place piles are limited by the ability of the driving rigs to extract the drive tube and they cannot be installed in very large diameters. They are unsuitable for river or marine works unless specially adapted for extending them through water and cannot be driven in situations of low headroom.

Replacement piles or bored piles. These are formed by drilling a borehole to the desired depth, followed by placing a cage of steel reinforcement and then placing concrete. It may be necessary to support the borehole by steel tubing (or casing) which is driven down or allowed to sink under its own weight as the borehole is drilled. Normally the casing is filled completely with easily workable concrete before it is extracted, when the concrete slumps outwards to fill the void.

In stiff cohesive soils or weak rocks it is possible to use a rotary tool to form an enlarged base to the piles which greatly increases the end-bearing resistance. Alternatively, men can descend the shafts of large-diameter piles to form an enlarged base by hand excavation(人工开挖). Reasonably dry conditions are essential to enable the enlarged bases to be formed without risk of collapse.

Care is needed in placing concrete in bored piles. In very soft ground there is a tendency to squeeze of the unset concrete, and if water is met under artesian head it may wash out the cement from the unset concrete. If water cannot be excluded from the pile borehole by the casing, no attempt should be made to pump it out before placing concrete. In these circumstances the concrete should be placed under water by tremie pipe (混凝土导管). Breaks in the concrete shafts of bored piles may occur if the concrete is lifted when withdrawing the casing, or if soil falls into the space above the concrete due to premature withdrawal of the casing.

Bored piles have the advantages that their length can be readily altered to suit varying ground conditions, the soil or rock removed during boring can be inspected and if necessary subjected to tests, and very large shaft diameters are possible, with enlarged base diameters up to 6m. Bored piles can be drilled to any desired depth and in any soil or rock conditions. They can be installed without appreciable noise or vibration in conditions of low headroom and without risk of ground heave.

Bored piles are unsuitable for obtaining economical skin friction and end bearing values in granular soils because of loosening of these soils by drilling. However, stable conditions can be achieved if the pile borehole is supported during the drilling operation by a bentonite slurry(膨润土泥浆). Boring in soft or loose soils results in loss of ground which may cause excessive settlement of adjacent structures. They are also unsuitable for marine works.

科技英语阅读与写作指南

科技英语写作——文体要求

科技英语写作是指有目的地写各种体裁的应用文或撰写科技论文。科学性是科技英语文章与其他文体的根本区别。其科学性首先表现为科技英语文章的内容是科学研究的成果，是客观存在的自然现象及其规律的反映。科技英语文章的科学性还表现为表达形式的科学性。其结构是清晰而严谨的，符合思维的一般规律，逻辑思维周密，语言简炼明确客观，格式比较固定。科技英语写作的文体要求主要有准确（Accuracy）、简洁（Brevity）、清晰（Clarity）三个方面的内容。

1. 准确

科技英语写作中，表达概念、判断一定要清楚明白，准确精当，不含糊其词，模棱两可。

这就要求作者一定要正确地运用英语的语法和句型。

例：原句：This group of chemical substances do not dissolve in alcohol, only one of which dissolves in ethanol.（自相矛盾）

修改：This group of chemical substances do not dissolve in alcohol except that one of them can do in ethanol.

原句：Multiphase flow is a new and developing discipline on the basis of hydrodynamics, heat and mass transfer, physic-chemistry and other disciplines.（性质判断错误，multiphase flow 为自然现象）

修改：The study of multiphase flow is a new and developing discipline on the basis of hydrodynamics, heat and mass transfer, physic-chemistry and other disciplines.

原句：The mechanism appears very often during the recrystallization of metals.（概念不清）

修改：The mechanism often works in the recrystallization of metals.

2. 简洁

科技英语文章尤其强调文章的简洁。在不影响表达的前提下尽可能使用简洁的句子、词组，同时，还应避免赘言和不必要的重复。

例：原句：In our experiment, we used a number of probes. The reason for that was to eliminate the problems and errors associated with wet chemical analysis.

修改：In our experiment, we used a number of probes so as to eliminate the problems and errors associated with wet chemical analysis.

原句：The precision of the experiment was affected by the noise of the engine nearby.

修改：The experimental precision was affected by the nearby engine noise.

原句：The rate of nuclear reaction is controlled by insertion of the control rods or removal of the control rods.

修改：The rate of nuclear reaction is controlled by insertion or removal of the control rods.

原句：It may seem reasonable to suggest that necrotic effects may possibly be due to involvement of some toxin-like substances.

修改：It is suggested that necrotic effects may be due to some toxin-like substances.

3. 清晰

科技英语写作的内容通常包括研究的目的和范围、研究的方法和步骤、研究的结果和推论等。在表述这些内容时作者的思维就要有逻辑性，作者的语言表达就要有连贯性。

例：原句：In soil, organic acids can dissolve Zn, the decrease of redox potential can enhance the effect of Mn. （缺少连接词）

修改：In soil, organic acids can dissolve Zn, while the decrease of redox potential can enhance the effect of Mn.

原句：A microcomputerized measuring system is developed. An I-V characteristic curve can be automatically acquired in 5 second with an accuracy of 0.05%. （突然改变主体）

修改：A microcomputerized measuring system is developed which can automatically produce an I-V characteristic curve with an accuracy of 0.05%.

原句：The accuracy of the new device is greater than the conventional one. （比较对象不一致）

修改：The accuracy of the new device is greater than that of the conventional one.

原句：When selecting proper parameters and memory directions in the operation, some new methods can be obtained, and the rate of convergence of the methods may be increased. （省略不当引起逻辑错误）

修改：When proper parameters and memory directions in the operation are selected, some new methods can be obtained, and the rate of convergence of the methods may be increased.

Lesson 10

Reinforced Concrete Beams

Singly Reinforced Beams

In the subject of applied mechanics, the behaviour of homogeneous beams has been dealt with. The basic formulae for pure flexure have been established as follows:

$$\frac{M}{I}=\frac{f}{y}=\frac{E}{R} \qquad M=\frac{fI}{y}=fZ \qquad \frac{M}{EI}=\frac{1}{R}\simeq\frac{d^2y}{dx^2}$$

[1] Using the above formulae, the stresses across the section, curvature, slopes and deflections at any point in the beam can be found, provided the material is elastic, obeys Hooke's law and Bernoulli's plane section hypothesis, and the beam is homogeneous and isotropic. In the case of shallow beams made of steel, the above approximations are known to be valid.

In the case of concrete, which is strong in compression and relatively weak in tension, a plain concrete beam cracks in the tension zone and fails suddenly. To augment the strength of such plain concrete beams, it has become customary to embed steel reinforcement in the tension zone, and hence the emergence and utilization of Reinforced Cement Concrete. Since steel has 15 to 30 times more strength than concrete, steel reinforcement has also been used in compression zones to reduce the size of flexural members. Depending on the quantity of reinforcement A_s used in the beam, its behaviour can be controlled. In a beam of rectangular cross-section, if there is reinforcement in the tension zone only, it is called a singly reinforced beam. In the case of beams, which have restrictions on depth (often imposed by the architect), there is need for reinforcing the tension and also the compression zone. Such beams are designated as doubly reinforced beams. Beams of simple rectangular cross-section are not used as frequently as beams and slabs which are cast together. In this case, a part of the slab acts along with the rectangular rib or web. If the slab projection is on one side of the web, the cross-section resembles an inverted 'L' and if the slab projects on both sides of the web, the cross-section resembles a 'T' shape. These are generally known as ell and tee beams. Laboratory tests indicate that when such a reinforced concrete beam is subjected to pure flexure, and the applied moment is gradually increased, the beam will deflect, develop cracks, shift its neutral axis, develop yielding of reinforcement and eventually fail due to excessive compressive strain in the extreme fibers.

The aim of the designer of reinforced concrete beams is to predict this entire spectrum of behaviour in mathematical terms, identify the parameters which influence this behaviour, and obtain the cracking, deflection and collapse limit loads.

LESSON 10

Analysis and design are really complementary in nature. Provided the nature of loading, the beam dimensions, the materials used and the quantity of reinforcement are known, the theory of reinforced concrete permits the analysis of stresses, strains, deflections, crack spacing and width and also the collapse load. However, the usual problem is to design a section to satisfy limiting crack widths, deflections and load carrying capacity and there are usually innumerable answers to a design problem. It is usual to estimate a cross-section based on one of the limiting states and analyse the beam for the satisfaction of the other limit states. Thus design is followed by analysis and a final section is obtained by a process of iteration. The design process becomes clear only when the process of analysis is learnt thoroughly. In the following, the methods of analysis for flexure will be emphasized.

In a reinforced concrete beam, the following behavioural sequence can be traced:

(a) Under small loads, the strains across a cross-section are small, the neutral axis is at the centroid of the uncracked section, the stresses are linearly related to strains and the deflection is proportional to load as in the case of isotropic, homogeneous, linearly elastic beam elements. This stage (Phase Ⅰ) persists up to cracking of concrete in the tension zone;

(b) as the load is increased, extensive cracking develops at distinct intervals of a purely flexurally loaded beam, the reinforcement bars come into play, steel strain increases, the neutral axis shifts at the zones of cracking and deflections and rotations increase at a faster rate, but it is found from experiments that plane-sections remain plane and normal. This second stage (Phase Ⅱ) is the normally observed behaviour of a beam in its service state; but the cracks are so fine that they can be noticed only at very close quarters; and

(c) the third stage of loading (Phase Ⅲ) starts with the yielding of steel reinforcement, considerable shift in the neutral axis position, non-linear deflection increase, extensive cracking and finally, the crushing of concrete ($\varepsilon_{cu}=0.0035$), which leads to the ultimate collapse of the beam, without further increase in load.

If the beam is reinforced rather heavily (over-reinforced), the steel may not yield; in which case the concrete in compression may crush and spall. Such failures are usually sudden and catastrophic. Most codes of practice do not permit over-reinforced beams to be designed deliberately. The next step is to develop mathematical models for these three different phases.

All mathematical formulations are based on a proper set of assumptions. The assumptions made for analysing the flexural behaviour of reinforced concrete beams are as follows:

(a) Plane sections remain plane;

(b) stress-strain behaviour is as prescribed by appropriate curves;

(c) concrete in tension may be neglected;

(d) there is no bond-slip between steel and concrete, i.e. strains in the reinforcement and concrete at the same location are the same. Stress in steel is the modular ratio times that of concrete ($m = E_s/E_c$); and

(e) there are no initial stresses in steel when it is embedded in concrete.

Failure Modes of Reinforced Concrete Beams

When a reinforced concrete beam is loaded to failure, three modes of bending failure are possible. The particular mode of failure is determined by the percentage of steel located in the tension zone. Two of these modes are brittle and one is ductile. Since the designer's prime concern is to produce ductile beams with a high capacity for energy absorption, beams must be proportioned to ensure that only the ductile failure mode is possible.

Case 1 The beam is over-reinforced and the failure mode is a sudden, brittle failure, which the engineer must carefully guard against in design. When the over-reinforced beam is loaded to failure, the failure is initiated by the crushing of the concrete followed by the sudden disintegration of the compression zone while the stress in the relatively large area of steel has not reached its yield point. To prevent a brittle failure, the reinforcement must yield while the strain in the concrete is less than the failure strain of 0.0035.

Case 2 The beam has a moderate percentage of steel, and the failure mode is initiated by a yielding of the steel while the strains in the concrete are relatively low. Such beams can continue to carry load and are able to undergo large deflections before final collapse occurs; this ductile mode of failure is the only acceptable mode.

Case 3 The beam is lightly reinforced with a very small percentage of steel, and the failure mode is also brittle. When the tensile stress in the concrete exceeds the modulus of rupture (the tensile strength), the concrete cracks and immediately releases the tensile force it carries; the lightly stressed steel must then absorb this increment of load. If the area of steel provided is too small to carry this added force, the steel will snap and total rupture of the section will occur suddenly.

To ensure ductile failures, upper and lower limits on the permitted area of reinforcing steel are established by the ACI Code. The lower limit ensures that enough steel will be used to prevent the steel from snapping suddenly and causing the beam to split. The upper limit on steel area prevents the design of over-reinforced beams.

Since the presence of shear force has little influence on the moment capacity of a cross section, shear is not considered in the design of members for bending.

New words

(1) curvature ['kə:vətʃə]   *n.* 曲率
(2) slope [sləup]   *n.* 转角，倾角；*v.* (使)顺斜
(3) deflection [di'flekʃən]   *n.* 挠度，变位
(4) hypothesis [hai'pɔθisis]   *n.* 假设
(5) valid ['vælid]   *a.* 有效的，有根据的，正确的
(6) augment [ɔ:g'ment]   *v.* 增加，增大；*n.* 增加
(7) restriction [ris'trikʃən]   *n.* 限制，约束

(8) modular ['mɔdjulə]　　　　　　　*a.* 模的，模数的，系数的
(9) iteration [,itə'reiʃən]　　　　　　*n.* 反复
(10) shift [ʃift]　　　　　　　　　　*v.* 移动

Phrases and Expressions

(1) applied mechanics　　应用力学
(2) plane section hypothesis　　平截面假定
(3) plain concrete beam　　素混凝土梁
(4) singly reinforced beam　　单筋梁
(5) doubly reinforced beam　　双筋梁
(6) pure flexure　　纯弯曲
(7) neutral axis　　中和轴
(8) collapse limit loads　　极限破坏荷载
(9) modes of bending failure　　受弯破坏形态
(10) over-reinforced beam　　超筋梁

Notes

[1] Using the above formulae, the stresses... can be found, provided... isotropic. provided 为连词，引导条件状语从句。全句可译为：如果材料是弹性的、服从虎克定律和伯努利平截面假定，以及梁是均质的、各向同性的，那么应用以上公式可以求出梁任一截面的应力、转角，任一点的曲率和位移。

Exercises

1. Fill in the blanks with proper words

(1) In the case of concrete, _____ is strong in compression and relatively weak in tension, a plain concrete beam cracks in the tension zone and fails suddenly.

(2) Since steel has 15 to 30 times more strength _____ concrete, steel reinforcement has also been used in compression zones to reduce the size of flexural members.

(3) In a beam of rectangular cross-section, _____ there is reinforcement in the tension zone only, it is called a singly reinforced beam.

(4) Beams of simple rectangular cross-section are not used _____ frequently as beams and slabs which are cast together.

(5) If the slab projection is _____ one side of the web, the cross-section resembles an inverted 'L' and if the slab projects on both sides of the web, the cross-section resembles a 'T' shape.

(6) Under small loads, the strains across a cross-section are small, the neutral axis is _____ the centroid of the uncracked section.

(7) This second stage (Phase Ⅱ) is the normally observed behaviour of a beam in its service state; but the cracks are so fine _____ they can be noticed only at very close quarters.

(8) If the beam is reinforced rather heavily (over-reinforced), the steel may not yield; _____ which case the concrete in compression may crush and spall.

(9) Most codes of practice do not permit over-reinforced beams _____ be designed deliberately.

(10) The particular mode of failure is determined _____ the percentage of steel located in the tension zone.

2. Translate the following phrases into Chinese/English.

  (1) plane section hypothesis   (6) 未裂梁截面形心
  (2) doubly reinforced beam   (7) 单筋梁
  (3) pure flexure   (8) 钢筋与混凝土的粘结滑移
  (4) over-reinforced beam   (9) 极限破坏荷载
  (5) modes of bending failure   (10) 少筋梁

3. Translate the following sentences into Chinese

(1) Using the above formulae, the stresses across the section, curvature, slopes and deflections at any point in the beam can be found, provided the material is elastic, obeys Hooke's law and Bernoulli's plane section hypothesis, and the beam is homogeneous and isotropic.

(2) Laboratory tests indicate that when such a reinforced concrete beam is subjected to pure flexure, and the applied moment is gradually increased, the beam will deflect, develop cracks, shift its neutral axis, develop yielding of reinforcement and eventually fail due to excessive compressive strain in the extreme fibres.

(3) The aim of the designer of reinforced concrete beams is to predict this entire spectrum of behaviour in mathematical terms, identify the parameters which influence this behaviour, and obtain the cracking, deflection and collapse limit loads.

(4) It is usual to estimate a cross-section based on one of the limiting states and analyse the beam for the satisfaction of the other limit states.

(5) Thus design is followed by analysis and a final section is obtained by a process of iteration. The design process becomes clear only when the process of analysis is learnt thoroughly.

(6) Under small loads, the stresses are linearly related to strains and the deflection is proportional to load as in the case of isotropic, homogeneous, linearly elastic beam elements.

(7) All mathematical formulations are based on a proper set of assumptions

(8) There is no bond-slip between steel and concrete, i.e. strains in the reinforcement and concrete at the same location are the same.

(9) When a reinforced concrete beam is loaded to failure, three modes of bending failure are possible. The particular mode of failure is determined by the percentage of steel located in the tension zone.

LESSON 10

(10) Since the designer's prime concern is to produce ductile beams with a high capacity for energy absorption, beams must be proportioned to ensure that only the ductile failure mode is possible.

4. Translate the following sentences into English.

(1) 在矩形截面梁中，仅在受拉区配有钢筋的梁称为单筋梁；在受拉、受压区都配有钢筋的梁称为双筋梁。

(2) 加荷的第三阶段开始于钢筋屈服、中和轴位置较大的上移、非线性变形增大、裂缝延伸，最后混凝土压碎，导致梁最终破坏。

(3) 当梁的配筋过多，破坏模式是突然的、脆性的破坏，这是工程师在设计中必须小心防止的破坏模式。

(4) 当梁配筋适中，破坏模式由钢筋屈服引起而混凝土中的应变较低；这种梁在最终倒塌前还能继续承担荷载，且能经受较大的变形。

(5) 为了保证延性破坏，规范规定了容许钢筋面积的上限和下限。下限保证配有足够的钢筋以防止钢筋拉断引起梁的折断，上限避免设计成超筋梁。

5. Fill in the blanks with the given words below.

by, for, if, in, on, since, than, to, to, while

Case 1 The beam is overreinforced and the failure mode is a sudden, brittle failure, which the engineer must carefully guard against in design. When the overreinforced beam is loaded to failure, the failure is initiated by the crushing of the concrete followed by the sudden disintegration of the compression zone while the stress in the relatively large area of steel has not reached its yield point. _____ prevent a brittle failure, the reinforcement must yield _____ the strain in the concrete is less _____ the failure strain of 0.0035.

Case 2 The beam has a moderate percentage of steel, and the failure mode is initiated _____ a yielding of the steel while the strains in the concrete are relatively low. Such beams can continue to carry load and are able _____ undergo large deflections before final collapse occurs; this ductile mode of failure is the only acceptable mode.

Case 3 The beam is lightly reinforced with a very small percentage of steel, and the failure mode is also brittle. When the tensile stress _____ the concrete exceeds the modulus of rupture (the tensile strength), the concrete cracks and immediately releases the tensile force it carries; the lightly stressed steel must then absorb this increment of load. _____ the area of steel provided is too small to carry this added force, the steel will snap and total rupture of the section will occur suddenly.

To ensure ductile failures, upper and lower limits _____ the permitted area of reinforcing steel are established by the ACI Code. The lower limit ensures that enough steel will be used to prevent the steel from snapping suddenly and causing the beam to split. The upper limit on steel area prevents the design of over-reinforced beams.

_____ the presence of shear force has little influence on the moment capacity of a cross section, shear is not considered in the design of members _____ bending.

Reading Material

Reinforced Concrete Columns

Introduction

Columns are members used primarily to support axial compressive loads and have a ratio of height to the least lateral dimension of 3 or greater. In reinforced concrete buildings, concrete beams, floors, and columns are cast monolithically, causing some moments in the columns due to end restraint. Moreover, perfect vertical alignment of columns in a multi-story building is not possible, causing loads to be eccentric relative to the center of columns. The eccentric loads will cause moments in columns. Therefore, a column subjected to pure axial loads dose not exist in concrete buildings. However, it can be assumed that axially loaded columns are those with relatively small eccentricity, e, of about $0.1h$ or less. Where h is the total depth of the column and e is the eccentric distance from the center of the column. Because concrete has a high compressive strength and is an inexpensive material, it can be used in the design of compression members economically.

Types of Columns

Columns may be classified based on the following different categories (Fig. 10.1):

1. Based on loading, columns may be classified as follows:

   a. Axially loaded columns, where loads are assumed acting at the center of the column section.

   b. Eccentrically loaded columns, where loads are acting at a distance e form the center of the column section. The distance e could be along the x or y axis, causing moments either about the x or y axis.

   c. Biaxially loaded columns, where the load is applied at any point on the column section, causing moments about both the x and y-axes simultaneously.

2. Based on length, columns may be classified as follows:

   a. Short columns, where the column's failure is due to the crushing of concrete or the yielding of the steel bars under the full load capacity of the column.

   b. Long columns, where buckling effect and slenderness ratio must be taken into consideration in the design, thus reducing the load capacity of the column relative to that

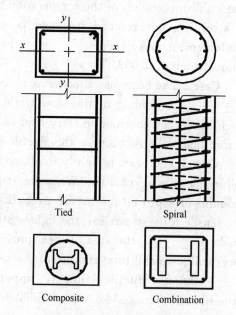

Fig. 10.1 Type of columns.

of a short column.

3. Based on the shape of the cross section, column sections may be square, rectangular, round, L-shaped, octagonal, or any desired shape with an adequate side width or dimensions.

4. Based on column ties, columns may be classified as follows:

a. Tied columns containing steel ties to confine the main longitudinal bars in the columns. Ties are normally spaced uniformly along the height of the column.

b. Spiral columns containing spirals (spring type reinforcement) to hold the main longitudinal reinforcement and to help increase the column ductility before failure. In general, ties and spirals prevent the slender, highly stressed longitudinal bars form buckling and bursting the concrete cover.

5. Based on frame bracing, columns may part of a frame that is braced against sidesway or unbraced against sidesway. Bracing may be achieved by using shear walls or bracings in the building frame. In braced frames, columns resist mainly gravity loads, and shear walls resist lateral loads and wind loads. In unbraced frames, columns resist both gravity and lateral loads, which reduce the load capacity of the columns.

6. Based on materials, columns may be reinforced, prestressed, composite (containing rolled steel sections such as I-sections), or a combination of rolled steel sections and reinforcing bars. Concrete columns reinforced with longitudinal reinforcing bars are the most common type used in concrete buildings.

Behavior of Axially Loaded Columns

When an axial load is applied to a reinforced concrete short columns, the concrete can be considered to behave elastically up to a low stress of about $(1/3)f'_c$. If the load on the column is increased to reach its ultimate strength, the concrete will reach the maximum strength and steel will reach its yield strength, f_y. The ultimate nominal load capacity of the columns can be written as follows:

$$P_u = 0.85 f'_c A_n + A_{st} f_y$$

where A_n and A_{st} = the net concrete and total steel compressive areas, respectively.

$$A_n = A_g - A_{st}$$

$$A_g = \text{gross concrete area}$$

Two different types of failure occur in columns, depending on whether ties or spirals are used. For a tied column, the concrete fails by crushing and shearing outward, the longitudinal steel bars fail by buckling outward between ties, and the column failure occurs suddenly, much like the failure of a concrete cylinder.

A spiral column undergoes a marked yielding, followed by considerable deformation before complete failure. The concrete in the outer shell fails and spalls off. The concrete inside the spiral is confined and provides little strength before the initiation of column failure. A hoop tension develops in the spiral, and for a closely spaced spiral, the steel may yield. A sudden failure is not expected. Fig. 10.2 shows typical load deformation curves for tied and spiral columns. Up to point a, both columns behave similarly. At point a, the longitudinal steel bars of the columns yield, and the spiral column shell spalls off. After the ultimate load is reached, a tied column fails suddenly (curve b), whereas a spiral column deforms appreciably before failure (curve c).

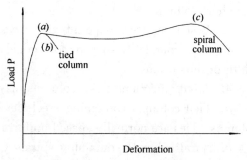

Fig. 10.2 Behavior of tied and spiral columns.

科技英语阅读与写作指南

科技英语写作——数与量的表达(1)

科技英语文体的特点要求表达数与量的概念时要十分准确,因此,在科技英语写作中,涉及到数与量方面的时候要十分注意。

英语的"times"一词,如果用在表示倍数增加的句型中,任何情况下,其含义都是一样的,就是表示"乘"的关系。英语中表示倍数增加的常见句型如下:

1. ...N times+名词词组
   ...N times+as...as...
   ...N times+-er than...
   ...-er than...by N times

以上结构表达的概念一样,意思是"…是…的 N 倍,或…比…多 $N-1$ 倍"。

Aluminium has nearly 5 times the thermal conductivity of cast iron.
铝的导热率几乎是铸铁的 5 倍。
This common high-alumina cement costs roughly three times as much as portland.
这种普通的高铝水泥价格大致为硅酸盐水泥的三倍。
Line AB is *five times longer* than Line CD.
AB 线比 CD 线长四倍。
Mercury weighs more than water by *about* 14 *times*.
水银比水约重 13 倍。

2. ...+double(treble/triple,quadruple)+...
   double 原意是"两倍、双倍",可理解为:增加一倍,翻一番或是…的两倍;
   treble/triple 原意是"三倍",可理解为:增加两倍或是…的三倍;
   quadruple 原意是"四倍",可理解为:增加三倍或翻两番。
   This country has *doubled* her annual output of steel in the past ten years.
   这个国家在过去十年中钢产量翻了一番。
   The city's industrial production in 1998 *trebled* that of 1978.
   1998 年该市的工业生产是 1978 年的三倍。
   The growth rate of GNP per capita for the country will be *quadrupled* by the year 2010.
   到 2010 年,这个国家人均国民生产总值增长率将翻两番。

3. 动词 increase 等＋(to) *N* times/fold
   动词 increase 等＋by *N* times
   动词 increase 等＋by a factor of *N*
   以上句型"times"含义都是一样的，都是表示"乘"的关系，即表示增加到什么程度，一般包括底数在内，意思是：增加到 *N* 倍或增加了 *N*－1 倍。

   By comparison with 1997, the foreign trade turnover of that country in 1998 *increased (to) 2.5 times.*
   和 1997 年相比，这个国家 1998 年的外贸总额增加了 1.5 倍。
   Total industrial output value *increased more than fourfold* in comparison with 1976.
   工业总产值比 1976 年增加了 3 倍多。
   A temperature rise 100℃ increases the conductivity of a semiconductor *by* 50 *times*.
   温度升高 100℃，半导体的导电率就增加到 50 倍。
   In this case, its gain will be increased *by a factor of* 5.
   在这种情况下，其增益将提高 4 倍。

4. ...as much (many...) again as...　　意思是：是…的两倍或比…多一倍
   ...half as much (many...) again as...　　意思是：是…的一倍半或比…多一半
   The bridge is as long again as that one.
   这座桥比那座桥长一倍。
   Wheel A turns *half as fast again as* Wheel B.
   A 轮转动速度比 B 轮快一半。

LESSON 11

Prestressing Methods

Prestressed members are often classified by how the steel is stressed and anchored to the concrete. The member is said to be pretensioned if the steel is positioned in the form and stressed before the concrete is cast. A member is said to be post-tensioned when the steel is stressed after the concrete has hardened to a specific design strength.

Pretensioning

Pretensioning is used primarily in precasting plants to mass-produce members whose size and weight are small enough to permit shipment to the site by truck. If pretensioning is carried out in the plant, the contractor is not required to supply equipment and trained personnel to prestress members in the field. In precast plants, members are commonly constructed on a long slab. These casting beds, which may be 400 to 500 ft long, permit a number of members to be pretensioned simultaneously (Fig. 11.1). Large abutments, positioned at each end of the casting bed, are constructed with fittings to stress and anchor the tendons. After tendons have been tensioned and anchored to the abutments, forms are erected. Next, regular reinforcing steel required for carrying diagonal tension associated with shear, for controlling crack width produced by moment, or for strengthening the anchorage zones is inserted into the form. Then concrete is cast and compacted. After the concrete reaches the required design strength, the tendons are cut. As the steel contracts, the force in the cable is transferred, primarily at the ends of the member, to the concrete by bond and by friction. As cables are elongated by tensioning, a lateral contraction of the tendon, due to the Poisson's ratio effect, takes place. After the tendons are cut and the reinforcement tries to return to its original unstressed dimensions, lateral expansion occurs. Wherever the reinforcement is encased in concrete, the lateral expansion creates high radial pressures between the concrete and the reinforcement. The radial pressures allow large values of friction to develop between the concrete and the tendon, thereby permitting effective anchorage of cable strand and small-diameter-wire tendons (Fig. 11.2). This method cannot be used to anchor large-diameter (3/4 in and above) high-strength bars because the available friction is not adequate to

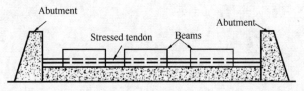

Fig. 11.1　Pretensioned beams constructed on a casting bed

anchor the large bar forces. Bearing plates must be used to anchor tendons with large forces.

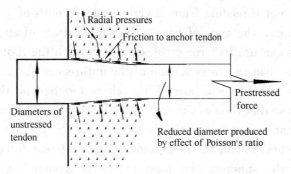

Fig. 11.2 Lateral expansion of the tendon after the jack is released induces high radial pressure.

Since steel forms and the capital costs of a prestressed plant are high, high-early-strength cement and steam curing are often used to accelerate the development of the concrete's strength in order to permit forms to be removed and reused as rapidly as possible. Under plant conditions, concretes with a compressive strength of 3 to 4 kips/in^2 can be routinely produced in approximately half a day.

Posttensioning

The other method of stressing the steel, posttensioning, is most logical when

1. Structures are too large to be pretensioned and shipped to the site.
2. [1] The required cable shape (often called the cable profile) cannot be produced, e.g., a curved cable, if the cable is heavily tensioned since a tensioned cable tends to straighten between the points at which the tension is applied.
3. The design requires that the tendons be stressed in stages.
4. A structure is fabricated in sections to limit the weight of the element and then joined to other components by posttensioning to form a unit.

To ensure that tendons are free to elongate when the steel is tensioned, post-tensioned construction requires the cable to remain unbonded until the concrete hardens. To prevent bond of the tendons to the concrete, cables may be enclosed in ducts that extend through the concrete or the tendons may be coated with grease or mastic and wrapped with paper. Ducts used to position tendons are often filled with cement grout after the tendons have been stressed and anchored. Grouting provides protection against corrosion and also raises the ultimate strength of a the tendon at the section of maximum moment.

A large variety of mechanical devices to anchor tendons to concrete have been developed for posttensioned construction by manufacturers of prestressing systems. [2] Fittings using wedges that lock the tendons to anchor plates by friction are frequently used to anchor tendons made of wire or strand. To minimize cable slipping when the jacking force is released and the wedges forced into position, the surface of the wedge in contact with the tendon is grooved to produce sharp projections that dig into the cable surface.

Large-diameter high-strength bars may be anchored by wedges or threaded connections. To prevent threading from lowering the strength of a bar by reducing the area of the end sections, the ends of bars to be threaded are often enlarged by forging (termed upsetting) to ensure that the cross section through the roots of the threads will be equal to or greater than the cross section of the unthreaded sections of the bars.

While engineers should be aware of the characteristics of the various types of prestressing systems so that their designs will provide adequate clearances for tendons and sufficient width for the end anchors, the designer typically specifies only the position of the centerline of the tendon and the magnitude of the prestress force. The contractor is then free to select the simplest and least expensive system supplying the required prestress.

Under certain design conditions members are both pretensioned and posttensioned. For example, if many identical members are required in a structure, economy may be achieved by using a prestressing plant to produce the members. Pretensioning would be designed to carry all forces applied to the member during shipping and erection. After the members have been assembled in the field, additional tendons can be posttensioned to produce continuity or create additional strength.

New Words

1. anchore [ˈæŋkə]   v. 锚固，锚定；n. 锚
2. cast [kɑːst]   v. 浇注，浇铸投，抛，投射
3. pretensioning [prəˈtenʃəniŋ]   n. 先张，预拉伸
4. contractor [kənˈtræktə]   n. 订约人，承包人
5. fitting [ˈfitiŋ]   n. [pl] 用具，装置，(接头)配件
6. abutment [əˈbʌtmənt]   n. 台座，拱座
7. tendon [ˈtendən]   n. 钢筋束，钢绞线
8. posttensioning [pəustˈtenʃəniŋ]   n. 后张，后加拉力
9. encase [inˈkeis]   vt. 装入，包住，围
10. grease [griːs]   n. 油脂；vt. 涂脂于
11. mastic [ˈmæstik]   n. 玛琦脂，胶粘剂
12. wedge [wedʒ]   n. 楔；vt. 楔入，楔进
13. groove [gruːv]   vt. 开槽于；n. 凹槽
14. thread [θred]   n. 线，细丝，螺纹
15. forging [ˈfɔːdʒiŋ]   n. 锻造(法)，锻件
16. upsetting [ʌpˈsetiŋ]   n. 镦锻，镦(粗)，加厚

Phrases and Expressions

1. prestressing methods   施加预应力的方法

LESSON 11

2. prestressing member 预应力构件
3. the casting bed 浇注台
4. be constructed with 用…建造
5. crack width 裂缝宽度
6. the anchorage zones 锚固区
7. the Poisson's ratio 泊松比
8. the lateral expansion 横向膨胀
9. high-strength bars 高强度钢筋
10. cement grout 水泥砂浆

Notes

[1] The required cable shape...cannot be produced,...since a tensioned cable tends to straighten between the points at which the tension is applied. since引导原因状语从句。全句可译为：因为受张拉的钢筋往往会在张拉点间变直，因此，如果钢筋承受很大的拉力，就很难做出所需的钢筋形状(常称为钢筋的外形)，如弧形。

[2] Fittings using wedges that...are frequently used to anchor tendons made of wire or strand. that引导定语从句修饰wedges。全句可译为：应用楔体由摩擦力把钢筋束固定到锚固板上的装置常常用来锚固由钢丝或钢绞线作成的钢筋束。

Exercises

1. Fill in the blanks with proper words.

(1) The member is said to be pretensioned if the steel is positioned in the form and stressed _____ the concrete is cast.

(2) A member is said to be post-tensioned when the steel is stressed _____ the concrete has hardened to a specific design strength.

(3) Pretensioning is used primarily in precasting plants to mass-produce members _____ size and weight are small enough _____ permit shipment to the site by truck.

(4) These casting beds, _____ may be 400 to 500 ft long, permit a number of members to be pretensioned simultaneously (Fig. 11.1).

(5) _____ tendons have been tensioned and anchored to the abutments, forms are erected.

(6) _____ the steel contracts, the force in the cable is transferred, primarily at the ends of the member, to the concrete by bond _____ by friction.

(7) _____ the reinforcement is encased in concrete, the lateral expansion creates high radial pressures between the concrete _____ the reinforcement.

(8) To ensure that tendons are free to elongate when the steel is tensioned, post-tensioned construction requires the cable _____ remain unbonded _____ the concrete hardens.

(9) _____ prevent bond of the tendons to the concrete, cables may be enclosed in ducts _____ extend through the concrete or the tendons may be coated with grease or mastic and wrapped with paper.

(10) For example, _____ many identical members are required in a structure, economy may be achieved _____ using a prestressing plant to produce the members.

2. Translate the following phrases into Chinese/English.

(1) prestressing members　　　　(6) 泊松比
(2) casting bed　　　　　　　　(7) 横向膨胀
(3) small-diameter-wire tendons　　(8) 水泥浆
(4) posttensioning member　　　　(9) 先张法构件
(5) crack width　　　　　　　　(10) 高强度钢筋

3. Translate the following sentences into Chinese.

(1) Prestressed members are often classified by how the steel is stressed and anchored to the concrete.

(2) If pretensioning is carried out in the plant, the contractor is not required to supply equipment and trained personnel to prestress members in the field.

(3) After the concrete reaches the required design strength, the tendons are cut in pretensioning.

(4) Since steel forms and the capital costs of a prestressed plant are high, high-early-strength cement and steam curing are often used to accelerate the development of the concrete's strength in order to permit forms to be removed and reused as rapidly as possible.

(5) The other method of stressing the steel, posttensioning, is most logical when structures are too large to be pretensioned and shipped to the site.

(6) Large-diameter high-strength bars may be anchored by wedges or threaded connections.

(7) The other method of stressing the steel, posttensioning, is most logical when the design requires that the tendons be stressed in stages.

(8) The contractor is free to select the simplest and least expensive system supplying the required prestress.

(9) After the tendons are cut and the reinforcement tries to return to its original unstressed dimensions, lateral expansion occurs.

(10) After the members have been assembled in the field, additional tendons can be posttensioned to produce continuity or create additional strength.

4. Fill in the blanks with the given words below.

by, from, of, or, or, that, to, to, through, with

A large variety _____ mechanical devices to anchor tendons to concrete have been developed for posttensioned construction by manufacturers of prestressing systems. Fittings using wedges _____ lock the tendons to anchor plates by friction are frequently used _____ anchor tendons made of wire _____ strand. _____ minimize cable slipping when the jacking force is released and the wedges forced into position, the surface of the wedge in contact _____ the tendon is grooved to produce sharp projections that dig into the cable surface.

Large-diameter high-strength bars may be anchored _____ wedges or threaded connections. To prevent threading _____ lowering the strength of bar by reducing the area of the end sections, the ends of bars to be threaded are often enlarged by forging (termed upsetting) to ensure that the cross section _____ the roots of the threads will be equal to _____ greater than the cross section of the unthreaded sections of the bars.

5. Translate the following sentences into English.
（1）如果在混凝土浇筑前将钢筋放入模板并预加应力，则构件称为先张法构件。
（2）这些 400 到 500 英尺长的浇筑台可使许多构件同时被预张拉。
（3）为了防止钢筋和混凝土粘结，钢筋可放在贯通混凝土的孔道内或者给钢筋涂上油脂或者玛琋脂并用纸包裹。
（4）钢筋张拉并锚固后，常用水泥浆灌注用于穿入钢筋的孔道。
（5）大直径、高强度的钢筋可以用楔块或螺纹型连接锚固。

Reading Material

Types of Reinforced Concrete Slab Construction

Reinforced concrete slab floors have taken many forms since their introduction. Some of these were clearly direct imitation of earlier floors made entirely of wood or of wood supported on steel or iron beams. Others were just as clearly invented, with no recognizable ancestors, to suit the properties of the materials—steel bars and plastic concrete.

Economics and development of methods of construction, the suitability of particular slabs for particular sets of requirements, and advances in the methods of analysis of slabs have all joined to shape the current practice, and these factors will just as surely continue to change the types of slabs that are built.

Slabs may be divided into two general categories: beamless slabs and slabs supported on beams located on all sides of each panel. There are many hybrid variants, and many otherwise beamless slabs have beams at the edges of the structure and around large openings such as those made for elevators and stairways.

Beamless slabs are described by the generic terms flat plates(平板) and flat slabs. The flat plate is an extremely simple structure in concept and construction, consisting of a slab of uniform thickness supported directly on columns, as shown in Fig. 11.3. The flat plate is a direct development from the earlier flat slab structure, which was characterized by the presence of capitals(柱帽) at the tops of the columns and usually also by drop panels(柱顶托板), or thickened areas of the slab surrounding each column. The basic form of the flat slab is shown in Fig. 11.4. The most common subtypes would be flat plates with drop panels and flat slabs without drop panels.

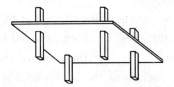

Fig. 11.3 the flat plate.

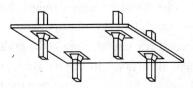

Fig. 11.4 the flat slab.

The choice between the use of flat slabs and flat plates is largely a matter of the magnitude of the design loading and of the spans. The strength of the flat plate structure is often limited by the strength in punching shear at sections around the columns, and they are consequently used with light loads, such as are found in residential and some office construction, and relatively short spans. The column capital and drop panel provide the shear strength necessary for larger loads and spans, and the flat slab is often the choice for heavily loaded industrial structures and for cases where large spans are necessary.

Slabs supported on beams on all sides of each panel are generally termed two-way slabs, and a typical floor is shown in Fig. 11.5. This system is a development from beam and girder systems, as shown in Fig. 11.6. In a beam and girder system, it was quite easy to visualize the path from load point to column as being from slab to beam to girder to column, and from this visualization then to compute realistic moments and shears for the design of all members. This system is still used with heavy timber and steel frame construction, especially when the column spacing becomes large. Removal of the beams, except those on the column lines, results in the two-way slab structure. If the beam spacing is reduced to 2 to 3 ft (0.6 to 0.9 m), the one-way joist floor system is the result. One of the problems with earlier slab and girder construction was that the slabs were assumed to be one-way slabs, with no bending parallel to the beams. However, since the ends of the subpanels were supported, moments parallel with the beams developed near the ends of the subpanels and negative-moment cracking often developed where the slabs joined the girders. Since this had not been anticipated, no reinforcement was provided, and many buildings from 1930 or before will be found in which the locations of the girders can be traced by the large unrestrained cracks that opened on the tops of the slabs.

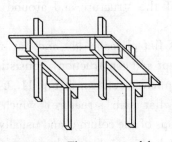

Fig. 11.5 The two-way slab.

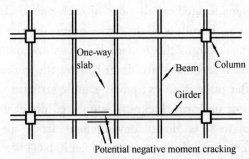

Fig. 11.6 Plan view of a beam and girder floor system.

LESSON 11

The waffle slab, a variant of the solid slab, may be visualized as a set of crossing joists(小梁), set at small spacings relative to the span, which support a thin top slab. The recesses(凹进处) in the slab, often cast using either removable or expendable(一次性的) forms, decrease the weight of the slab and allow the use of a large effective depth without the accompanying dead load. The large depth also leads to a stiff structure. Waffle slabs are usually used in situations demanding spans larger than perhaps about 30 ft (10m).

Waffle slabs may be designed as either flat slabs or two-way slabs, depending on just which recesses are omitted to give larger solid areas. The solid areas near the column in the flat plate arrangement is comparable to a drop panel or column capital, as it provides a path for shear transfer and extra compression area in the highly stressed negative-moment regions surrounding the columns. The solid areas where the recesses have been omitted along the column lines in the two-way slab configuration are equivalent to beams since they are areas of concentrated flexural stiffness, even though they do not extend below the general lower surface of the slab.

The joists around each recess are designed as beams for the forces attributable to a width of slab equal to the joist spacing, and they may easily be reinforced for shear if necessary. The larger the number of joists per span, the better is the approximation of the behavior of a solid slab, and a minimum of six to eight joists would seem necessary if the slab is to be designed as a slab rather than as a series of crossing beams.

A further variation of a waffle slab is a hollow slab in which the holes are made by placing terra-cotta tiles(空心砖), precast concrete boxes, or other fillers on the formwork, placing the reinforcing bars between the filler units, and covering the fillers with cast-in-place concrete. The lower surface of the slab may be either flat or have recesses, depending on the fillers used, and in some cases the fillers are the full depth of the slab. In a two-way configuration, the fillers along the column lines are omitted, and the beams may extend below the slab as well.

Unlike the flat slab, the two-way slab became a viable(可行的) structural system only after suitable analyses had been developed. However, the system remained a captive of the assumptions made in the analyses. It was assumed that the beams were nondeflecting, and the beams were then designed for the reactions the slab applied to the rigid supports. As a result of the magnitude and distribution of reactions computed, in combination with the additional restrictions imposed by the use of the working stress design method, the beams that were used in two-way slabs were either quite deep and stiff or had to be heavily reinforced in compression as well as tension.

Slabs supported on walls rather than beams are used in bearing-wall buildings. The walls are treated as flexurally rigid beams, and the walls may or may not resist moments transmitted from slab to wall, depending on both the wall construction and on the details of the connections. Many of the modern precast building systems are bearing-wall structures in which the slabs are supported by walls along most edges.

The prestressed concrete flat plate is a cast-in-place structure in which most of the reinforcement is in the form of post-tensioned tendons. The tendons are placed in a grid with steel parallel to the column lines in both directions. The chief advantage of this form of construction is in crack and deflection control. The prestressing forces cause compression stresses directly opposing the tensile stresses caused by dead and live loads, and as a result the slab will be nearly crack-free at service load levels. Since cracking is delayed, the full section remains effective, and as a consequence deflections at service load levels may be considerably less than in a reinforced concrete flat plate of the same thickness and span. The absence of cracking helps keep the slab watertight. In addition, the use of draped post-tensioned tendons, which cause an upward distributed loading within much of the spans, will reduce the deflections significantly. Proper selection of the steel profile and force may lead to a floor that undergoes only very small long-term deflection changes. The Compression forces in the plane of the slab which result from prestressing also enhance the shear strength of the slab. Some reinforcing bars are usually used in addition to the post-tensioned tendons. These bars would be placed over the columns at the very least, and often in other locations as well. The tendons may be either bonded or unbonded.

One-way floors, consisting of precast, prestressed concrete members placed side by side and spanning between beams or girders, are also commonly used for floors. The precast members are typically of double- or single-tee section or a hollow core plank, and a cast-in-place concrete topping slab is generally placed over the precast members to provide a smooth surface and additional stiffness and strength. Such one-way floors can be analysed and designed using ordinary beam theory.

科技英语阅读与写作指南

科技英语写作——数与量的表达(2)

在科技英语中，倍数的减少、分数百分数的增减的表达与汉语表达不尽相同，因此在进行科技英语写作时应特别注意。

英语"times"一词可用来表示倍数的减少，但需要注意的是，英语可以说"小/少几倍"，而汉语不习惯这么说，所以只能用分数来表示。常见的句型如下：

1. A is N times smaller than B

    A is N times as small as B

    A is smaller than B by N times

    这三种表达方式的含义是相同的，汉语意思为"A是B的N分之一"或"A比B小N分之$N-1$"

    This bridge is 3 *times shorter* than that one.

    这座桥的长度是那座桥的三分之一。或：这座桥比那座桥短三分之二。

    The wire is shorter than that one *by* 4 *times*.

    这根导线比那根短四分之三。

    The power output of the machine is *twice less* than its input.

    该机器的输出功率比输入功率小二分之一。

2. 动词 reduce 等＋(to/by)N times

LESSON 11

动词 reduce 等＋by a factor of *N*

动词 reduce 等＋*N* times ＋ as much (many...)as

这三种表达方式的含义是相同的，应理解为为"减少到 *N* 分之一"或"减少了 *N* 分之 *N*－1"

The voltage has *dropped five times*.

电压降低了五分之四。

According to the Department of Health，mortality rates from heart disease *decreased three times* from the 1960s to the 1990s.

根据卫生部的报告，心脏病的死亡率从 60 年代至 90 年代下降了三分之二。

3. 动词 increase，reduce 等 ＋(by)分数/百分数

本句型后面的数词为净增加数，意思是"增加(减少)几分之几"

This oilfield has increased its annual output of crude oil *by an average of* 25 *per cent* in the past five years.

这个油田的原油产量在过去 5 年中平均增长 25％。

The introduction of new equipment in this factory has reduced the cost of production (*by*) *one third*.

由于引进了新设备，这家工厂的生产成本降低了三分之一。

4. be＋分数/百分数＋-er than...

be＋分数/百分数＋over/up on/above...

本句型后面的数词为净增加数，意思是"增加(减少)几分之几"

The output value of agricultural output for this year was 8 *percent higher* than that for last year.

今年农业总产值比去年增加 8％。

The output value of chemical fertilizer in the first quarter was 18 *percent above* that of the same period in 1998.

第一季度化肥总产值比 1998 年同期增长了百分之十八。

The output of cars in the country last year was 24 *percent less* than in 1999.

去年这个国家小汽车产量比 1999 年下降了 24％。

5. 动词 increase，reduce 等＋(from)...to＋分数/百分数

本句型后面的数词已包括底数，意思是"增加(减少)到几分之几"

According to a new census report，from 1958 to 1992，women's share of management jobs *increased from* 3 *percent to* 32 *percent*.

根据一份新的调查报告，从 1958 年到 1992 年从事领导管理工作的妇女由 3％上升到 32％。

By using this new process the loss of metal *was reduced to* 20％.

采用这种新工艺，使金属损耗率降为 20％。

LESSON 12

Prestressed Concrete Bridges (1)

Prestressed concrete has been used extensively in U.S. bridge construction since its first introduction from Europe in the late 1940s. Literally thousands of highway bridges of both precast, prestressed concrete and cast-in-place post-tensioned concrete have been constructed in the United States. Railroad bridges utilizing prestressed concrete have become common as well. The use and evolution of prestressed concrete bridges is expected to continue in the years ahead.

Short-span Bridges

Short-span bridges, as shown in Fig. 12.1, for the purposes of this discussion, will be assumed to have a maximum span of 45 ft (13.7m). It should be understood that this is an arbitrary figure, and there is no definite line of demarcation between short, moderate and long spans in highway bridges. Short-span bridges are most efficiently made of precast prestressed-concrete hollow slabs, I-beams, solid slabs or cast-in-place solid slabs and T-beams of relatively generous proportions.

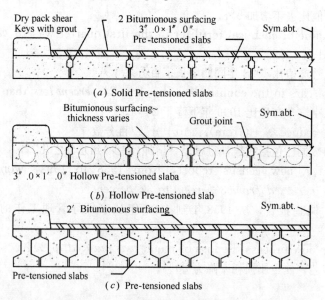

Fig. 12.1 Half-sections of typical prestressed-concrete short-span.

Precast solid slabs are most economical when used on very short spans. The slabs can be made in any convenient width, but widths of 3 or 4 ft (0.9 to 1.2m) have been common. Keys frequently are cast in the longitudinal sides of the precast units. After the slabs have been erected and the joints between the slabs have been filled with concrete, the keys transfer live load shear forces between the adjacent slabs.

Precast hollow slabs used in short-span bridges may have round or square voids. They too are generally made in units 3 to 4 ft(0.9 to 1.2m) wide with thicknesses from 18 to 27 in (45.7 to 68.6cm). Precast hollow slabs can be made in any convenient width and depth and frequently are used in bridges having spans from 20 to 50 ft (6.1 to 15.2m). Longitudinal shear keys are used in the joints between adjacent hollow slabs in the same way as with solid slabs. [1] Hollow slabs may or may not be used with a composite, cast-in-place concrete topping, but the use of a leveling course of some type normally is required as a means of obtaining an acceptable appearance and levelness.

Transverse reinforcement normally is provided in precast concrete bridge superstructures for the purpose of tying the structure together in the transverse direction. [2] Well-designed ties ensure that the individual longitudinal members forming the superstructure will act as a unit under the effects of the live load. In slab bridge construction, transverse ties most frequently consist of threaded steel bars placed through small holes formed transversely through the member during fabrication. Nuts frequently are used as fasteners at each end of the bars. In some instances, the transverse ties consist of post-tensioned tendons placed, stressed and grouted after the slabs have been erected. The transverse tie usually extends from one side of the bridge to the other.

The shear forces imposed on the stringers in short-span bridges frequently are too large to be resisted by the concrete alone. Hence, shear reinforcement normally is required. The amount of shear reinforcement required may be relatively large if the webs of the stringers are relatively thin.

Concrete diaphragms, reinforced with post-tensioned reinforcement or nonprestressed reinforcement, normally are provided transversely at the ends and at intermediate locations along the span in stringer-type bridges. The diaphragms ensure the lateral-distribution of the live loads to the various stringers and prevent individual stringers from displacing or rotating significantly with respect to the adjacent stringers.

No generalities will be made here about the relative cost of each of the above types of constructions; construction costs are a function of many variables which prohibit meaningful generalizations. However, it should be noted that the stringer type of construction requires a considerably greater construction depth than that is required for solid, hollow or channel slab bridge superstructures. Stringer construction does not require a separate wearing surface, as do the precast slab types of construction, unless precast slabs are used to span between the stringers in lieu of the more commonly used cast-in-place reinforced concrete deck. Stringer construction frequently requires smaller quantities of superstructure materials than do slab bridges (unless the spans are very short). The construction time needed to complete a bridge is greater with stringer framing than with the slab type of framing.

Bridges of Moderate Span

Again for the purposes of this discussion only, moderate spans for bridges of prestressed concrete are defined as being from 45 to 80 ft (13.7 to 24.4m). Prestressed concrete bridges in this span range generally can be divided into two types: stringer-type bridges and slab-type bridges. The majority of the precast prestressed concrete bridges constructed in the United States have been stringer bridges using I-shaped stringers, but a large number of precast prestressed concrete bridges have been constructed with precast hollow-box girders (sometimes also called stringers). Cast-in-place post-tensioned concrete has been used extensively in the construction of hollow-box girder bridges—a form of construction that can be considered to be a slab bridge.

Stringer bridges, which employ a composite, cast-in-place deck slab, have been used in virtually all parts of the United States. These stringers normally are used at spacing of about 5 to 6 ft (1.5 to 1.8m). The cast-in-place deck is generally from 6.0 to 8.0 inch (15.2 to 20.3cm) in thickness. This type of framing is very much the same as that used on composite-stringer construction for short-span bridges.

Diaphragm details in moderate-span bridges are generally similar to those of the short spans, with the exception that two or three interior diaphragms sometime are used, rather than just one at midspan as in the short-span bridge.

As in the case of short-span bridges, the minimum depth of construction in bridges of moderate span is obtained by using slab construction, which may be either solid-box or hollow-box in cross section. Average construction depths are required when stringers with large flanges are used in composite construction, and large construction depths are required when stringers with small bottom flanges are used. Composite construction may be developed through the use of cast-in-place concrete decks or with precast concrete decks. Lower quantities of materials normally are required with composite construction, and the dead weight of the superstructures normally is less for stringer construction than for slab construction.

New Words

1. demarcation [ˌdiːmɑːˈkeiʃən] n. 划分
2. slab [slæb] n. 厚平板，梁板
3. key [kei] n. 销子，楔子，键
4. joint [dʒɔint] n. 接缝，接合点
5. topping [ˈtɔpiŋ] n. 上部，面层
6. tie [tai] n. 拉杆，结，扣
7. nut [nʌt] n. 螺母，螺帽
8. fastener [ˈfʌstənə] n. 扣件，使系牢之物
9. stringer [ˈstriŋə] n. 纵梁
10. web [web] n. 腹板，梁腹
11. diaphragm [ˈdaiəfræm] n. 横隔板
12. lieu [ˈljuː] n. 场所
13. spacing [ˈspeisiŋ] n. 间隔，间距
14. flange [flændʒ] n. 翼缘

15. deck [dek]　　　　　　　　　　　　　　　　*n.* 桥面，甲板
16. girder [ˈɡəːdə]　　　　　　　　　　　　　*n.* 纵梁，大梁，桁梁

Phrases and Expressions

1. half-section　半幅
2. shear key　剪力键
3. shear reinforcement　抗剪钢筋
4. I-shaped stringer　工字形截面纵梁
5. in lieu of　作为(…)的替代
6. leveling course(layer)　整平层
7. threaded steel bar　螺纹钢筋
8. wearing surface (or course)　磨耗层
9. stringer-type bridge　纵梁桥
10. slab-type bridge　板式桥
11. hollow-box girder　空心箱梁
12. interior diaphragms　内横隔板

Notes

[1] Hollow slabs may or may not be used with …, but the use of … is required as a means of obtaining an acceptable appearance and levelness. as a means of 意为"作为……方法"。全句可译为：空心板和复合现浇混凝土桥面可以一起使用，也可以不在一起使用，但是要求使用整平层，以获得满意的外观和平整度。

[2] Well-designed ties ensure that…members…will act as a unit under the effects of the live load. 全句可译为：设计良好的横向联系能保证组成上部结构的每个纵向构件在活载作用下作为一个整体工作。

Exercises

1. Fill in the blanks with proper words.

（1）Short-span bridges, as shown in Fig. 12.1, _____ the purposes of this discussion, will be assumed to have a maximum span of 45 ft (13.7m).

（2）Prestressed concrete has been used extensively in U.S. bridge construction _____ its first introduction _____ Europe _____ the late 1940s.

（3）Short-span bridges are most efficiently made _____ precast prestressed-concrete hollow slabs, I-beams, solid slabs _____ cast-in-place solid slabs _____ T-beams of relatively generous proportions.

（4）The slabs can be made _____ any convenient width, but widths of 3 or 4 ft (0.9 to 1.2m) have been common.

（5）Longitudinal shear keys are used _____ the joints _____ adjacent hollow slabs in the same way as with solid slabs.

（6）Transverse reinforcement normally is provided in preast concrete bridge superstructures for the purpose _____ tying the structure together _____ the transverse direction.

（7）Concrete diaphragms, reinforced _____ post-tensioned reinforcement or nonprestressed reinforcement, normally are provided transversely _____ the ends and at intermediate locations along the span _____ stringer-type bridges.

（8）Stringer construction does not require a separate wearing surface, _____ do the precast slab types of construction.

（9）The cast-in-place deck is generally from 6.0 to 8.0 inch (15.2 to 20.3cm) _____ thickness.

（10）Average construction depths are required when stringers _____ large flanges are used in composite construction, _____ large construction depths are required when stringers with small bottom flanges are used.

2. Translate the following phrases and expressions into Chinese /English.

  （1）shear force   （6）工字形截面纵梁
  （2）precast units   （7）螺纹钢筋
  （3）wearing surface   （8）抗剪钢筋
  （4）lateral distribution   （9）槽形板
  （5）shear key   （10）空心板

3. Translate the following sentences into Chinese.

（1）The use and evolution of prestressed concrete bridges is expected to continue in the years ahead.

（2）Literally thousands of highway bridges of both precast, prestressed concrete and cast-in-place post-tensioned concrete have been constructed in the United States.

（3）It should be understood that this is an arbitrary figure, and there is no definite line of demarcation between short, moderate and long spans in highway bridges.

（4）After the slabs have been erected and the joints between the slabs have been filled with concrete, the keys transfer live load shear forces between the adjacent slabs.

（5）In slab bridge construction, transverse ties most frequently consist of threaded steel bars placed through small holes formed transversely through the member during fabrication.

（6）The shear forces imposed on the stringers in short-span bridges frequently are too large to be resisted by the concrete alone.

（7）The diaphragms ensure the lateral-distribution of the live loads to the various stringers and prevent individual stringers from displacing or rotating significantly with respect to the adjacent stringers.

（8）It should be noted that the stringer type of construction requires a considerably greater construction depth than that is required for solid, hollow or channel slab bridge superstructures.

（9）The majority of the precast prestressed concrete bridges constructed in the

United States have been stringer bridges using I-shaped stringers, but a large number of precast prestressed concrete bridges have been constructed with precast hollow-box girders.

(10) Average construction depths are required when stringers with large flanges are used in composite construction, and large construction depths are required when stringers with small bottom flanges are used.

4. Fill in the blanks with the given words below.

    and, by, either, for, in, in, in, through, with, with

  As in the case of short-span bridges, the minimum depth of construction _____ bridges of moderate span is obtained _____ using slab construction, which may be _____ solid-box or hollow-box _____ cross section. Average construction depths are required when stringers _____ large flanges are used _____ composite construction, _____ large construction depths are required when stringers with small bottom flanges are used. Composite construction may be developed _____ the use of cast-in-place concrete decks or _____ precast concrete decks. Lower quantities of materials normally are required with composite construction, and the dead weight of the superstructures normally is less _____ stringer construction than for slab construction.

5. Translate the following sentences into English.
  (1) 预应力混凝土实心板适宜于非常短跨径的桥梁。
  (2) 这座桥是由一些空心板组成的结构。
  (3) 作用在纵梁上的剪力如此之大，以至于需要设置剪力钢筋。
  (4) 与实心板桥相比，空心板桥上部结构的恒载一般要小些。
  (5) 采用预应力混凝土的公路桥已经变得越来越普及。

Reading Material

Prestressed Concrete Bridges (2)

Long-Span Bridges

Prestressed concrete bridges having spans of the order of 100 ft are of the same general types of construction as structures having moderate span length, with the single exception that solid slabs are not used for long spans. The stringer spacings are frequently greater (with stringers at 7 to 9 ft) as the span lengths of bridges increase. Because of dead weight considerations, precast hollow-box construction generally is employed for spans of this length only when the depth of construction must be minimized. Cast-in-place post-tensioned hollow-box bridges with simple and continuous spans frequently are used for spans on the order of 100 ft and longer.

  Simple, precast, prestressed stringer construction would be economical in the

United States in spans up to 300 ft under some conditions. However, only limited use has been made of this type of construction on spans greater than 100 ft. For very long simple spans, the advantage of precasting frequently is nullified(抵消；使无意义)by the difficulties involved in handling, transporting and erecting the girders, which may have depths as great as 10 ft and weight over 200 tons. The exceptions to this occur on large projects where all of the spans are over water of sufficient depth and character that precast beams can be handled with floating equipment, when custom girder launchers can be used and when segmental construction techniques can be used.

The use of cast-in-place, post-tensioned, box-girder bridges has been extensive. Although structures of these types occasionally are for spans less than 100 ft, they more often are used for spans in excess of 300 ft. Structurally efficient in flexure, especially for continuous bridges, the box girder is torsionally stiff and hence an excellent type of structure for use on bridges that have horizontal curvature. Some governmental agencies use this form of construction almost exclusively in urban areas where appearance from underneath the superstructure, as well as from the side, is considered important.

Segmental Bridges(拼装式桥梁)

Bridges that are constructed in pieces of various configurations, connected together in some way, frequently are referred to as segmental bridges. The segments may be cast-in-place or precast, elongated units, such as portions of stringers or girders, or relatively short units that are as wide as the completed bridge superstructure.

The Esbly Bridge in France is an example of one of the earliest precast concrete segmental bridges. This bridge is one of five bridges that were made with the same dimensions and utilized the same steel molds for casting the concrete units. All of the bridges span the River Marne, and because of the required navigational clearances and the low grades on the roads approaching the bridges, the depth of construction at the center of each span was restricted. The bridges were formed of precast elements, 6 ft long and were made in elaborate molds by first casting and steam-curing the top and bottom flanges in which the ends of the web reinforcement were embedded. The flanges were then jacked apart and held apart by the web forms while the web concrete was cast and cured. Releasing and stripping the web forms resulted in the prestressing of the webs. The 6-ft-long elements were temporarily post-tenioned in the factory into units approximately 40 ft long. The 40 ft units were transported to the bridge site, raised into place and post-tensioned together longitudinally, after which the temporary posttensioning was removed. Each span consists of six ribs or beams that were post-tensioned together transversely after they were erected. Hence, the beams are triaxially prestressed. The completed Esbly Bridge consists of a very flat, two hinged, prestressed concrete arch with a span of 243 ft and a depth at the midspan of about 3 ft.

Cast-in-place prestressed concrete segmental construction, in which relatively short, full-width sections of a bridge superstructure are constructed cantilevered from both sides of a pier, originated in Germany shortly after World War II. This procedure sometimes is referred to as balanced cantilever construction. The well-known, late German engineer U. Finsterwalder is credited with being the originator of the technique. The basic construction sequence used in this method is illustrated in Fig. 12.2 which shows that segments, erected one after another on each side of a pier, form cantilevered spans. The construction sequence normally progresses from pier to pier, from one end of the bridge to the other, with the ends of adjacent cantilevers being jointed together to form a continuous deck. The individual segments frequently are made in lengths of 12 to 16 ft in cycles of four to seven days. The method has been used in the United States for bridges having spans as long as 750 ft.

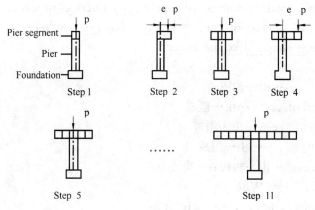

Fig. 12.2 Erection sequence for segmental bridges using the cantilever.

The segmental construction technique also has been used with precast segments. The technique originated in France and has been used in the construction of bridges having spans in excess of 300 ft. The eminent French engineer Jean Muller is credited with originating precast segmental bridge construction using match-cast segments. The precast segments may be erected in balanced cantilever, similar to the method described above for cast-in-place segmental bridges constructed in cantilever, or by using the span-by-span technique. Precast segment have been made in precasting plants located on the construction site as well as off site. The segments frequently are stored for a period of weeks or months before being moved to the bridge site and erected—a factor having favorable effects on concrete strength, shrinkage and creep. Construction of precast segmental bridge superstructures normally progresses at a rapid rate once the erection process begins. The erection of precast concrete segments normally does not commence, however, until such time as a large number of segments have been precast and stockpiled（储蓄，贮存） because the erection normally can progress at a faster rate than the production of the segments.

科技英语阅读与写作指南

科技英语写作——物体形状、结构、连接

在第一单元里我们说过科技英语文章的内容大多是科学研究的成果，是客观存在的自然

现象及其规律的反映。因此，在科技英语写作中，语言应规范准确，物体的描述、计量单位、符号、图文、表格、数据等的使用，都应力求准确无误。从本单元至第十五单元，我们将通过实例介绍一些较为重要的句型结构。

1. 物体形状的表达

  be + adj.（+in shape/form）（形状）是…的，是…形的
  be shaped like… 形状像…
  have the shape of… 具有…形状
  take the shape of… 呈…的形状

  Most of the early modern domes are nearly hemispherical in shape.
  In weightlessness, a drop of liquid takes the shape of a sphere.
  This steel tube is shaped like the letter "U".

2. 物体结构的表达

  …consist of… …由…组成
  …be composed of… …由…组成
  …be made up of… …由…组成
  …be formed by… …由…组成
  …comprise… …由…构成；…构成…
  …constitute… …构成…
  The elements of… are… …的成分是…
  The components of… are… …的成分是…

  The roof of the Sports Palace in Mexico City for the 1968 Olympics consists of 22 intersecting trussed steel arches spanning 433 ft.
  For the taller buildings, the majority are composed of interactive elements in three-dimensional arrays.
  Purlin sections are usually made up of channels, junior beams, or coldformed sections.
  Ferrite and carbon comprise mild steel / Mild steel comprises ferrite and carbon.
  The elements of soda (Na_2CO_3) are sodium, carbon and oxygen.
  The components of a hi-fi music system are the tuner, the recorder, the amplifier, the record-player and two separate speakers.

3. 物体连接的表达

  …be connected to / with… …与…相连接
  …be attached to… …附在(贴在，挂在)…上，…附属于…
  …be suspended from… …从…上悬下来(垂下来，挂下来)
  …be supported by… …由…支撑
  …be anchored to… …固定在…上
  …be tied into… …与…相连
  …fit into… …能塞进…，…与…相配
  …be detached from… …与…相脱离，…与…不连

  Labels are attached to the luggage.

No interior cranes are needed but light mechanical equipment may be suspended form the roof.

The girts are connected to the outside flange of the columns.

Care must be taken to ensure that masonry units are well tied into the column core to avoid shedding of the masonry.

The 440-ft dome rests on the tension ring which is supported by vertical columns.

The 52-ft deep radial cantilever steel trusses are anchored to the 11-story central circular core.

A square thing does not fit into a round hole.

Foundations

Spread Footing Foundations

A spread footing (also known as a *footer* or simply a *footing*) is an enlargement at the bottom of a column or bearing wall that spreads the applied structural loads over a sufficiently large soil area. Typically, each column and each bearing wall has its own spread footing, so each structure may include dozens of individual footings.

Spread footings are by far the most common type of foundation, primarily because of their low cost and ease of construction. They are most often used in small-to medium-size structures on sites with moderate to good soil conditions.

Spread footings may be built in different shapes and sizes to accommodate individual needs, as shown in Fig. 13.1. These include the following:

Square spread footings (or simply *square footings*) have plan dimensions of $B \times B$. The depth from the ground surface to the bottom of the footing is D and the thickness is T. Square footings usually support a single centrally-located column.

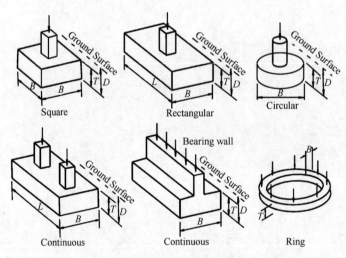

Fig. 13.1 Spread footing shapes.

Rectangular spread footings have plan dimensions of $B \times L$, where L is the longest dimension. These are useful when obstructions prevent construction of a square footing with a sufficiently large base area and when large moment loads are present.

Circular spread footings are round in plan view. These are most frequently used as foundations for light standards, flagpoles, and power transmission lines. If these foundations extend to a large depth (i. e. , D/B greater than about 3), they may behave more like a deep foundation.

Large cylindrical above ground storage tanks also will behave as a circular foundation. Although the walls may be supported on an annular-shaped continuous footing (a *ring footing*) and the roof may be supported by columns founded on square footings, the contents of the tank will be distributed evenly across the tank floor.

Continuous spread footings (also known as *wall footings or strip footings*) are used to support bearing walls.

Combined footings are those that support more than one column. These are useful when columns are located too close together for each to have its own footing. Sometimes it is necessary to build spread footings very close to a property line, another structure. Because such a footing cannot be centered beneath the column, the load is eccentric. This can cause the footing to rotate and thus produce undesirable moments and displacements in the column.

[1] One solution to this problem is to use a strap footing (also known as a *cantilever footing*), which consists of an eccentrically loaded footing under the exterior column connected to the first interior column using a grade beam. This arrangement, which is similar to a combined footing, provides the necessary moment in the exterior footing to counter the eccentric load. Sometimes grade beams connect all of the spread footing; provide a more rigid foundation system.

Bored Concrete Piles and Steel Piles

Bored concrete piles are concrete columns cast inside the soil in a hole. The hole is drilled with various types of drilling tools whose choice depends the kind of soil in question. Bored piles are especially useful for applications in which vibration caused by driving should be eliminated. Piles with diameters of 300 to 500 mm, 10 to 30 m long and with design loads of 200 to 400 kN are in use. Piles with diameters larger than 600 mm are termed drilled piers. The bored piles have the following advantages: (1) they are installed by drilling, which is preferred in stiff clays, and wherever adjacent buildings and the inside of structures are apt to be damaged by vibration produced by driving; (2) they may be installed in practically unlimited lengths; (3) since they do not displace the soil, they are not accompanied by heave; and (4) they can be spaced as close as $1.75d$ apart.

However, compared to the driven piles, they have a limited bearing capacity unless they bear on a rock. This *limited bearing capacity* is contingent to the fact that they produce no soil displacement and, consequently, the soil adjacent to the shaft and below the base is not compacted. Moreover, they are frequently installed incorrectly and this circumstance impairs their reliability.

The steel piles are *steel columns* driven into the ground. They are capable of withstanding hard driving thanks to their strength and to the fact that they displace only a small volume of soil, the latter property makes them suitable for driving through hard soils and to great depths.

The steel piles with relatively thin walls penetrate the soil without setting up heavy vibrations which are detrimental to adjacent buildings. They can easily be spliced or cut off and this property is advantageous whenever their length varies considerably due to the irregularity of the surface, for example, in driving to a rock. It is also this property that makes them well adapted to driving in a limited headroom, for they can be driven in short lengths and readily spliced by welding during the installation.

On the other hand, steel piles are expensive, and their use is confined to cases in which their large bearing capacity can be exploited to the full, for example, when they are end-bearing on a rock. In addition, they are adapted to hard driving and depths over 15m, and provide excellent service under heavy lateral loads, as in marine structures, where their parts which protrude into the air double as columns.

The *durability of steel in the ground*, which is sometimes a matter of dispute, was studied in Sec. 12.2 and found to be sufficient. No failure of steel piles driven into the ground, which can be attributed to corrosion, has been recorded, except in organic, acid and chemical plants. When steel piles are used for marine or river structures, their sections extending above the low water should be protected by concrete jackets. In waterfront structures, the protective coatings and/or cathodic protection systems are always recommended.

Steps in Choosing a Foundation

The design of a foundation method depends on several factors which, in areas where no previous experience with foundations is available, cannot be determined without trial. As a rule, several solutions are possible.

There are several factors involved in the choice of an appropriate type of foundation. Questions which we wish to answer is how to transmit the load of the superstructure to the subsoil, how to construct the chosen type of foundation and how to built it at a reasonable cost. The purpose of foundations is to transfer the required load safely to the subsoil; therefore, a foundation should be designed to perform this task without detrimental deformation of the superstructure or failure of the supporting soil or rock under the effect of static load, dynamic load, seepage forces, scour, etc.

In choosing the method of foundation, the designer generally adopts the procedure of:

(1) obtaining information concerning the type of the superstructure involved and the loads acting thereon;

(2) procuring geological exploration;

(3) investigating the engineering properties of the soil in question;

(4) studying the customary types of foundations in relation to the load or structure, sensitivity to settlement, case of construction and eliminating the unsuitable types;

(5) designing the chosen type proceeding from detailed soil mechanics data and computations;

(6) estimating the cost,

(7) evaluating the time required for construction.

New Words

1. accommodate [əˈkɔmədeit]   v. 适应，供应，提供
2. splice [splais]   v. 接合
3. flagpole [ˈflæɡpəul]   n. 旗杆
4. heave [hi:v]   v. 隆起
5. obstruction [əbˈstrʌkʃən]   n. 阻塞，障碍物
6. waterfront [ˈwɔ:təfrʌnt]   n. 水边码头区，滨水地区
7. procure [prəˈkjuə]   v. 获得，取得
8. cathodic [kəˈθɔdik]   a. 阴极的，负极的
9. subsoil [ˈsʌbsɔil]   n. 地基土，天然地基
10. annular [ˈænjulə]   a. 环的，环
11. contingent [kənˈtindʒənt]   a. 可能发生的，附随的；n. 偶然的事情
12. headroom [ˈhedru:m]   n. [建] 净空，头上空间
13. jacket [ˈdʒækit]   n. 套，护封；vt. 给…装护套
14. seepage [ˈsi:pidʒ]   n. 渗流，渗出的量

Phrases and Expressions

1. spread footing   扩展基础
2. deep foundation   深基础
3. continuous spread footing   连续扩展基础
4. strip footing   条形基础
5. combined footings   联合基础
6. grade beam   基础梁
7. bored concrete pile   钻孔混凝土桩
8. bearing wall   承重墙
9. cathodic protection   阴极保护，阴极防蚀
10. helical blade   螺旋叶片
11. screw pile   螺旋桩
12. seepage force   渗透力
13. drilled piers   钻孔墩（桩）

Notes

[1] One solution to this problem is to use a strap footing (...), which consists of... beam. which 引导非限制性定语从句修饰 strap footing；从句中的 connected to 修饰

the exterior column。全句可译为：解决这个问题的一种方法是使用条形基础（也称为悬臂基础），这种基础是由外柱下的偏心基础通过基础梁与第一个内柱相连组成的。

Exercises

1. Fill in the blanks with proper words.

(1) Spread footings are by far the most common type of foundation, primarily because of their low cost and _____ of construction.

(2) These are useful when obstructions prevent construction of a square footing with a sufficiently large base area and when large _____ loads are present.

(3) Combined footings are useful when columns are located too _____ together for each to have its own footing.

(4) Because such a footing cannot be centered beneath the column, the load is _____.

(5) Bored piles are especially useful for applications in which _____ caused by driving should be eliminated.

(6) Continuous spread footings (also known as wall footings or strip footings) are used to support bearing _____.

(7) A foundation is the supporting part of a structure which transmits the _____ load to the foundation soil or rock. Foundations are divided into spread and deep foundations.

(8) In contrast to concrete and steel which are man-made in the desired and prescribed quality to suit the structure, soils and rocks are made by _____ in a random manner.

2. Translate the following phrases into Chinese/English

(1) grade beam   (6) 偏心荷载
(2) spread foundation   (7) 动荷载
(3) bored concrete piles   (8) 承重墙
(4) strip footing   (9) 基础底面
(5) deep foundation   (10) 联合基础

3. Translate the following sentences into Chinese

(1) Because of the character of these information, combined with the impact of cost, foundation engineering is more all art than a science.

(2) The purpose of foundations is to transfer the required load safely to the subsoil; therefore, a foundation should be designed to perform this task without detrimental deformation of the superstructure or failure of the supporting soil or rock under the effect of static load, dynamic load, seepage forces, scour, etc

(3) This arrangement, which is similar to a combined footing, provides the necessary moment in the exterior footing to counter the eccentric load.

(4) Sometimes grade beams connect all of the spread footing; provide a more rigid foundation system.

LESSON 13

(5) Bored concrete piles are concrete columns cast inside the soil in a hole.

(6) One solution to this problem is to use a strap footing (also known as a *cantilever footing*), which consists of an eccentrically loaded footing under the exterior column connected to the first interior column using a grade beam.

(7) Typically, each column and each bearing wall has its own spread footing, so each structure may include dozens of individual footings.

(8) They are most often used in small-to medium-size structures on sites with moderate to good soil conditions.

4. Fill in the blanks with the given words below.

by, for, in, in, inside, on, to, unless, with

Bored concrete piles are concrete columns cast _____ the soil in a hole. The hole is drilled _____ various types of drilling tools whose choice depends the kind of soil _____ question. Bored piles are especially useful _____ applications _____ which vibration caused _____ driving should be eliminated. Piles with diameters of 300 to 500mm, 10 to 30m long and with design loads of 200 to 400kN are in use. Piles with diameters larger than 600mm are termed drilled piers. Compared to the driven piles, they have a limited bearing capacity _____ they bear _____ a rock. This *limited bearing capacity* is contingent to the that they produce no soil displacement and, consequently, the soil adjacent _____ the shaft and below the base is not compacted. Moreover, they are frequently installed incorrectly and this circumstance impairs their reliability.

5. Translate the following sentences into English

(1) 扩展基础可以做成不同的形式和尺寸，以适应不同的需要。

(2) 扩展基础就是将柱基或墙基扩大，从而将作用其上的结构荷载传递给分布于足够大的地基土面积上。

(3) 联合基础用于支承一个以上的柱子。当柱子太近而无法使用独立基础时，联合基础就很有用。

(4) 钢桩就是打入地基中的钢柱。

(5) 钻孔桩通过钻孔成桩，钻孔更适合于硬黏土以及打桩振动易于损坏附近建筑物和结构的地方。

Reading Material

Shear Failure and Parameters of Soil

A simple equation and theory relating the shear strength of soil to the applied normal stress was first suggested by Coulomb in 1776. The cohesive resistance to shearing is assumed to be constant for a given soil and independent of the applied stress, while the frictional resistance varies directly with the magnitude of the normal stress developed on the shear slip surface. A straight-line equation for the limiting shear stress is given thus:

$$\tau_f = c + \sigma_n \tan\phi \tag{13.1}$$

where c = cohesion

σ_n = normal stress on slip surface

ϕ = angle of internal friction

From the graphical representation of Coulombs equation it will be seen that the value of the cohesion (c) is the intercept on the shear stress axis and the slope of the line is $\tan\phi$.

It is now generally accepted that soil shear strength in fact is related to effective stress and that the strength envelope is curved; the Coulomb expression therefore represents a straight-line estimate for a given range of stresses:

$$\tau_f = c' + \sigma_n' \tan\phi' \tag{13.2}$$

where c' = apparent cohesion referred to effective stress

σ_n' = effective normal stress on the slip surface = $\sigma_n - u$

u = pore pressure acting on the slip surface

ϕ' = angle of internal friction referred to effective stress

The shear strength parameters c' and ϕ' would have constant values for a given soil, providing that the void ratio, density and pore pressure also remained constant for different values of normal stress. This cannot be the case, either in the field or during laboratory tests, since under drained loading the volume will change and under undrained loading the pore pressure will change. It is therefore necessary to refer measured values to the type of test and conditions under which they were measured.

Measurement of Shear Strength and Practical Parameters

The purpose of shear strength testing is to establish empirical values for the shear strength parameters. The conditions of drainage during the test are of great significance and influence the measured values considerably. It is important that measured values of cohesion and angle of friction are referred to the test conditions. Shear strength tests are carried out in two main stages involving the following types of drainage conditions.

Undrained tests

In undrained tests no drainage of porewater is allowed, so that any increase in total stress produces a corresponding increase in pore pressure. In the case of fully saturated soils (pore pressure coefficient $B=1$), the increase in pore pressure will be equal to the increase in total stress; and so no increase in effective stress takes place.

$$\text{If } \Delta u = \Delta \sigma_n, \text{ then } \Delta \sigma' = 0 \tag{13.3}$$

Giving: $\tau_f = c_u$.

where c_u = undrained cohesion (undrained shear strength).

Since no account is taken of the pore pressure, the undrained strength measured in this way is referred only to total stress and is reliable only if the test specimen is known to be saturated; for a saturated soil, $\phi_u = 0$. The value of c_u also depends on the void ratio (or specific volume) of the soil and corresponds to the ultimate (critical state) stress; a higher peak stress is not developed.

Consolidated-undrained tests

In this procedure the test specimen is first allowed to consolidate under conditions of constant isotropic stress and full drainage, after which the axial load is increased with no drainage allowed. The initial consolidation stage brings the soil to a prescribed state of volume and pore pressure, from which subsequent changes in volume or pore pressure may be accurately measured.

Consolidated-undrained tests are used to obtain the effective stress parameters c' and ϕ' and to obtain volume change and stiffness characteristics. If the undrained shear strength parameters are evaluated they should be referred to as c_{cu}, and ϕ_{cu}.

Drained tests

As in consolidated-undrained tests, the test specimen is first consolidated under conditions of constant isotropic stress and full drainage. When the consolidation stage is complete, the axial load is increased at a rate slow enough to ensure that no increase in pore pressure takes place. The increase in effective stress is therefore equal to the increase in total stress ($\Delta\sigma' = \Delta\sigma$).

Peak stresses develop in dense or heavily consolidated soil giving rise to the failure envelope:

$$\tau_f = c' + \sigma_n' \tan\phi_f' \tag{13.4}$$

Where φ_f' = peak angle of friction

For normally consolidated soils the failure envelope based on ultimate effective stress passes through the origin, i.e. $c' = 0$, so that:

$$\tau_f = \sigma \tan\phi_c' \tag{13.5}$$

where ϕ_c' = critical angle of friction

For residual conditions involving large strains the failure envelope is slightly curved at low normal stresses and c_r' tends toward zero. The residual angle of friction (ϕ_r') is therefore stress dependent, but the following relationship is often used:

$$\tau_f = \sigma_n' \tan\phi_r' \tag{13.6}$$

Types of shear test

A variety of shear tests is available, some for use in the laboratory and some for use in situ. These are summarily listed below, with those of some importance being described in later sections. They all have one common characteristic in that they are tests on samples; whether the tests are carried out in situ or, on samples brought to the laboratory. In order that reliable results might be produced it is essential that samples are properly representative of the site materials that may be encountered in the construction process. Great care should be taken in obtaining, packaging and transporting samples from site to laboratory; especially where undisturbed samples are required, in which the in-situ structure, density and moisture content must be preserved.

Mohr-Coulomb Failure Criterion

In the case of a shear slip failure or continuous yielding, the Mohr circle containing the normal and shear stresses on the slip plane is clearly a limiting circle. Limiting circles at different values of normal stress will all touch a common tangent which is called a failure envelope. The equation of this failure envelope (usually referred to as Coulomb's equation)is:

$$\tau_f = c' + \sigma' \tan\phi'$$

where ϕ' = angle of friction or the angle of shearing resistance
c' = apparent cohesion.

From the geometry of the Mohr-Coulomb construction the angle of failure is

$$\alpha_f = \frac{1}{2}(90° + \phi') = 45° + \frac{\phi'}{2}$$

If a number of samples of the same soil can be brought to a state of shear slip failure or continuous yielding and the principal stresses (σ'_1 and σ'_3) are measured, the Mohr-Coulomb construction may be determine the failure envelope and thus values for the parameters c' and ϕ'.

A large majority of problems in soil mechanics design require shear strength parameters relating to limiting values and stresses on slip surfaces. In such cases, the Mohr-Coulomb failure criterion may be used in the interpretation of triaxial test results.

Several (usually three) specimens of the same soil are tested at different values of cell pressure (σ_3) and a Mohr circle (or semi-circle) is drawn for each peak or ultimate 'failure' stress. A common tangent to these failure circles is then drawn and, providing there is a reasonable goodness of fit, this may be taken as the strength envelope for the soil from which values of cohesion (c') and angle of friction (ϕ') may be scaled. A minimum of three circles will be required to give a reliable result.

科技英语阅读与写作指南

科技英语写作——物体测量

1. 计量

...is / measures...＋单位＋tall (high, deep, long, wide) …的高度(深度、长度、宽度)为

...is / measures...＋单位＋in height (in depth, in length, in width) …的高度(深度、长度、宽度)为

...has a height (depth, length, width) of...＋单位 …的高度(深度、长度、宽度)为

...is/measures as tall(high, deep, long, wide)as...＋单位 …有…高(深、长、宽)

...has/covers an area of...＋单位 …的面积为…

...has a/an＋表场所、用途词＋space of...＋单位 …的面积为…

...is/measures＋数字＋单位＋by＋数字＋单位 …的长…宽…

...is/measures＋数字＋单位＋by＋数字＋单位＋by＋数字＋单位 …的长…宽…高…

The structural system measures 94 ft wide, 196 ft long, and 601 ft high.

The new overpass is 48m in width.

The new library has a floor space of 18,000 square metres.

The plan dimensions of the building are 120 ft. by 216 ft.

The pond <u>measures as deep as</u> 16 feet in the middle.

This college <u>covers an area of</u> 500 mu.

2. 精确度

    to an accuracy of...   精度达…，达…的精度

    with an accuracy of...   精度达…

    within the accuracy of...   在…的精度范围内

    be accurate to...   精度达…，精确到…

    be accurate within...   精度在…的范围之内

    This apparatus <u>is accurate within</u> microseconds.

    The components can be positioned <u>with an accuracy of</u> 0.01 inch.

    Readings can be obtained <u>to an accuracy of</u> one micron.

    The scales <u>are accurate to</u> half a gram.

    The error is <u>within the accuracy of</u> the analysis.

3. 比例与比率

    The ratio of... to... is... to...   …与…的比是…比…

    The ratio between... and... is... to...   …与…的比是…比…

    The proportion of... to... is... to...   …与…的比是…比…

    ...and... are in the proportion of... to...   …与…的比是…比…

    ...is mixed/formed in a proportion of... to...   …以…的比例混合/组成

    ...is directly/inversely proportional to...   …与…成正/反比

    ...is in direct/inverse proportion to...   …与…成正/反比

    <u>The ratio between</u> students of science <u>and</u> students of engineering <u>is</u> 3∶2.

    The height <u>is directly proportional to</u> the rate of climb which must be designed to permit the concrete to reach sufficient strength.

    The water and land on earth are <u>in the proportion of three to one.</u>

    Floor and water have to <u>be mixed in a proportion of</u> 1,000 ml to 1b.

    There is a relationship between the cross-sectional area of a rope and its strength. It strength is <u>in direct proportion to</u> its cross-sectional area.

4. 最大与最小

    maximize...   把…增加/扩大到最大限度，使…达到最高限度

    minimize...   使…减(缩)到最小(少)，使…达到最低限度

    The maximum/minimum... is...+单位   …的最大/最小…为…

    ...have the maximum/minimum...of...+单位   …的最大/最小…为…

    The upper/lower limit of... is...+单位   …的最高/最低极限为…

    In this case, a central core is preferred as it <u>maximizes</u> the amount of high rental perimeter space.

    The bracing is used to aid in aligning the frame in the erection, <u>to minimize vibration</u> and to reduce the unsupported length of main members.

    <u>The upper limit of</u> temperature in this district <u>is</u> about 39℃.

    The boiler <u>has the maximum</u> pressure <u>of</u> 500 1b per sq. inch.

Lesson 14

The Cable-stayed Bridge System

Introduction

During the past decade cable-stayed bridges have found wide application, especially in Western Europe, and to a lesser extent in other parts of the world.

The renewal of the cable-stayed system in modern bridge engineering was due to the tendency of bridge engineers in Europe, primarily Germany, to obtain optimum structural performance from material, which was in short supply during the post-war years.

[1] Cable-stayed bridges are constructed along a structural system which comprises an orthotropic deck and continuous girders which are supported by stays, i.e. inclined cables passing over or attached to towers located at the main piers.

The idea of using cables to support bridge spans is by no means new, and a number examples of this type of construction were recorded a long time ago. Unfortunately, the system in general met with little success, due to the fact that the statics were not fully understood and that unsuitable materials such as bars and chains were used to form the inclined supports or stays. [2] Stays made in this manner could not be fully tensioned and in a slack condition allowed large deformations of the deck before they could participate in taking the tensile loads for which they were intended.

Wide and successful application of cable-stayed systems was realized only recently, with the introduction of high-strength steels, orthotropic type decks, development of welding techniques and progress in structural analysis. The development and application of electronic computers opened up new and practically unlimited possibilities for the exact solution of these highly statically indeterminate systems and for precise statical analysis of their three-dimensional performance.

Existing cable-stayed bridges provide useful data regarding design, fabrication, erection and maintenance of the new system. With the construction of these bridges many basic problems encountered in their engineering are shown to have been successfully solved. However, these important data have apparently never before been systematically presented.

The following factors helped make the successful development of cable-stayed bridges possible: (1) The development of methods of structural analysis of highly statically indeterminate structures and application of electronic computers; (2) The development of orthotropic steel decks; (3) Experience with previously built bridges containing basic elements of cable-stayed bridges; (4) Application of high strength steels, new methods of fabrication and erection; (5) The ability to analyze such structures through model studies.

Basic Concepts

The application of inclined cables gave a new stimulus to construction of large bridges. The importance of cable-stayed bridges increased rapidly and within only one decade they have become so successful that they have taken their rightful place among classical bridge systems. It is interesting to note how this development which has so revolutionized bridge construction, but which in fact is no new discovery, came about.

The beginning of this system, probably, may be traced back to the time when it was realized that rigid structures could be formed by joining triangles together.

Although most of these earlier designs were based on sound principles and assumptions, the girder stiffened by inclined cables suffered various misfortunes that regrettably resulted in abandonment of the system. Nevertheless, the system in itself was not at all unsuitable. The solution of the problem had unfortunately been attempted in the wrong way.

On the one hand, the equilibrium of these highly indeterminate systems had not been clearly appreciated and controlled, and on the other, the tension members were made of timber, round bars or chains. They consisted therefore of low-strength material which was fully stressed only after a substantial deformation of the girder took place. This may explain why the renewed application of the cable-stayed system was possible only under the following conditions: (1) The correct analysis of the structural system; (2) The use of tension members having under dead load a considerable degree of stiffness due to high prestress and beyond this still sufficient capacity to accommodate the live load; (3) The use of erection methods which ensure that the design assumptions are realized in an economic manner.

The renaissance of the cable-stayed system, however, was finally successfully achieved only during the last decade.

Modern cable-stayed bridges present a three-dimensional system consisting of stiffening girders, transverse and longitudinal bracings, orthotropic-type deck and supporting parts such as towers in compression and inclined cables in tension. The important characteristics of such a three-dimensional structure are the full participation of the transverse construction in the work of the main longitudinal structure. This means a considerable increase in the moment of inertia of the construction which permits a reduction in the depth of the girders and economy in steel.

Structural Advantages

The introduction of the cable-stayed system in bridge engineering has resulted in the creation of new types of structures which possess many excellent characteristics and advantages. Outstanding among these are their structural characteristics, efficiency and wide range of application. The basic structural characteristics and reasons for the rapid development and success of cable-stayed bridges are as outlined below.

Cable-stayed bridges present a space system, consisting of stiffening girders, steel or concrete deck and supporting parts as towers acting in compression and inclined cables in tension. By their structural behavior cable-stayed systems occupy a middle position between the girder type and suspension type bridges.

The main structural characteristic of this system is the integral action of the stiffening girders and prestressed or post-tensioned inclined cables, which run from the tower tops down to the anchor points at the stiffening girders. Horizontal compressive forces due to the cable action are taken by the girders and no massive anchorages are required. The substructure, therefore, is very economical.

Introduction of the orthotropic system has resulted in the creation of new types of superstructure which can easily carry the horizontal thrust of stay cables with almost no additional materials, even for very long spans.

In old types of conventional superstructures the slab, stringers, floor beams and main girders were considered as acting independently. Such superstructures were not suitable for cable-stayed bridges. With the orthotropic type deck, however, the stiffened plate with its large cross-sectional area acts not only as the upper chord of the main girders and of the transverse beams, but also as the horizontal plate girder against wind forces, giving modern bridges much more lateral stiffness than the wind bracings used in old systems. In fact, in orthotropic systems, all elements of the roadway and secondary parts of the superstructure participate in the work of the main bridge systems. This results in reduction of the depth of the girders and economy in the steel.

Another structural characteristic of this system is geometrically unchangeable under any load position on the bridge, and all cables are in a state of tension. This characteristic of cable-stayed systems permits them to be built from relatively light flexible elements-cables.

The important characteristic of such a three-dimensional bridge is the full participation of the transverse structural parts in the work of the main structure in the longitudinal directions. This means a considerable increase in the moment of inertia of the construction, which permits a reduction of the depth of the girders and a consequent saving in steel.

The orthotropic system provides the continuity of the deck structure at the towers and in the center of the main span. The continuity of the bridge superstructure over many spans has many advantages and is actually necessary for good cable-stayed bridges.

Considering the range of applications in the domain of highway bridges, cable-stayed bridges fill the gap that existed between deck type and suspension bridges. Orthotropic deck plate girders showed superiority over other systems in the case of medium spans. For long spans, however, they required considerable girder depth. The cable-stayed bridge provides a solution to this problem, based on a structural system comprising an orthotropic plate deck and a continuous girder.

LESSON 14

New Words

1. renewal [ri'nju(:)əl]   n. 复兴，恢复
2. stay [stei]   n. 拉索，支撑；v. 支持
3. attach [ə'tætʃ]   vt. 缚上，系上，附上…的
4. pier [piə]   n. 桥墩，桥台
5. slack [slæk]   a. 松弛的
6. sound [saund]   a. 可靠的，完善的
7. stiffen ['stifn]   vt. 加劲
8. bracing ['breisiŋ]   n. 支撑，支柱，系杆
9. regrettably [ri'gretəbli]   ad. 抱歉地，遗憾地
10. renaissance [rə'neisəns]   n. 复活，新生
11. thrust [θrʌst]   n. 推力，轴向(压)力
12. roadway ['rəudwei]   n. 车道，道路；路面，桥面
13. girder ['gə:də]   n. 纵梁，大梁，桁梁

Phrases and Expressions

1. cable-stayed bridge   斜拉桥
2. be in short supply   供应短缺
3. continuous girder   连续梁
4. suspension type bridge   悬吊型桥
5. girder type bridge   梁式桥
6. orthotropic deck   正交各向异性板桥
7. transverse and longitudinal bracing   横向和纵向支撑
8. highly statically indeterminate system   高次超静定体系

Notes

[1] Cable-stayed bridges are…, i.e. inclined cables passing over or attached to towers located at the main piers. 本句中的 passing over or attached to 作后置定语修饰 inclined cables；located at the main piers 作后置定语修饰 towers。全句可译为：斜拉桥是按如下结构体系建造的，它包括正交各向异性桥面板和由通过位于主墩上的索塔顶部或固定于索塔顶部的倾斜缆索支承的连续梁组成。

[2] Stays… could not be fully tensioned and in a slack condition allowed large deformations of the deck before… they were intended. could not be fully tensioned 和 allowed 的主语均为 stays。全句可译为：这种拉索不能充分拉紧，而处于松弛状态的拉索在参与承担所期望承担的受拉荷载之前容许桥面发生很大变形。

Exercises

1. Fill in the blanks with proper words.

（1）Stays made in this manner could not be fully tensioned and _____ a slack condition allowed large deformations of the deck before they could participate in taking the tensile loads _____ which they were intended.

（2）Unfortunately, the system in general met _____ little success, due to the fact that the statics were not fully understood _____ that unsuitable materials such as bars and chains were used to form the inclined supports or stays.

（3）Wide and successful application of cable-stayed systems was realized only recently, _____ the introduction of high-strength steels, orthotropic type decks, development of welding techniques and progress _____ structural analysis.

（4）During the past decade cable-stayed bridges have _____ wide application, especially in Western Europe, and to a _____ extent in other parts of the world.

（5）Existing cable-stayed bridges provide useful data _____ design, fabrication, erection and maintenance of the new system.

（6）Modern cable-stayed bridges present a three-dimensional system consisting of stiffening girders, transverse and longitudinal bracings, orthotropic-type deck and supporting parts such as towers _____ compression and inclined cables _____ tension.

（7）_____ their structural behavior cable-stayed systems occupy a middle position _____ the girder type and suspension type bridges.

（8）The main structural characteristic of this system is the integral action of the stiffening girders and prestressed _____ post-tensioned inclined cables, which run from the tower tops down to the anchor points _____ the stiffening girders.

（9）The full participation of the transverse structural parts _____ the work of the main structure in the longitudinal directions means a considerable increase _____ the moment of inertia of the construction.

（10）Orthotropic deck plate girders showed superiority _____ other systems _____ the case of medium spans.

2. Translate the following phrases into Chinese/English.

　　（1）highly statically indeterminate systems　　　（6）斜拉桥
　　（2）orthotropic deck　　　　　　　　　　　　　（7）梁式桥
　　（3）suspension bridges　　　　　　　　　　　　（8）横向和纵向支撑
　　（4）three-dimensional structure　　　　　　　　（9）横向刚性
　　（5）high-strength steel　　　　　　　　　　　　（10）连续梁

3. Translate the following sentences into Chinese.

（1）Unfortunately, the system in general met with little success, due to the fact that the statics were not fully understood and that unsuitable materials such as bars and chains were used to form the inclined supports or stays.

LESSON 14

(2) Although most of these earlier designs were based on sound principles and assumptions, the girder stiffened by inclined cables suffered various misfortunes which regrettably resulted in abandonment of the system.

(3) On the one hand, the equilibrium of these highly indeterminate systems had not been clearly appreciated and controlled, and on the other, the tension members were made of timber, round bars or chains.

(4) The important characteristics of such a three-dimensional structure is the full participation of the transverse construction in the work of the main longitudinal structure.

(5) The importance of cable-stayed bridges increased rapidly and within only one decade they have become so successful that they have taken their rightful place among classical bridge systems.

(6) In old types of conventional superstructures the slab, stringers, floor beams and main girders were considered as acting independently.

(7) The main structural characteristic of this system is the integral action of the stiffening girders and prestressed and post-tensioned inclined cables, which run from the tower tops down to the anchor points at the stiffening girders.

(8) Modern cable-stayed bridges present a three-dimensional system consisting of stiffening girders, transverse and longitudinal bracings, orthotropic-type deck and supporting parts such as towers in compression and inclined cables in tension.

(9) In orthotropic systems, all elements of the roadway and secondary parts of the superstructure participate in the work of the main bridge systems.

(10) Stays made in this manner could not be fully tensioned and in a slack condition allowed large deformations of the deck before they could participate in taking the tensile loads for which they were intended.

4. Fill in the blanks with the given words below.

all, although, and, by, by, in, in, nevertheless, on, when

The beginning of this system, probably, may be traced back to the time _____ it was realized that rigid structures could be formed _____ joining triangles together. _____ most of these earlier designs were based _____ sound principles _____ assumptions, the girder stiffened _____ inclined cables suffered various misfortunes that regrettably resulted _____ abandonment of the system. _____, the system in itself was not at _____ unsuitable. The solution of the problem had unfortunately been attempted _____ the wrong way.

5. Translate the following sentences into English.

(1) 电子计算机的应用使斜拉桥这样的高次超静定体系的精确分析成为可能。

(2) 随着高强度钢和正交各向异性板桥面的出现以及焊接技术和结构分析技术的发展，近年来斜拉桥才得到了广泛和成功的应用。

(3) 已有的斜拉桥为这一新体系的设计、建造、安装和养护提供了有益的数据。

(4) 随着这些桥梁的修建，桥梁工程中的很多基础问题都得到了成功解决。

(5) 斜拉桥的特点是这种结构可将斜拉索的原理和正交各向异性板桥面结合起来，故其具有跨径大、结构厚度小和用料省的优点。

Reading Material

Highway Bridges

A bridge may be defined as a drainage structure that has a span of more than 6m (20ft). As a further distinguishing feature, bridges spans usually, although not always, rest on separate abutments, whereas culverts are regarded as integral structures. Although the term "bridge" is usually associated with structures that are required to carry the roadbed over an established waterway, it may also be somewhat loosely applied to grade separation structures and elevated highways in urban areas (viaducts(高架桥)).

Bridge Location

In modern practice, bridges of relatively short span are located to conform with the general location of the highway, which has been previously determined. That is, the tentative location for the highway is established after an analysis of all the economic and engineering factors involved, and the bridge engineer is given the problem of providing an economical and adequate bridge design to conform to the roadway location. In some cases, the location of a suitable stream crossing may be the most important single factor influencing the location of the highway in a given section; such is usually the case when long bridge spans are involved.

The ideal location for a bridge crossing is, of course, one in which the crossing is made at right angles to the centerline of the stream at the nearest point, where the alignment of the approach pavement is straight, where the approach grade is slight, and where soil conditions are adequate for the installation of the most economical foundation for the span involved. This ideal combination of circumstances is encountered all too infrequently, except in structures of short span, and many bridges have been located on skew(歪斜的) crossings, vertical curves or with curving alignment. In such cases, considerations related to the general roadway location may still be regarded as controlling factors, and the required adjustments in the location of the bridge are made with these requirements in mind.

Many times, alternative locations of a proposed bridge may seem to offer somewhat similar advantages. A careful comparison must then be made of the several possible locations. The final decision should be based on a complete analysis, including factors related to traffic safety and operating conditions, fulfillment of the purpose of the road (e.g., the direct connection of population centers) and economics. Any complete analysis must include both the bridge and the approaches to it. A comparison of this type will generally result in the selection of one of the possible sites as the most desirable.

Once the general location is determined, the selected site must be subjected to careful scrutiny. This examination may be extremely detailed or somewhat cursory, depending largely on the size and importance of the contemplated structure. A complete survey of the bridge site may include an examination of the channel for some distance above and below the bridge crossing, a complete topographic map of the site, and an extensive soil survey of the area, including securing undisturbed soil samples where required and determining the required waterway opening and the requirements of navigation on large streams.

Although the preceding paragraphs have dealt largely with waterway crossings, similar factors govern the design of grade separation structure and the bridge portions of complex interchanges. Obviously, a grade separation structure designed to carry the roadway over an existing railroad presents the location engineer and designer with similar problems, as does the design of a highway overpass. Similarly, the general location of an elevated highway in an urban area is usually determined on the basis of maximum serviceability to traffic (and availability of right-of-way) so that the engineer must prepare a design suitable to conditions in a rather limited area.

Design of Waterway Opening

In many locations the natural stream channel is somewhat constricted by the bridge structure and roadway approaches. In the interests of economy, the roadway is frequently placed on an embankment on either side of the bridge span, the distance between abutments is reduced as much as possible, and piers may be placed in the stream channel. All these things serve in many cases to reduce severely the area through which the water must pass, particularly when the stream is at flood stage. Two results may immediately be noticed: during flood stage the velocity of the water through the bridge opening may be considerably increased, with resultant danger to bring structure through scour at abutments and piers, and the elevation of the water on the upstream side may be increased, with the result that the area subjected to flooding above the bridge site is increased and adjacent property is subjected to overflow beyond the limits of the normal floodplain. It thus seems axiomatic that the bridge must be designed to pass the flow occurring at flood stage without excessive velocity and without damage to property located above the bridge crossing. Estimating flood flows is best done by study of stream-gagging records but is sometimes based on observation of high water marks, the behavior of structures located on the same stream and hydrologic computations.

Bridge openings are also normally designed to pass floating debris(碎片，残骸) carried in the channel at normal and flood states. On navigable streams, requirements of navigation must be evaluated and provided for. Generally speaking, navigable streams are spanned by high-level crossings or movable bridges.

Bridge Types

For permanent bridges, the most commonly used materials are steel and concrete. General categories of steel bridges are briefly described in the following paragraphs:

Suspension bridges are used for very long spans or for shorter spans where intermediate piers cannot be built.

Girder bridges come in two basic varieties: plate and box girders. Plate girders are usually used for medium spans. They generally are continuous structures with maximum depth of girder over the piers and minimum depth at midspan. The plate girders generally have an I cross section; they are arranged in lines that support stringers, floorbeams, and, generally, a cast-in-place concrete deck. The girders are shop-fabricated by welding; field connections generally are by high-strength bolts. Welded-steel box girder structures are generally similar to plate girder spans except for the configuration of the bridge cross section.

Rigid frames are used occasionally, most often for spans in the range of 23 to 30m (75 to 100ft) and for grade-separation structures.

Arch bridges are used for longer spans at locations where intermediate piers cannot be used and where good rock is available to withstand the thrusts at the arch abutments. A variation in the arch bridge is the tied arch, in which a horizontal tie that carries the roadway takes much of the horizontal thrust inherent in the arch form.

Truss bridges are built in many forms and in many locations for medium and long spans. Both deck and through trusses are built, with cantilever and continuous trusses being the most common.

Concrete bridges come in nearly as great a variety as do steel bridges. Following are various types now in the use and some examples of outstanding concrete structures:

Conventional reinforced concrete is used primarily for short spans, with a variety of innovation from the customary cast-in-place, slab-and-beam design.

Precast, prestressed concrete bridges are popular in the bridge engineering for short simple spans; they generally consist of prestressed I beams or box girders that support a cast-in-place deck.

Cast-in-place prestressed concrete has been used for long span bridges in Europe and in a few locations in the United States. It was stressed by a longitudinal movement of the pier bases produced by jacking after the superstructure was completed.

科技英语阅读与写作指南

科技英语写作——定义，分类与功能用途

1. 定义

　　...be defined as...　　…是…
　　...means/signifies...　　…的意思是…
　　...refers to...　　…是指…
　　...is considered to be...　　…是…
　　By...I/we mean...　　我/我们说…指的是…
　　By...is meant...　　…是…的意思

The unit weight or density of a material <u>is defined as</u> the weight of a given piece of the material divided by its volume.

<u>By</u> mechanical system, <u>we mean</u> a collection of particles and rigid bodies as distinguished

from a system whose members may deform.

The soil structure <u>refers to</u> the geometric configuration of the particles in a soil aggregate and has a profound effect on the physical properties of the soil.

<u>By</u> inflation <u>is meant</u> the depreciation of money and the rise of prices.

2. 分类

  There are two/several types（kinds，classes，groups，varieties）of... …有…种/类

  ... are of two types …分为两类

  We can classify（divide, group）... into... 我们可以把…分为…

  ... can be divided(classified, categorized，grouped)into …可以把…分为…

  ... falls into... …分为…

  Dead loads are defined as fixed，nonmovable loads of a permanent nature <u>which can be divided into two categories</u>.

  <u>There are basically two main groups</u> for the typical cantilever systems.

  We can <u>classify</u> bearings according to their position on the shaft.

  The most commonly used structural systems used in high-rise buildings <u>can be categorized into</u> seven types

  Engines <u>are basically of two types</u> according to the kind of fuel they use.

  Vehicles <u>fall into</u> three categories according to their use.

3. 功能用途

  ... be used for... …的用途是…

  ... be capable of doing... …能做…

  The function of... is to do... …的功能是…

  ... serve to do... …用来做…

  ... act as... …的功用是…

  ... function as... …的功用是…

  ... be a/an instrument(tool，device)for doing... …是用来…的器具

  After separation occurs，the panel <u>acts as</u> a diagonal strut with an effective width w less than that of the full panel.

  In this case，the brickwork or blockwork is considered only to <u>function as</u> permanent formwork，and is ignored in strength calculations.

  Localized areas to <u>be used for</u> storage or heavy filing loads are often unknown at the time of preliminary design.

  The dynamo <u>serves to</u> generate electricity.

  <u>The function of</u> a deep foundation <u>is</u> to carry building loads beneath a stratum of material deemed unsatisfactory to a satisfactory bearing stratum.

  The critical path method has <u>become a useful tool for</u> planning the construction of a project.

LESSON 15

Concrete placement

The principles governing proper placement of concrete are:

Segregation must be avoided during all operations between the mixer and the point of placement, including final consolidation and finishing.

The concrete must be thoroughly consolidated, and should fill all angles and corners of the forms.

Where fresh concrete is placed on hardened concrete, a good bond must be developed.

The temperature of fresh concrete must be controlled from the time of mixing through final placement, and protected after placement.

Methods of Placing

Concrete may be conveyed from a mixer to point of placement by any of a variety of methods and equipment, if properly transported to avoid segregation. Selection of the most appropriate technique for economy depends on jobsite conditions, especially project size, equipment, and the contractor's experience. In building construction, concrete usually is placed with hand-or power-operated buggies; dropbottom buckets with a crane; inclined chutes; flexible and rigid pipe by pumping; shotcrete, in which either dry materials and water are sprayed separately or mixed concrete is shot against the forms; and for underwater placing, tremie chutes (closed flexible tubes). For mass-concrete construction, side-dump cars on narrow-gage track or belt conveyers may be used. For pavement, concrete may be placed by bucket from the swinging boom of a paving mixer, directly by dump truck or mixer truck, or indirectly by trucks into a spreader.

Excess Water

Even within the specified limits on slump and water-cementitious materials ratio, excess water must be avoided. In this context, excess water is present for the conditions of placing if evidence of water rise (vertical segregation) or water flow (horizontal segregation) occurs. Excess water also tends to aggravate surface defects by increased leakage through form openings. The result may be honeycomb, variations in color, or soft spots at the surface.

In vertical formwork, water rise causes weak planes between each layer deposited. In addition to the deleterious structural effect, such planes, when hardened, contain voids through which water may pass.

In horizontal elements, such as floor slabs, excess water rises and causes a weak laitance layer at the top. This layer suffers from low strength, low abrasion resistance, high shrinkage, and generally poor quality.

Consolidation

The purpose of consolidation is to eliminate voids of air and to ensure intimate complete contact of the concrete with the surfaces of the forms and the reinforcement. Intense vibration, however, may also reduce the volume of desirable entrained air; but this reduction can be compensated by adjustment of the mix proportions.

Powered internal vibrators are usually used to achieve consolidation. For thin slabs, however, high-quality, low-slump concrete can be effectively consolidated, without excess water, by mechanical surface vibrators. For precast elements in rigid external vibration is highly effective. External vibration is also effective with in-place forms, but should not be used unless the formwork is specially designed for the temporary increase in internal pressures to full fluid head plus the impact of the vibrator.

Except in certain paving operations, vibration of the reinforcement should be avoided. Although it is effective, the necessary control to prevent overvibration is difficult. Also, when concrete is placed in several lifts of layers, vibration of vertical rebars passing into partly set concrete below may be harmful. Note, however, that revibration of concrete before the final set, under controlled conditions, can improve concrete strength markedly and reduce surface voids. This technique is too difficult to control for general use on field-cast vertical elements, but it is very effective in finishing slabs with powered vibrating equipment.

Concreting Vertical Elements

The interior of columns is usually congested; it contains a large volume of reinforcing steel compared with the volume of concrete, and has a large height compared with its cross-sectional dimensions. Therefore, though columns should be continuously cast, the concrete should be placed in 2-to 4-ft-deep increments and consolidated with internal vibrators. These should be lifted after each increment has been vibrated. If delay occurs in concrete supply before a column has been completed, every effort should be made to avoid a cold joint. When the remainder of the column is cast, the first increment should be small, and should be vibrated to penetrate the previous portion slightly.

In all columns and reinforced narrow walls, concrete placing should begin with 2 to 4 in of grout. Otherwise, loose stone will collect at the bottom, resulting in the formation of honeycomb. This grout should be proportioned for about the same slump as the concrete or slightly more, but at the same or lower water-cementitious material ratio. ([1]Some engineers prefer to start vertical placement with a mix having the same proportions of water, cement, and fine aggregate, but with one-half the quantity of coarse aggregate, as in the design mix, and to place a starting layer 6 to 12 in deep.) When concrete is placed for walls, the only practicable means to avoid segregation is to place no more than a 24-in layer in one pass. Each layer should be vibrated separately and kept nearly level.

For walls deeper than 4 ft, concrete should be placed through vertical. The concrete should not fall free more than 4 ft or segregation will occur, with the coarse aggregate ricocheting off the forms to lodge on one side. Successive layers after the initial layer should be penetrated by internal vibrators for a depth of about 4 to 6 in to ensure complete integration at the surface of each layer. Deeper penetration can be beneficial (revibration), but control under variable jobsite conditions is too uncertain for recommendation of this practice for general use.

[2] The results of poor placement in walls are frequently observed: sloping layer lines; honeycombs, leaking, if water is present; and, if cores are taken at successive heights, up to a 50% reduction in strength from bottom to top. Some precautions necessary to avoid these ill effects are:

Do not move concrete laterally with vibrators.

For deep, long walls, reduce the slump for upper layers 2 to 3 in below the slump for the starting layer.

On any delay between placing of layers, vibrate the concrete thoroughly at the interface.

Inspection of Concrete Placement

Concrete should be inspected for the owner before, during, and after casting. Before concrete is placed, the formwork must be free of ice and debris and properly coated with bond-breaker oil. The rebars must be in place, properly supported to bear any traffic they will receive during concrete placing. Conduit, inserts, and other items to be embedded must be in position, fixed against displacement.[3] Construction personnel should be available, usually carpenters, bar placers and other trades, if piping or electrical conduit is to be embedded, to act as form watchers and to reset any rebars, conduit, or piping displaced.

As concrete is cast, the slump of the concrete must be observed and regulated within prescribed limits, or the specified strengths based on the expected slump may be reduced. An inspector of placing who is also responsible for sampling and making cylinders, should test slump, temperatures, and unit weights, during concreting and should control any field adjustment of slump and added water and cement. The inspector should also ascertain that handling, placing, and finishing procedures that have been agreed on in advance are properly followed, to avoid segregated concrete. In addition, the inspector should ensure that any emergency construction joints made necessary by stoppage of concrete supply, rain, or other delays are properly located and made in accordance with procedures specified or approved by the engineer.

Inspection is complete only when concrete is cast, finished, protected for curing, and attains full strength.

LESSON 15

New Words

1. segregation [ˌsegriˈgeiʃən]   n. 分凝，离析
2. shotcrete [ʃɔtkrit]   n. 喷射混凝土
3. buggy [ˈbʌgi]   n. 手推车，小货车
4. dropbottom [drɔpˈbɔtəm]   n. 底卸式，活底
5. bucket [ˈbʌkit]   n. 桶，铲斗，料罐
6. chute [ʃuːt]   n. 斜道，斜槽，槽
7. tremie [ˈtremi]   n. （水下灌注用）混凝土导管
8. spreader [ˈspredə]   n. 延辗机，铺料机
10. aggravate [ˈægrəveit]   vt. 使恶化，加重
11. laitance [ˈleitəns]   n. 浮浆，浮渣
12. abrasion [əˈbreiʒən]   n. 磨损
13. entrain [inˈtrein]   vt. 使空气以气泡状存在于混凝土中
14. rebar [riˈbɑː]   n. 钢筋，螺纹钢筋
15. debris [ˈdebriː, ˈdeib-]   n. 碎片，岩屑
16. conduit [ˈkɔndit]   n. 管道，导管
17. bugholes [ˈbʌghəulz]   n. 凹痕
18. ricochet [ˈrikəʃet]   n. 跳飞，跳弹；v. （使）跳飞
19. deleterious [ˌdeliˈtiəriəs]   a. 有害的
20. lodge [lɔdʒ]   n. 门房，小屋

Phrases and Expressions

1. fresh concrete   新浇混凝土，未结硬混凝土
2. hardened concrete   硬化混凝土
3. mass concrete   大体积（块）混凝土
4. swinging boom   起重机回转臂，吊车旋转杆
5. paving mixer   铺路拌和机
6. dump truck   自动倾卸卡车
7. mixer truck   混凝土搅拌车
8. side dump   侧卸（式）
9. laitance layer   （水泥）浆沫层
10. surface vibrator   平面振实器，表面式振捣器
11. construction joint   施工缝
12. bar placer   钢筋工

Notes

[1] Some engineers prefer to start . . . , as in the design mix, and to place a starting

layer 6 to 12 in deep. 有些工程师在浇筑竖向构件时，喜欢用与设计混凝土相同配比的水、水泥、细骨料，但粗骨料只用一半的量，作为先浇混凝土，浇筑 6～12 英寸高。

[2] The results of poor placement in walls are frequently observed:... from bottom to top. 全句可译为：经常遇到的墙体浇筑时的不良施工后果有：层面倾斜、蜂窝、漏浆，若沿高度连续取芯，从底部到顶部的强度降低达 50%。

[3] Construction personnel should be available,..., or piping displaced. 全句可译为：当铺设水管或电线管道时，施工人员必须到位，通常有木工、钢筋工及其他工种，对模板进行检查，对移动了的钢筋、电线或管子重新放置。

Exercises

1. Fill in the blanks with proper words.

（1）Segregation must be avoided during all operations between the mixer and the point of _____, including final consolidation and finishing.

（2）Where fresh concrete is placed against or on hardened concrete, a good _____ must be developed.

（3）Concrete may be conveyed from a mixer to point of placement by any of a variety of methods and equipment, if properly transported to avoid _____.

（4）Even within the specified limits on _____ and water-cementitious materials ratio, excess water must be avoided.

（5）The purpose of consolidation is to _____ voids of air and to ensure intimate complete contact of the concrete with the surfaces of the forms and the reinforcement.

（6）The interior of columns is usually congested; it contains a large volume of reinforcing steel compared with the volume of concrete, and has a large _____ compared with its cross-sectional dimensions.

（7）Concrete should be inspected for the owner before, _____, and after casting.

（8）As concrete is cast, the slump of the concrete must be observed and regulated within prescribed _____.

（9）When the remainder of the column is cast, the first increment should be small, and should be vibrated to _____ the previous portion slightly.

2. Translate the following phrases into Chinese/English

（1）construction joint 　　（6）坍落度
（2）hardened concrete 　　（7）水下浇筑
（3）laitance layer　　　　　（8）水灰比
（4）mass concrete 　　　　（9）平面振实器
（5）bar placer 　　　　　　（10）粗骨料

3. Translate the following sentences into Chinese

（1）Where fresh concrete is placed on hardened concrete, a good bond must be developed.

（2）Before concrete is placed, the formwork must be free of ice and debris and properly coated with bond-breaker oil.

(3) Construction personnel should be available, usually carpenters, bar placers and other trades, if piping or electrical conduit is to be embedded, to act as form watchers and to reset any rebars, conduit, or piping displaced.

(4) In addition, the inspector should ensure that any emergency construction joints made necessary by stoppage of concrete supply, rain, or other delays are properly located and made in accordance with procedures specified or approved by the engineer.

(5) In vertical formwork, water rise causes weak planes between each layer deposited.

(6) In some factory buildings, settlement effects are unimportant, but when the interior finish is marble, trouble may be encountered if settlement is not taken care of in advance.

(7) In horizontal elements, such as floor slabs, excess water rises and causes a weak laitance layer at the top.

(8) Any total overall measuring done after loading will have to be corrected by calculated deformations based on the modulus of elasticity of the column material.

(9) The temperature of fresh concrete must be controlled from the time of mixing through final placement, and protected after placement.

4. Fill in the blanks with the given words below.

also, by, by, for, in, in, on, to, within, with

As concrete is cast, the slump of the concrete must be observed and regulated _____ prescribed limits, or the specified strengths based _____ the expected slump may be reduced. An inspector of placing who is also responsible _____ sampling and making cylinders, should test slump, entrained air, temperatures, and unit weights, during concreting and should control any field adjustment of slump and added water and cement. The inspector should _____ ascertain that handling, placing, and finishing procedures that have been agreed on _____ advance are properly followed, _____ avoid segregated concrete. _____ addition, the inspector should ensure that any emergency construction joints made necessary _____ stoppage of concrete supply, rain, or other delays are properly located and made in accordance _____ procedures specified or approved _____ the engineer.

5. Translate the following sentences into English

(1) 钢筋必须设备到位，适当支撑以承受浇筑混凝土过程中受到的任何运输作用。

(2) 检验员还必须确保混凝土运送、浇筑和抹光程序按事先要求进行，避免混凝土离析。

(3) 只有在混凝土浇筑、抹光、养护完成，并完全达到强度时检验才结束。

(4) 更深的贯入效果会更好（复捣），但在不同的场地条件下其效果是难以确定的，因此，不作为一般工程实践的建议。

(5) 在所有柱子和钢筋混凝土窄墙浇筑时，要先用2～4英寸的水泥浆。否则，游离的石子就会聚集在底部，从而形成蜂窝。

Reading Material

Soil Improvement

Another way of dealing with weak or compressible soils is to improve them. Some soil improvement techniques have been used for many years, whereas others are relatively new. This section discusses some of the more common methods.

Removal and Replacement

Sometimes poor soils can simply be removed and replaced with good quality compacted fill. This alternative is especially attractive if the thickness of the deposit is small, the groundwater table is deep, and good quality fill material is readily available.

Surcharge Fills

Covering poor soils with a temporary surcharge fill, as shown in Fig. 15.1, cause them to consolidate more rapidly. When the temporary fill is removed, some or all of the soil is now overconsolidated, and thus stronger and less compressible. This process is known as preloading or precompression.

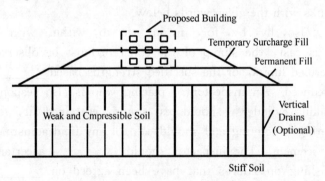

Fig. 15.1 Soil improvement by preloading

    Engineers have primarily used preloading to improve saturated silts and clays because these soils are most conductive to consolidation under static loads. Sandy and gravelly soils respond better to vibratory loads.

    If the soil is saturated, the time required for it to consolidate depends on the ability of the excess pore water to move out of the soil voids. This depends on the thickness of the soil deposit, its coefficient of permeability, and other factors, and can be estimated using the principle of soil mechanics. The time required could range from only a few weeks to 30 years or more.

    The consolidation process can be accelerated by an order of magnitude or more by installing vertical drains in the natural soil, as shown in Fig. 15.1. These drains provide a pathway for the excess water to escape more easily.

    Preloading is less expensive than some other soil improvement techniques, especially when the surcharge soils can be moved from place to place, thus preloading the site in sections. Vertical drains, if needed, may double the cost.

Vibro-Compaction and Vibro-Replacement

Sandy and gravelly soils consolidate most effectively when subjected to vibratory loads. This is especially true at depths of about 10 ft (3m) because of the greater overburden stress.

Engineers in Germany recognized this behavior and developed depth vibrators in the 1930s. These methods were refined during the 1970s and now are frequently used throughout the world.

Some of these depth vibrators are essentially vibratory pile hammers attached to a length of steel pipe. Known as a terra probe(水下振砂器), this device is vibrated into the ground, densifying the adjacent soils, and then retracted. This process is repeated on a grid pattern across the site until all of the soil has been densified.

Another technique uses a probe with a built-in vibrator that is lowered into the ground, also on a grid pattern. The probe is known as a vibroflot(振浮压实器) and the technique is called *vibroflotation*. The vibroflots are also equipped with water jets to aid penetration and improve soil compaction.

Both of these techniques may be classified as vibro-compaction methods because they compact the soils in-situ using vibration. In either case, additional sandy soil is added to assist the compaction process. Another closely related method is vibro-replacement, which uses the vibrator to create a shaft, and then the shaft is backfilled with gravel to form a stone column. This technique may be used in cohesive soils and is primarily intended to provide load bearing members that extend through the weak soils. The stone column also acts as a vertical drain, thus helping to accelerate consolidation settlements.

Dynamic Consolidation(动力固结)

The Soviets tried dropping heavy weights to stabilize loess in the 1930s. However, this method did not become widely accepted until the French developed *dynamic consolidation* (also known as *heavy tamping*) in 1970. This technique consists of dropping 5 to 40 ton weights, called *pounders*, from heights of 20 to 100ft (6-30m). The impact of the falling weight compacts the soil to significant depths. This tamping process is repeated on a grid pattern, and then the upper soils are smoothed and compacted using conventional earthmoving and compaction equipment.

Dynamic consolidation has been effectively used with a wide range of soil types. It is relatively inexpensive, but it also generates large shock waves and therefore cannot be used close to existing structures.

Reinforcement Using Geosynthetics(土工织物)

Soil is similar to concrete in that both materials are strong in compression but weak in tension. Fortunately, both can be improved by introducing tensile members to form a composite material. Steel bars are used to form reinforced concrete, which is vastly superior to plain concrete. Likewise, various metallic and nonmetallic materials can be used to reinforce soil.

Engineers most frequently use materials known as geosynthetics to reinforce soils. Although most of these applications have been in the context of retaining structures and earth slopes, strategically placed tensile reinforcement could also provide flexural strength in soil beneath spread footings.

科技英语阅读与写作指南

科技英语写作——表格与插图

1. 常用词语

  figure 图，插图   illustration 插图，图解   diagram 图表
  graph 曲线图，图表   sketch 简图   flowchart 流程图
  curve 曲线图   cross-section 剖面图   distribution 分布图
  table 图表   three-dimension graph 三维图

2. 常用句型

The table shows the changes in the number of... over the period from... to...
该表格描述了在…至…间…数量的变化。
The graph provides some interesting data regarding...
该图为我们提供了有关…有趣数据。
This is a curve graph which describes the trend of...
这个曲线图描述了…的趋势。
From the table/chart/diagram/figure, we can see clearly that...
从图表我们可以很清楚(明显)看到…
It is clear/apparent from the chart that...
从图表我们可以很清楚(明显)看到…
This table shows the changing proportion of a & b from... to...
该表格描述了…到…间 a 与 b 的比例关系。
The graph, presented in a pie chart, shows the general trend in...
该图以圆形图形式描述了…总的趋势。
As can be seen from the graph, the two curves show the fluctuation of...
如图所示，两条曲线描述了…的波动情况。
Over the period from... to... the... remained level.
在…至…期间，…基本不变。
In the 3 years spanning from 1995 through 1998...
1995 年至 1998 三年里…
The number of... remained steady/stable from (month/year) to (month/year).
…月(年)至…月(年)…的数量基本不变。
The statistics provided by Fig. 5 shows that...
表 5 提供的数据表明…
The number sharply went up to...

数字急剧上升至…
The percentage of… stayed the same between… and…
…至…期间…的比率维持不变。
The figures peaked at… in(month/year)
…的数目在…月(年)达到顶点，为…
The percentage remained steady at…
比率维持在…
The percentage of… is slightly larger/smaller than that of…
…的比例比…的比例略高(低)。
The situation reached a peak(a high point at) of …%
…的情况(局势)到达顶(高)点，为…百分点。
The figures reached the bottom/a low point/hit a trough.
数字(情况)达到底部(低谷)。
There is an upward trend in the number of…
…数字呈上升趋势。
From… to… the rate of decrease slows down.
从…到…，下降速率减慢。
From this year on, there was a gradual decline in the…, reaching a figure of…
从这年起，…逐渐下降至…
…(year) witnessed/saw a sharp rise in…
…年…急剧上升。

LESSON 16

Concrete Formwork

Cost of Concrete Formwork

Formwork has a decided influence on the cost of concrete in place and may indeed be responsible for a very large part of the cost, ranging from 20% to 60%.

There are five principal items to be considered in arriving at the cost of concrete in place:

1. Formwork
2. Steel reinforcement
3. Concrete
4. Finishing
5. Curing

The most costly items are the first three listed. The concrete usually bought from a ready-mix plant and the cost per cubic yard varies only a small amount owing to differences in strength and the distance it must be hauled. The labor cost for placing will vary some, owing mostly to the height to which it must be lifted and the complexity of the structure.

The cost of reinforcement will vary with the amount used. This cost can be lessened if the depth of the section is increased, thus providing a longer lever arm that would require less area of reinforcement for the same moment. Finishing and curing are relatively minor items.

Formwork is the only item where the cost can be materially controlled. If the beam and column size are repeated enough, then the forms can be used over and over again, from three to five times, and even more. Every time the forms are reused the cost per cubic yard is reduced. The forms have only to be assembled into panels one time regardless of the number of uses; the only work that has to be repeated for each additional use is the erection, stripping, and cleaning of the panel. Thus it is evident that the designer, by the judicious use of column and beam sizes, can have a great deal of influence on the cost of the forms.

Design Considerations

Formwork must be capable of sustaining construction loads consisting of the weight and side pressure of the green concrete, equipment, personnel, and so on; it must also be rigid enough to maintain its shape without undue deflection; and it must be economical in terms of final cost, while at the same time being strong enough to withstand construction hazards.

Forms should be designed by conventional engineering practices to resist the forces resulting from the known loads. [1] If designed by experience or guesswork, the forms might be too light and subject to an expensive failure. On the other hand, the forms could be stronger than necessary and cost too much.

When forms are to be used many times, that part of the form in contact with the concrete must be of a good grade of material, which will have a high first cost but will be economical due to more than one use. If the finished surface of the concrete must be smooth and free of blemishes, the use of a very high grade of material will minimize expensive finishing.

To attain maximum economy in formwork, the highest practical unit stresses for the form material should be used. When the concrete is just cast, it is more or less fluid and exerts considerable side pressure on the forms. In several hours time after the concrete has set up, the side pressure will cease and the beam with its reinforcement will carry its own dead load plus the superimposed live loads; and stresses in the formwork will be practically nothing. Thus the forms will be subjected to maximum stresses for a very short period of time. [2] Wood is capable of absorbing large overloads if the stresses are of short duration, and because of this the allowable stresses based on constant loads of long duration may be increased by, say one third, as long as the forms, which are to be reused, are protected from abuse and excessive exposure to weather. However, it must be noted that the allowable deflections in formwork will many times govern the design for the reason that if the weight of the fresh concrete deflects the member too much, either horizontally or vertically, the finished concrete will set up in the deflected shape.

Some ways by which the cost of formwork may be kept at a minimum are the following:

1. Have the structural and architectural designers prepare their plans at the same time so that they may both be compatible with an economical system of formwork.

2. Keep the structural system uncomplicated so that the formwork may be simple and economically erected and removed.

3. Use the same size of columns over a whole building, if possible, or at least over several floors. This will permit the reuse of beam and column forms without alteration.

4. Space the columns uniformly, if possible, or if not, retain the same pattern floor to floor.

5. Space columns, if possible, to fit the use of plywood sheets for decking without cutting.

6. Use the same width for column and column-supported girders to eliminate the cutting and fitting of girder forms into column forms.

7. Specify beams of the same size and depth for each floor, and choose the depth that will permit the use of standard lumber sizes for beam sides.

Of course, it will not be feasible to let the attempt to achieve maximum formwork economy completely override all other considerations; however, any economies within the framework of the architectural and structural requirements should be implemented.

Cause of Failures

Failures that occur during concrete construction are principally formwork failures, which ordinarily happen when the concrete is being placed. When the forms are filled with wet concrete, there is a top-heavy effect and the formwork system is not inherently a stable structure. Some unusual application of a force may cause one member to fail, and if its stress is not absorbed by the other members, failure may occur. However, good design and construction practice and reasonable care can provide both safety and efficiency.

Removing the shores and formwork before the concrete has gained enough strength may cause sagging and hairline cracks that will be a serious maintenance problem later, and even failure may occur.

There are other causes for formwork failure besides the too early removal of formwork and shores. As stated before, the formwork must support all vertical and lateral loads until such time as these loads can be picked up by the hardened concrete. Care should be exercised to control the unsymmetrical placement of fresh concrete in forms, which can produce disastrous results.

Impact loads on formwork can produce very bad result. Some of these impact loads are caused by the dumping of large loads from powered buggies into the form, especially on large amounts of fresh concrete recently deposited. Care should be taken in moving any type of equipment about the forms so as not to produce impact.

Inadequate horizontal and cross bracing are among the principal causes of formwork accidents. If vertical shores are not properly braced, the loss of one or two shores, being accidentally knocked out of place, will most likely set up a chain reaction causing the loss of an entire floor. Vibrations due to the movement of concrete buggies and vibrators can also cause failure if the shores are not properly braced.

Faulty formwork is not always the reason for construction failures, which may be caused when the earth support of one or more columns fails. Another source of trouble sometimes makes its presence felt when the temperature drops sharply during a pouring of concrete, causing the setting time to be considerably lengthened. In this case the pouring should be slowed down to prevent a build-up of lateral pressure from overloading the forms.

New Words

1. stripping ['stripiŋ]   n. 抽锭，脱模，拆模
2. alteration [ˌɔːltə'reiʃən]   n. 变更，变更
3. dump [dʌmp]   vi. 卸货[料]; vt. 倾卸，倾倒
4. formwork ['fɔːmwəːk]   n. 模板，支模
5. undue [ˌʌn'djuː]   a. 过度的，过分的，不适当的
6. guesswork ['gesweːk]   n. 臆测，猜测

7. blemish [ˈblemiʃ]	n. 污点, 瑕疵; vt. 损害, 玷污
8. girder [ˈgəːdə]	n. 大梁, 钢桁的支架
9. lumber [ˈlʌmbə]	n. 木材, 锯材
10. feasible [ˈfiːzəbl]	a. 可行的, 切实可行的
11. override [ˌəuvəˈraid]	vt. 压倒, 制服, 践踏
12. shore [ʃɔː]	n. 支撑 [柱]; vt. 支撑, 支持

Phrases and Expressions

1. concrete formwork   混凝土模板工程
2. high grade of material   高等级材料
3. undue deflection   过大变形
4. side pressure   侧压力
5. constant load   不变荷载, 恒荷载
6. allowable stress   容许应力
7. plywood sheet   胶合板
8. hairline cracks   微裂缝

Notes

[1] If designed by experience or guesswork,... by experience or guesswork 中省略了 the forms are. 全句可译为: 如果凭经验和猜测做设计, 模板可能太弱而遭受严重损失。另一方面, 如果模板过强, 成本就会很大。

[2] Wood is capable of absorbing large overloads if ... to weather. based on constant loads of long duration 作定语修饰 the allowable stresses。全句可译为: 如果应力持续时间短, 木材可以承受较大的超载, 因此只要重复使用的模板免于滥用和过分暴露在露天中, 长期恒载下的允许应力可以增加, 比如三分之一。

Exercises

1. Fill in the blanks with proper words.

   (1) Formwork must be capable of sustaining construction loads consisting _____ the weight and side pressure of the green concrete, equipment, personnel, _____ so on.

   (2) Formwork must be economical _____ terms of final cost, _____ at the same time being strong enough to withstand construction hazards.

   (3) _____ the other hand, the forms could be stronger _____ necessary and cost too much.

   (4) When forms are to be used many times, that part of the form in contact _____ the concrete must be of a good grade of material, _____ will have a high first cost but will be economical due to more than one use.

   (5) Have the structural and architectural designers prepare their plans at the same

time _____ that they may both be compatible _____ an economical system of formwork.

(6) Space the columns uniformly, if possible, _____ if not, retain the same pattern floor to floor.

(7) Failures that occur during concrete construction are principally formwork failures, _____ ordinarily happen when the concrete is being placed.

(8) When the forms are filled _____ wet concrete, there is a top-heavy effect and the formwork system is not inherently a stable structure.

(9) However, good design and construction practice _____ reasonable care can provide both safety _____ efficiency.

(10) Some of these impact loads are caused _____ the dumping of large loads from powered buggies into the form, especially on large amounts _____ fresh concrete recently deposited.

2. Translate the following phrases into Chinese/English.

(1) live load (6) 混凝土模板工程
(2) allowable stress (7) 高等级材料
(3) impact load (8) 侧压力
(4) chain reaction (9) 不变荷载
(5) hairline crack (10) 胶合板

3. Translate the following sentences into Chinese.

(1) Forms should be designed by conventional engineering practices to resist the foces resulting from the known loads.

(2) If the finished surface of the concrete must be smooth and free of blemishes, the use of a very high grade of material will minimize expensive finishing.

(3) Keep the structural system uncomplicated so that the formwork may be simple and economically erected and removed.

(4) Use the same size of columns over a whole building, if possible, or at least over several floors. This will permit the reuse of beam and column forms without alteration.

(5) Space columns, if possible, to fit the use of plywood sheets for decking without cutting.

(6) Use the same width for column and column-supported girders to eliminate the cutting and fitting of girder forms into column forms.

(7) Specify beams of the same size and depth for each floor, and choose the depth that will permit the use of standard lumber sizes for beam sides.

(8) Some unusual application of a force may cause one member to fail, and if its stress is not absorbed by the other members, failure may occur.

(9) Care should be exercised to control the unsymmetrical placement of fresh concrete in forms, which can produce disastrous results.

(10) Vibrations due to the movement of concrete buggies and vibrators can also cause failure if the shores are not properly braced.

4. Fill in the blanks with the given words below.

layer 6 to 12 in deep. 有些工程师在浇筑竖向构件时，喜欢用与设计混凝土相同配比的水、水泥、细骨料，但粗骨料只用一半的量，作为先浇混凝土，浇筑6～12英寸高。

［2］The results of poor placement in walls are frequently observed：… from bottom to top. 全句可译为：经常遇到的墙体浇筑时的不良施工后果有：层面倾斜、蜂窝、漏浆，若沿高度连续取芯，从底部到顶部的强度降低达50％。

［3］Construction personnel should be available，…，or piping displaced. 全句可译为：当铺设水管或电线管道时，施工人员必须到位，通常有木工、钢筋工及其他工种，对模板进行检查，对移动了的钢筋、电线或管子重新放置。

Exercises

1. Fill in the blanks with proper words.

（1）Segregation must be avoided during all operations between the mixer and the point of _____ , including final consolidation and finishing.

（2）Where fresh concrete is placed against or on hardened concrete, a good _____ must be developed.

（3）Concrete may be conveyed from a mixer to point of placement by any of a variety of methods and equipment, if properly transported to avoid _____.

（4）Even within the specified limits on _____ and water-cementitious materials ratio, excess water must be avoided.

（5）The purpose of consolidation is to _____ voids of air and to ensure intimate complete contact of the concrete with the surfaces of the forms and the reinforcement.

（6）The interior of columns is usually congested; it contains a large volume of reinforcing steel compared with the volume of concrete, and has a large _____ compared with its cross-sectional dimensions.

（7）Concrete should be inspected for the owner before, _____, and after casting.

（8）As concrete is cast, the slump of the concrete must be observed and regulated within prescribed _____.

（9）When the remainder of the column is cast, the first increment should be small, and should be vibrated to _____ the previous portion slightly.

2. Translate the following phrases into Chinese/English
　　（1）construction joint　　　　（6）坍落度
　　（2）hardened concrete　　　　（7）水下浇筑
　　（3）laitance layer　　　　　　（8）水灰比
　　（4）mass concrete　　　　　　（9）平面振实器
　　（5）bar placer　　　　　　　　（10）粗骨料

3. Translate the following sentences into Chinese

（1）Where fresh concrete is placed on hardened concrete, a good bond must be developed.

（2）Before concrete is placed, the formwork must be free of ice and debris and

LESSON 15

New Words

1. segregation [ˌsegriˈgeiʃən] n. 分凝，离析
2. shotcrete [ʃɔtkrit] n. 喷射混凝土
3. buggy [ˈbʌgi] n. 手推车，小货车
4. dropbottom [drɔpˈbɔtəm] n. 底卸式，活底
5. bucket [ˈbʌkit] n. 桶，铲斗，料罐
6. chute [ʃuːt] n. 斜道，斜槽，槽
7. tremie [ˈtremi] n. (水下灌注用)混凝土导管
8. spreader [ˈspredə] n. 延辗机，铺料机
9. aggravate [ˈægrəveit] vt. 使恶化，加重
10. laitance [ˈleitəns] n. 浮浆，浮渣
11. abrasion [əˈbreiʒən] n. 磨损
12. entrain [inˈtrein] vt. 使空气以气泡状存在于混凝土中
13. rebar [riˈbɑː] n. 钢筋，螺纹钢筋
14. debris [ˈdebriː, ˈdeib-] n. 碎片，岩屑
15. conduit [ˈkɔndit] n. 管道，导管
16. bugholes [ˈbʌghəulz] n. 凹痕
17. ricochet [ˈrikəʃet] n. 跳飞，跳弹；v. (使)跳飞
18. deleterious [ˌdeliˈtiəriəs] a. 有害的
19. lodge [lɔdʒ] n. 门房，小屋

Phrases and Expressions

1. fresh concrete   新浇混凝土，未结硬混凝土
2. hardened concrete   硬化混凝土
3. mass concrete   大体积(块)混凝土
4. swinging boom   起重机回转臂，吊车旋转杆
5. paving mixer   铺路拌和机
6. dump truck   自动倾卸卡车
7. mixer truck   混凝土搅拌车
8. side dump   侧卸(式)
9. laitance layer   (水泥)浆沫层
10. surface vibrator   平面振实器，表面式振捣器
11. construction joint   施工缝
12. bar placer   钢筋工

Notes

[1] Some engineers prefer to start ..., as in the design mix, and to place a starting

after, as, if, or, or, on, the, to, which, up

To attain maximum economy in formwork, _____ highest practical unit stresses for the form material should be used. When the concrete is just cast, it is more _____ less fluid and exerts considerable side pressure on the forms. In several hours time _____ the concrete has set up, the side pressure will cease and the beam with its reinforcement will carry its own dead load plus the superimposed live loads; and stresses in the formwork will be practically nothing. Thus the forms will be subjected _____ maximum stresses for a very short period of time. Wood is capable of absorbing large overloads _____ the stresses are of short duration, and because of this the allowable stresses based _____ constant loads of long duration may be increased by, say one third, as long _____ the forms, _____ are to be reused, are protected form abuse and excessive exposure to weather. However, it must be noted that the allowable deflections in formwork will many times govern the design for the reason that if the weight of the fresh concrete deflects the member too much, either horizontally _____ vertically, the finished concrete will set _____ in the deflected shape.

5. Translate the following sentences into English
 (1) 模板必须具有足够的刚度以保持其形状，没有过度变形。
 (2) 当模板要被多次使用，与混凝土接触的那部分模板必须是优质材料的，优质材料初次使用成本高，但因不止一次使用最终将是经济的。
 (3) 在刚浇筑时，混凝土近乎流体，会对模板施加很大的侧压力。
 (4) 良好的设计和施工方法以及合理的管理能够保证安全性和有效性。
 (5) 作用于模板上的冲击荷载会引起非常严重的后果。有些冲击荷载是由机动车向模板内倾卸大荷载引起的，特别是向大量新近浇筑的湿混凝土倾卸时。

Reading Material

Factory Design and Construction

Factory Design

Factory design is interesting to most civil engineers because it includes the design of many important services, and the engineer is the main designer, not a mere helper as he is for a multi-storey building. He must design the roads and the drains, possibly the water supply and the heating or air conditioning and provide for the power and telephone cables and gas pipes. If possible he will try at least to get the main roads and drains in position before the main construction starts. This will make the site much easier to travel over, and by keeping it drier will probably reduce the damage to vehicles.

Provided that a factory is of one storey, it can usually be well lit from the roof except in hot climates, but if it is more than one storey high, day-lighting of the lower storeys in any large-span building becomes difficult or impossible. For this reason, some US factory designers have built factories without windows, entirely air-conditioned. And as spans increase this will become unavoidable for the internal rooms. In fact, it is now quite common to place bathrooms internally so that they do not waste the valuable space for windows that would be more useful to a living-room. In temperate climates, the air-conditioning equipment should be designed to provide cooled air in summer and warm air in winter.

Roof lighting can be through transparent sheets in an ordinary sheeted sloping roof, or through a sawtooth(锯齿形的) roof which would be north-facing in norther continents or south-facing in southern. A monitor roof enables the lights to be either vertical or on the roof slope and also provides excellent ventilation. Glass is still the commonest material used for admitting light because it is the cheapest, but in hot countries it is unsuitable. In a sheeted roof occasional sheets may be replaced with a translucent(半透明的) or transparent material, either glass fiber which is translucent, or one of the transparent plastics materials, which may be colourless or tinted red, yellow, etc. All these large sheets can be corrugated(波状的) to allow them to span over distances of about 2m.

One difficulty in every building for heavy industry is the arrangement of the supports for an overhead crane. The crane is carried by a bridge across the building, and the bridge runs on rails, one along each wall. These two rails are carried on crane beams which pass the full length of the building, being carried on the main columns, usually at about 10m above ground level, so that the crane can command the whole of the work area. This means that the roof structure and the columns cannot be fully detailed until the main design of the crane is known. Crane makers are usually happy to give details of the dimensions of their cranes and bridges to structural engineers, so this does not usually cause much delay. However, each column must be designed to carry about three quarters of the crane weight plus three quarters of its hook load, as well as half the bridge weight. The roof columns must also carry the structure load (which is much smaller) and they will be about 10m long plus the crane height.

The columns will be eccentrically loaded since the part of the column above the crane must be offcentre from the crane girder. Precast concrete columns have been successfully cast to carry crane beams of this type though it was once thought that they would be too big and complicated for precasting. A successful design for the overhead crane and its supports will help the reputation of a civil engineering designer.

Factory Construction

Factory construction, the design and construction of single-storey buildings of large span often hundreds of meters long, is a typical task of the civil engineer. Though architects often supervise these projects, they succeed generally because the architect and the civil engineering designer work together, with understanding of the client's needs.

For light industry which is not noisy, the roofing and cladding(覆层) generally consist of factory-made sheets, of which hundreds of types exist, made of corrugated or troughed(槽状的)or flat steel, plywood, aluminium, or asbestos(石棉)-cement. The waterproof skin on the outside of some of them may also be of copper sheet, tarred felt or steel. Some of these cladding or roofing units are expensive, especially the sandwich units which contain a middle layer of highly efficient thermal insulator, such as expanded polystyrene(聚苯乙烯)or glass fiber.

The insulation must be completely protected from the condensation of water out of the air from the hotter side of the cool insulating material. Thus in a hot climate the condensation will be on the inner face of the insulator and in a cold climate on its outer face. The insulation must be protected from moisture or it will rapidly lose its insulating power as the moisture enters it. As it loses insulating power, the condensation will increase, more moisture will enter and the insulation will be completely lost, quite apart from the unpleasantness of dampness in the wall.

It is therefore essential to prevent not only moisture but also air from entering the insulation, and this is done by a waterproof sheet of polythene(聚乙烯)or metal or other material, called a vapour barrier. It must be sealed at the joints to prevent air leaking through and condensation occurring inside. The civil engineer should therefore ask whether the cladding is for use in a hot or a cold climate, and the maker will usually be happy to provide a possible buyer with all this information.

For noisy factories, such as those which house heavy industry (car factories, etc.), cladding sheets are not good because noise passes through them. Any heavy walling is better because the deadening(衰减)of sound depends on the weight of the wall. Brickwork has been the universal material in Britain in the past but modern civil engineering contractors have precast large concrete units of 4m～5m and placed them with powerful cranes. Such walls are quickly built provided that the organization of the site is good, and the cranes are available and able to get to the lifting point. If the units are too large for one crane, they are sometimes lifted by two cranes working together. The alternative is to reduce the height of the wall unit, keeping its length equal to the column spacing, since this construction is simple and looks good. If the crane is very small and the units are only about 15cm high, it may be advisable to lay a thin mortar joint between the units so as to keep out the wind. For the very large units, the mortar joint is less important since the joints are fewer.

科技英语阅读与写作指南

科技英语写作——题名

　　题名是科技英语论文的必要组成部分，它是作者表达论文特定内容，反映研究范围和深度的最精炼的概括，它要求用最简洁、恰当的词组反映文章的基本内涵与特色。准确、简练、清晰的题名能把论文的主题明白无误地告诉读者，并且使之具有画龙点睛，启迪读者兴趣的功能。一般情况下，题名中应包括文章的主要关键词。

1. 题名的结构：英文题名以短语为主要形式，尤以名词短语最常见，即题名基本上由一个或几个名词加上其前置和(或)后置定语构成。如果出现动词，一般是分词或动名词形式。各个词的顺序很重要，词序不当，会导致表达不准。题名一般不应是陈述句形式，因为题名主要起标示作用，而陈述句容易使题名具有判断式的语义；而且陈述句不够精练和清晰。少数情况(评述性、综述性和驳斥性)下可以用疑问句做题名，因为疑问句可有探讨性语气，易引起读者兴趣。但疑问句作题名一般不宜用于学术性论文。

  例：Comparisons of Friction Models in Bulk Metal Forming
    Application of Microprocessors on Processing of Chemical Heat-treatment

2. 题名的字数：题名不应过长。国际上不少著名期刊都对题名的用字有所限制。论文题名用字不宜超过20个汉字，外文题名不超过10个实词。使用简短题名而语意未尽时，可用副题名。副题名与题名之间可用冒号分开。

  例：Meeting California's Air-Quality Goals：The Role of New Technologies and Fuels

3. 题名中的冠词：目前按国际上的习惯，题名中可以省去定冠词和不定冠词。

  例：The Effect of Groundwater Quality on the Wheat Yield and Quality.
    其中两处的冠词 the 均可不用。

4. 题名中的缩略词：题名应避免使用不常见的缩略词、字符和公式等，以便读者检索。

5. 题名的书写格式：题名字母的大小写有以下3种格式。

  (1) 全部字母大写。

  例：EMBRITTLE AND FRACTURE OF STEELS

  (2) 每个实词的首字母大写，但冠词、连词、介词全部小写。

  例：The Deformation and Strength of Concrete Dams with Defects

  (3) 题名第1个词的首字母大写，其余字母均小写。

  例：Prediction of wash load rate by bed load function

  目前(2)格式用得最多，而(3)格式也为很多期刊采用。

6. 作者与作者单位的英译：

  (1) 作者。中国人名按汉语拼音拼写，姓在前，名在后，姓首字母大写；双名之间无连字符，但首字母大写，复姓同样。其他非英语国家人名按作者自己提供的罗马字母拼法拼写。

  例：Wang Wei(王维)
    Fang Zhongda(方忠达)
    Zhuge Yushan(诸葛玉山)

  目前我国很多期刊采用下面的格式，即姓氏在前全大写，名在后首字母大写，双名连写，中间加连字符。

  例：WANG Wei(王维)
    FANG Zhong-da(方忠达)
    ZHUGE Yu-shan(诸葛玉山)

  (2) 单位。单位名称要写全(由小到大)，写出一、二级单位，城市和邮政编码，结尾处应加"China"。另外，单位英译一定要采用本单位统一的译法(即本单位标准译法)。

  例：School of Civil Engineering, Xi'an University of Architecture and Technology, Xi'an 710055, China
    西安建筑科技大学土木工程学院，西安　710055

Behavior of Beam-Columns

Introduction

Beam-columns are structural members subjected to combined axial forces and bending moments. The bending moments that are present in a beam-column consist of two types: *primary bending moments* which arise from moments applied or induced at the ends of the member and/or moments from transverse loadings on the member; *secondary bending moments* which arise as a result of the axial force acting through the lateral displacement of the member. The so-called $P—\delta$ *moments* are moments caused by the axial force acting through the lateral displacement of the member relative to its chord (Fig. 17.1a), whereas the $P—\Delta$ *moments* are moments caused by the axial force acting through the relative lateral displacement of the two ends of the member (Fig. 17.1b).

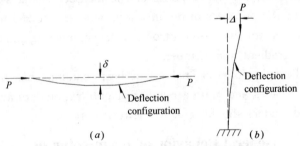

Fig. 17.1 Secondary P—delta Effects
(a) $P—\delta$ Effect; (b) $P—\Delta$ Effect

Secondary moments generally produce detrimental effects to slender compression members and so they must be accounted for in design. The nature and the manner in which these secondary moments are incorporated in the *analysis* and *design* of structural members in frames will be addressed in this section.

Beam-columns can be considered as the basic element of a structural frame. *Beams* and *columns* are special cases of beam-columns. [1] In the case of beams, the effect of axial force on the primary bending moments is negligible, but in the case of beam-columns this effect may be such as to add significant additional moments to the primary moments. At the present time, the design methodology for frames is based essentially on the behavior of individual members that comprise the frame rather than on the entire frame itself, i.e. the design is performed on a *member level*. Thus the usual procedure for a frame design is first to carry out an elastic frame analysis and to determine the axial force and bending moments on each member. [2] The design of each member is then carried out one at a time by using an ultimate strength *interaction equation* that expresses a safe combination of axial force and bending moments that the member can sustain. A detailed discussion of these beam-column design interaction equations will be given later. At the present time, it suffices to say that the design of a structural frame is merely a selection of members that comprise the frame. Realistically, a frame should be designed based on an interactive system behavior rather than on a collection of individual behaviors of beam-columns. Nevertheless, this will require a considerable change in the concept and philosophy of structural design which is currently not feasible; however, with the present rapid infusion of computing into structural engineering, such a challenge may be achieved in the next decade.

Although a structural frame is designed at the member level, the member is by no means treated as a totally isolated element. It is easily conceivable that an isolated member behaves rather differently from a framed member because of the interaction effect that always exists among adjacent members of a frame. To account for this interaction approximately, the concept of *effective length* has been widely used in present engineering practice.

In addition to member interaction in a frame, it is well known that the behavior of a member depends on the types of loadings on the member. Different loadings will produce different moment patterns and the response of the member changes according to these moment patterns. For the purposes of design, a parameter referred to as the *equivalent moment factor* (the C_m factor) has been introduced in engineering practice to account for the effect of moment gradient in a member.

The study of the behavior and analysis of beam-columns has been the subject of intense research for decades and quite a number of publications are available in the open literature. Interested readers should refer to the related books.

General Behavior of Beam-columns

The general behavior of a beam-column can best be studied by investigating the load-deflection relationship of the member. Fig. 17.2 shows an I-shaped member subjected to an axial force P and end moments M_0. Suppose P is applied first and then held constant. The moments are subsequently applied and increased monotonically about the major principal axis of the cross-section. The variation of M_0 with end rotation θ_0 is then plotted. This M_0-θ_0 curve is shown as a full line in Fig. 17.2. The curve is nonlinear almost from the start because of the $P-\delta$ effect. The axial force acts through the displacement caused by the applied end moments creating an additional rotation at the ends. The $P-\delta$ effect becomes more and more significant as the applied end moments increase. At point A, the combined effect of the primary

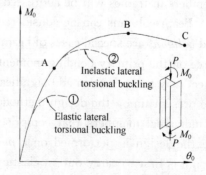

Fig. 17.2 Behavior of a beam-column.

moment M_0 and the secondary P—δ moment causes yielding of the most severely stressed fibers of the cross-section. This yielding reduces the stiffness of the member. This is reflected in the further decrease in slope of the M_0-θ_0 curve beyond point A. As deformation increases, the P—δ moment also increases. This secondary moment will share a proportionately larger portion of the moment capacity of the cross-section. Eventually, at point B, the rate of increase of the internal resisting moment of the cross-section is just equal to the rate of increase of the applied moment M_0 and the P—δ moment. Beyond point B, any further increase in deflection must be accompanied by a decrease in applied moment M_0 as the rate of increase of the P—δ moment becomes much faster than the rate of increase of the internal moment of the cross-section. Failure of the member by the formation of a *plastic hinge* occurs at point C when the moment-carrying capacity of the cross-section is finally exhausted.

In the foregoing discussion, it is tacitly assumed that other forms of failure do not occur before the formation of a plastic hinge. If the member is slender and the cross-section is torsionally weak, *lateral torsional buckling* may occur. Lateral torsional buckling may occur in the elastic range (curve 1) or in the inelastic range (curve 2) depending on the slenderness of the member. A member with a high slenderness ratio will experience *elastic* lateral torsional buckling, whereas a member with an intermediate slenderness ratio will experience *inelastic* lateral torsional buckling. Lateral torsional buckling will not occur if the slenderness ratio of the member is low or if the member is bent about the minor principal axis of the cross-section. Lateral torsional buckling will also be absent regardless of the slenderness ratio in members for which the moments of inertia of the cross-sections are equal for both principal axes (e. g. a square box section) or for cross-sections with axisymmetry (e. g. circular sections). Lateral torsional buckling is an important design criterion for steel members since it is clear from Fig. 17.2 that the occurrence of lateral torsional buckling reduces the maximum load-carrying capacity of the member.

Another form of failure which may occur in the member is *local buckling*. Local buckling is the buckling of component elements of the cross-section. An element with a high width to thickness ratio is very susceptible to local buckling. Like lateral torsional buckling, local buckling may occur in the elastic or inelastic range. The effect of local buckling is to reduce the load-carrying capacity of the cross-section. Local buckling is accounted for in design by the use of a reduced width for the buckled element.

The analysis of beam-columns is an inherent complicated problem. To trace a load-deflection curve, like that shown in Fig. 17.2, one must resort to some type of approximate or numerical technique. This is because the differential equations governing the inelastic behavior of a beam-column are highly nonlinear even for the simplest loading case. Although a number of methods are available for the analysis of beam-columns, they all involve some form of simplifying assumptions to make the problem tractable.

New Words

1. induce [in'dju:s]   vt. 引起，促使，导致
2. chord [kɔ:d]   n. 弦
3. detrimental [ˌdetri'mentl]   a. 不利的，有害的
4. incorporate [in'kɔ:pəreit]   v. 合并
5. methodology [meθə'dɔlədʒɪ]   n. 方法学(论)
6. suffice [sə'fais]   vi. 足够，有能力；vt. 使满足
7. feasible ['fi:zəbl]   a. 可行的，切实可行的
8. infusion [in'fju:ʒən]   n. 导入，引入，渗入
9. conceivable [kən'si:vəbl]   a. 可能的，想得到的
10. adjacent [ə'dʒeisənt]   a. 邻近的，接近的
11. gradient ['greidiənt]   a. 倾斜的   n. 梯度，倾斜度
12. exhausted [ig'zɔ:stid]   a. 耗尽的，疲惫的
13. tacitly ['tæsitli]   adv. 肃静地，沉默地
14. axisymmetry [æksi'simitri]   n. 轴对称
15. susceptible [sə'septəbl]   a. 易受影响的，易感动的
16. resort [ri'zɔ:t]   vi. 求助，采取(某种手段等)
17. tractable ['træktəbl]   a. 易驾驭的，易处理的

Phrases and Expressions

1. primary bending moment   主弯矩，一阶弯矩
2. secondary bending moment   次弯矩，二阶弯矩
3. interaction equation   相关公式
4. equivalent moment factor   等效弯矩系数
5. plastic hinge   塑性铰
6. the moment of inertia of a cross-section   截面惯性矩
7. width to thickness ratio   宽厚比
8. lateral torsional buckling   弯扭屈曲
9. local buckling   局部屈曲
10. numerical technique   数值方法
11. differential equation   微分方程

Notes

[1] In the case of beams, the effect of axial force... is negligible, but in the case of beam-columns this effect may be such as to add... to the primary moments. be such as to 意为"如此…以至于"，全句可译为：对梁来说，轴力对主弯矩的影响可以忽略不记，但对梁柱这种影响会对主弯矩增加显著的附加弯矩。

[2] The design of each member is then carried out one at a time…sustain. 本句中第一个 that 引导定语从句修饰 interaction equation，第二个 that 引导另一个定语从句修饰 bending moments。全句可译为：然后应用极限强度相关公式进行每一构件的设计（每次一个构件）。相关公式表示了该构件可以承受的轴力和弯矩的安全组合。

Exercises

1. Fill in the blanks with proper words.
   （1）At the present time, the design methodology for frames is based essentially on the behavior of individual members that comprise the frame _____ on the entire frame itself.
   （2）Realistically, a frame _____ designed based on an interactive system behavior rather than on a collection of individual behaviors of beam-columns.
   （3）It is easily conceivable _____ an isolated member behaves rather differently from a framed member because of the interaction effect _____ always exists among adjacent members of a frame.
   （4）For the purposes of design, a parameter referred to as the *equivalent moment factor* has been introduced in engineering practice to account for the effect of moment _____ in a member.
   （5）The P-δ effect becomes more and more significant _____ the applied end moments increase.
   （6）This secondary moment will share a proportionately larger _____ of the moment capacity of the cross-section.
   （7）In the foregoing discussion, it is tacitly assumed _____ other forms of failure do not occur before the formation of a plastic hinge.
   （8）Lateral torsional buckling will not occur _____ the slenderness ratio of the member is low or if the member is bent about the minor principal axis of the cross-section.
   （9）Although a number of methods are available for the analysis of beam-columns, they all involve some form of simplifying assumptions _____ the problem tractable.
   （10）Lateral torsional buckling is an important design _____ for steel members since the occurrence of lateral torsional buckling reduces the maximum load-carrying capacity of the member.
2. Translate the following phrases into Chinese/English.
   （1）primary bending moment
   （2）interaction equation
   （3）the moment of inertia of a cross-section
   （4）differential equations
   （5）load-deflection curve
   （6）次弯矩
   （7）等效弯矩系数
   （8）塑性铰
   （9）宽厚比
   （10）数值方法
3. Translate the following sentences into Chinese.

(1) The general behavior of a beam-column can best be studied by investigating the load-deflection relationship of the member.

(2) The bending moments that are present in a beam-column consist of two types: *primary bending moments* and *secondary bending moments*.

(3) The so-called $P\text{-}\delta$ *moments* are moments caused by the axial force acting through the lateral displacement of the member relative to its chord.

(4) In the case of beams, the effect of axial force on the primary bending moments is negligible, but in the case of beam-columns this effect may be such as to add significant additional moments to the primary moments.

(5) A detailed discussion of these beam-column design interaction equations will be given later.

(6) To account for this interaction approximately, the concept of *effective length* has been widely used in present engineering practice.

(7) Different loadings will produce different moment patterns and the response of the member changes according to these moment patterns.

(8) The general behavior of a beam-column can best be studied by investigating the load-deflection relationship of the member.

(9) Failure of the member by the formation of a *plastic hinge* occurs at point C when the moment-carrying capacity of the cross-section is finally exhausted.

(10) The study of the behavior and analysis of beam-columns has been the subject of intense research for decades and quite a number of publications are available in the open literature.

4. Fill in the blanks with the given words below.

by, for, for, of, of, or, to, to, which, with

Another form of failure _____ may occur in the member is *local buckling*. Local buckling is the buckling _____ component elements _____ the cross-section. An element _____ a high width _____ thickness ratio is very susceptible _____ local buckling. Like lateral torsional buckling, local buckling may occur in the elastic _____ inelastic range. The effect of local buckling is to reduce the load-carrying capacity of the cross-section. Local buckling is accounted _____ in design _____ the use of a reduced width _____ the buckled element.

5. Translate the following sentences into English.

(1) 梁柱是承受轴力和弯矩复合作用的结构构件。

(2) 虽然框架结构是在构件水平上设计的，但绝不是把构件看作完全独立的构件。

(3) 二阶弯矩对细长的受压构杆一般产生不利影响，因此设计中必须予以计算。

(4) 众所周知，除了框架中构件的相互作用外，构件的性能与构件上荷载的类型有关。

(5) 大长细比的构件将经历弹性弯扭屈曲，而中等长细比的构件将经历非弹性弯扭屈曲。

Reading Material
Introduction to Second-order Analysis of Frames

In a structural analysis, when the equilibrium and kinematic relationships are written with respect to the undeformed (or original) geometry of the structure, the analysis is referred to as a *first-order analysis*. On the other hand, when the equilibrium and kinematic relationships are written with respect to the deformed geometry of the structure, the analysis is referred to as a *second-order analysis*. Second-order analysis is always necessary for the stability consideration of structures. When a structure becomes unstable under a system of forces, it often assumes a configuration which deviates (偏离) quite noticeably from its undeformed configuration. In fact, in a bifurcation (分岔) analysis, the critical load is obtained as the eigenvalue (特征值) of the characteristic equation of the governing differential equation written with respect to the deformed configuration of the structure. In a load-deflection analysis, the nonlinear load-deflection curve can be traced only if the change of geometry of the structure is taken into account.

Unlike a first-order analysis in which the solutions can be obtained in a rather simple and direct manner, a second-order analysis often entails an iterative type procedure to obtain solutions. This is due to the fact that the deformed geometry of the structure is not known during the formulation of the equilibrium and kinematic relationships. Thus, the analysis usually proceeds in a step-by-step incremental manner. The deformed geometry of the structure obtained from a preceding cycle of calculations is used as the basis for formulating the equilibrium and kinematic relationships for the current cycle of calculations. There are various iterative schemes available for the solution of second-order problems. The four most commonly used schemes are: (1) the load control method, (2) the displacement control method, (3) the arc length control method, and (4) the work control method.

Generally speaking, nonlinearities in structures exist in two forms: *geometrical nonlinearity*(几何非线性)and *material nonlinearity*. For framed structures, geometrical nonlinearity gives rise to the P-delta effects that are properly reflected in the term "second-order analysis". The nature and manner by which these effects are taken into account in design have been discussed before. It is important to mention here that the presence of a compressive axial force in a member is detrimental (有害的) to the strength of the member. This is because this force tends to reduce the flexural rigidity of the member. Geometrical nonlinearity is particularly important for tall and slender frames subjected to high gravity loadings. The geometrical nonlinear effect can be taken into account in analysis by the use of stability stiffness functions in a beam-column formulation or by the use of a geometrical (or initial stress) stiffness matrix in a finite element formulation. These two formulations are discussed in detail in the following sections.

Material nonlinearity arises when yielding occurs or if the stress-strain behavior exhibits a nonlinear characteristic. For steel framed structures, material nonlinearity arises when yielding spreads through the cross-section (plastification) and along the member length (plastic zone) as the moment in the cross-section increases from the initial yield moment M_y to the full plastic moment M_p. Depending on the degree of accuracy one desires, two models of material nonlinear frame analysis can be used. The first model, known as the *concentrated plasticity (plastic hinge) model*, ignores the progressive yielding that takes place in the cross-section and in the member. The second and more sophisticated model, known as the *distributed plasticity (plastic zone) model*, takes into consideration the spread of yield in the cross-section and along the member length. The analyses of plane rigid frames using these models are the subject of this chapter. Methods of simplified second-order plane frame analysis with rigid beam-to-column connections are presented in the following chapter.

Fig. 17.3 shows a schematic comparison of the load-deflection behavior of a plane frame using these refined and simplified models and their combinations. The broken straight line is obtained by a first-order elastic analysis ignoring the effects of both the change of geometry and the yielding of the material. The broken curve is a second-order elastic analysis that includes only the effect of the change of geometry, and instability. The curve approaches asymptotically(渐近地) to the elastic critical value which can be obtained directly by an eigenvalue analysis. The piecewise linear curve without a

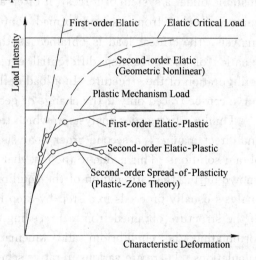

Fig. 17.3 Load-deflection behavior of plane frame.

descending branch represents a first-order elastic-plastic hinge analysis when the effects of the change of geometry are ignored. Its peak value is the plastic limit load that can be obtained directly by a simple plastic analysis. The piecewise linear curve with a descending branch shows the result of a second-order elastic-plastic hinge analysis allowing a simple plastic analysis for the change of geometry which is associated with the increase of sway deflection (or the P-Δ effect). Finally, when the spread of plastic zones, residual stresses, initial imperfections and strain hardening are all accounted for, the full smooth curve is obtained by a second-order spread-of-plasticity analysis. The peak load of this curve gives the true strength or the load-carrying capacity of the plane frame.

If the P-delta effects are to be considered in a structural analysis, it is necessary to perform a second-order analysis on the structure based on the large displacement-small strain theory. For simplicity, we first ignore the yielding of the material and focus our attention on the elastic behavior of the structure. In the following three sections, we discuss three practical approaches to second-order elastic analysis of frameworks: (1)the beam-column approach using the modified slope-deflection equations, (2)the finite element approach using the energy theorem, and (3)the pseudo(假的，伪的) load approach using the analogy between a beam-column and a beam problem.

科技英语阅读与写作指南

科技英语写作——英语摘要

科技英语论文中的摘要又称概要、内容提要。摘要是以提供文献内容梗概为目的，不加评论和补充解释，简明、确切地记述文献重要内容的短文。摘要应具有独立性和自明性，并且拥有与文献同等量的主要信息，即不阅读全文，就能获得必要的信息。摘要的主要功能是：让读者尽快了解论文的主要内容，以补充题名的不足，为科技情报文献检索数据库的建设和维护提供方便。科技英语论文的摘要基本要素包括研究目的、方法、结果和结论。

1. 本文的目的或要解决的问题

   常用句型

   The aim of this research is to carry out the critical experiment and obtain...

   The purpose of this paper is to explain theoretically the problem of...

   Our project aims to study/survey/evaluate/determine...

   The main objective of this study is to determine...

   This paper seeks to justify...

   The work presented in this paper focuses on several aspects of the following...

   The purpose for this study is to show that...

   This report presents evidence to show that the conventional method...

   In the experiments reported here, we determined a new method for reducing/improving...

2. 解决问题的方法及过程

   常用句型

   The experiments on... were carried out by using...

   Experiments on... were performed to measure... under different conditions.

   The accuracy of the solutions is tested by comparing them with...

   The tests were carried out on a...

   The tests were designed to determine...

   We undertook many experiments to support the hypothesis which...

   Methods of analysis are based on...

   A simplified diagram of... is taken as reference.

   The assumptions are evaluated by comparison with measurement results.

3. 研究的主要结果

   常用句型

   ... has been greatly improved.

   The agreement with the corresponding results from... is obtained.

   The data obtained appear to be very similar to those reported earlier by...

   Our work involving studies of... prove to be encouraging.

   The problem of... is solved.

...is realized by using...

...was constructed which can be used in...

This paper provides an ideal source of...

With the application of..., ...may be decreased by...

4. 研究得出的结论

常用句型

It is concluded that...

Finally we come to the conclusion that...is feasible.

In summing up it may be stated that...

The results are generally supportive of...

These findings of the research have led the author to the conclusion that...

These results suggest that...

The result can be expected to be of great use...

The data reported here suggest that...

The result obtained has important application in...

LESSON 18

Welding and Common Types of Welds

Introduction

Welding can be thought of as the fusing of two pieces of metal together to form a continuous, rigid plate. The earliest welding was probably accomplished by craftsman and artists in ancient times. There are many modern day welding techniques, although the two basic categories are gas and arc welding. These modern techniques can trace their roots back to the late nineteenth century when arc welding was first patented and used on a limited scale.

Generally, all welding processes will have the following common elements:
- Base metals
- Heat source
- Electrode or Welding Rod
- Shielding Mechanism

The base metals are simply the pieces to be joined together. They are joined together using some type of heat source. In structural steel welding this heat source is most frequently generated through an electric arc that creates a confined temperature in excess of 6000°F. In gas welding the heat source is generated through the burning of gas (typically acetylene and oxygen) at the end of a welder's "torch". In both cases, the heat source melts not only the base metal, but also an electrode or welding rod. As the electrode or welding rod is melted, it is deposited as additional steel into the area of the weld. The electrode or welding rod may be thought of as the "weld metal".

The weld must also be protected from coming in contact with the surrounding air during its cooling period. This is usually accomplished through some type of shielding mechanism. This shielding can be accomplished by a gaseous cloud or by immersion of the electrode into a material generally referred to as flux. Flux is a material that will help prevent the intrusion of undesirable contaminants into the pool of molten weld. A common contaminant, which hopefully is minimized by good welding techniques, is air or other gases. If air is allowed to penetrate the weld during its cooling period, it can greatly reduce the strength and quality of the weld due to pitting or high porosity. Flux can be either a loose, granular material through which the electrode is moved—or it can be contained on a coating that shrouds the electrode. Such a coating would then melt as the electrode is consumed thereby creating a gaseous cloud.

The use of welding is very popular in steel construction because it has a number of advantages. Among them are a savings produced by the reduction of splicing plates, the ease of welding odd shapes (i.e. pipes), and the ease of implementing field changes. Disadvantages of welding include their fatigue behavior and quality assurance. The former of these disadvantages has led to the development of fatigue criteria and special details in practically all welded structures.

As mentioned earlier, the most common method of welding structural steel is arc welding. The two most basic types of arc welding are the shielded metal arc welding (SMAW) process and the submerged arc welding (SAW) process.

The shielded metal arc welding (SMAW) process is the traditional type of welding that is manually produced. [1] The generation of heat is from an electric arc and the electrode, usually designated by a term such as E70XX, is melted into the weld area to fuse together with the base metal. In the electrode designation, E70XX, the 70 represents the ultimate tensile strength (ksi) of the electrode. The subscript symbols (XX) may reflect a variety of things such as coating, positions, and other characteristics. In general, A36 steel can be used successfully with either E60XX or E70XX electrodes. Further designations can be found in the American Welding Society's *Structural Welding Code*.

The submerged arc welding (SAW) process also uses an electric arc for its heat source. This method is used most often in a fabrication shop and is accomplished by an automated welding machine. The machine will lay down a coating of granular flux through a feeding tube that advances in front of an uncoated electrode. This covering of loose flux provides a shielding mechanism to protect the weld from contaminant intrusion while cooling. This type of weld is very advantageous when welding long lengths (such as web to flange connections on plate girders) and is considered to be superior because of the uniform quality characteristics, mechanical properties, and speed of production. The designation for submerged arc welding (SAW) is somewhat different than that for the SMAW method; a standard designation includes the combination of the flux and electrode. A SAW weld might be F7X-E7XX, where the first part stands for its flux and its tensile strength and the latter part represents the electrode and its corresponding properties.

Common Types of Welds

There are many different ways to classify welds based on the type of weld, the welding position, and the type of end treatment in which a plate may be fabricated to better adapt to the welding procedure. In this section we will be concerned with identifying the characteristics and terminology for the common weld types.

The most common type of weld is the *fillet weld*, comprising probably 85% of all welds that are produced. These welds are used to join two pieces of steel that form a perpendicular corner where the weld is placed and can be used in many different types of connections (Fig. 18.1). The abundance of fillet welds is due in part to their ease of production because of the "pocket" formed by the perpendicular edges. This pocket serves as a holder of the molten steel and eliminates the requirement for additional backup plates. Fillet welds also require less precise alignment of the members to be connected, in contrast to the stringent alignment required for groove-welded members.

The most common fillet weld is the *equal leg fillet weld*, where the leg dimensions are the same length. The different parts of the fillet weld are shown in Fig. 18.2. The most important part of the fillet weld, as far as design is concerned, is the throat dimension. The throat dimension is the shortest length from the root of the weld to its face. This distance is critical because, although fillet welds have a generally rounded face, the throat distance is the probable line of failure through the weld. In an equal leg fillet weld this throat distance will be $0.707 \times$ *the leg*. If a fillet weld should be asymmetrical (having unequal legs), the throat distance should be calculated as the perpendicular distance from the face of the weld to its root using trigonometric principles. Fillet welds are called out by their leg size in equal leg welds (i.e. a $3/8''$ fillet weld has a leg $3/8''$ long).

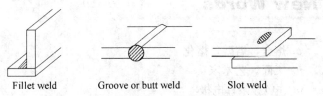

Fig. 18.1 Schematic illustration of fillet, groove, and slot welds.

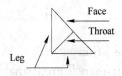

Fig. 18.2 Standard fillet weld terminology.

The other common type of weld is a *groove or butt weld*. This weld is used when connecting two plates that lie in the same plane and is meant to transfer the load in that plane from one member to the other (Fig. 18.1). A groove weld is referred to as a full penetration groove weld if the weld extends the full thickness of the plate being joined and it is referred to as a partial penetration groove weld if the weld does not extend the full thickness. The partial penetration groove welds may occur in a situation where access to the welding area is restricted and can only be accomplished from one side. A groove weld has many other variations based on the depth of the weld, the edge fabrication of the plates, and the configuration of the plates to be welded. Such configurations may include single and double U, V, or J welds as illustrated in Fig. 18.3. In any case, groove welds are more difficult to produce and should be avoided if possible because of the cost associated with additional plate fabrication and weld production. The additional cost is incurred because the weld is not confined in a pre-made "pocket" such as the fillet weld.

The critical throat distance in a full penetration groove weld is defined by the AISC to be the thickness of the thinnest plate joined. That is to say, if a $1/4''$ thick plate was to be groove welded to a $1/2''$ thick plate, the throat distance of the groove weld would be $1/4''$.

The last type of weld shown in Fig. 18.1, is the *slot* or *plug weld*. These welds are typically used in a lap connections where weld material is placed in standard or slotted holes that have been prepunched in the steel members. These welds increase the shear resistance of the connected parts and inhibit potential buckling of the members along their interface.

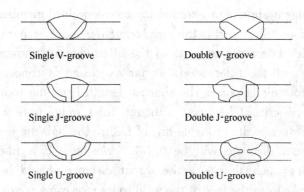

Fig. 18.3　Types of common groove welds.

New Words

1. fuse [fju:z]　　　　　　　　 v. 熔合，熔融，熔化
2. craftsman [ˈkrɑːftsmən]　　　n. 工匠，艺术家
3. electrode [iˈlektrəud]　　　　n. (电)焊条，电极
4. acetylene [əˈsetiliːn]　　　　n. 乙炔，电石气
5. flux [flʌks]　　　　　　　　n. 焊剂，焊药，钎剂
6. intrusion [inˈtruːʒən]　　　　n. 侵入，闯入，侵扰
7. contaminant [kənˈtæminənt]　n. 致污物，污染物
8. splice [splais]　　　　　　　v. 接合，拼接，粘接
9. implement [ˈimpliment]　　　vt. 实现，贯彻，执行
10. fillet [ˈfilit]　　　　　　　　n. 角焊缝，倒角
11. stringent [ˈstrindʒənt]　　　 a. 严格的，精确的
12. alignment [əˈlainmənt]　　　n. 定位，对中
13. groove [gruːv]　　　　　　　n. (焊接接头的)坡口
14. butt [bʌt]　　　　　　　　　n. 平接，对接
15. slot [slɔt]　　　　　　　　　n. 缝，狭槽，细长的孔
16. plug [plʌg]　　　　　　　　vt. 堵，塞，插栓；n. 塞子，插销
17. lap [læp]　　　　　　　　　n. 搭接，重叠
18. prepunch [priːˈpʌntʃ]　　　vt. 预先打孔

Phrases and Expressions

1. gas welding　气焊
2. arc welding　电弧焊
3. base metal　主体金属
4. the pool of molten weld　熔(焊)池
5. splicing plate　拼接板

6. special details　　特殊构造
7. shielded metal arc welding　　手工电弧焊，气体保护金属极电弧焊
8. submerged arc welding　　埋弧焊
9. American Welding Society　　美国焊接学会
10. Structural Welding Code　　结构焊接规范
11. fillet weld　　角焊缝
12. backup plate　　垫板
13. groove or butt weld　　坡口焊或对接焊缝
14. full penetration groove weld　　焊透的对接焊缝
15. partial penetration groove weld　　部分焊透的对接焊缝
16. slot or plug weld　　槽焊缝或塞焊缝

Notes

[1] The generation of heat is from an electric arc and the electrode, usually designated by a term such as E70XX, is melted into the weld area to fuse together with the base metal. 全句可译为：热量的产生来自电弧，焊条被熔化到焊接区与主体金属融合成一体。焊条通常用 E70XX 这样的符号标记。

Exercises

1. Fill in the blanks with proper words.
   (1) Welding can be thought of as the fusing _____ two pieces of metal together to form a continuous, rigid plate.
   (2) The modern welding techniques can trace _____ roots back to the late nineteenth century when arc welding _____ first patented and used on a limited scale.
   (3) The electrode or welding rod may _____ thought of as the "weld metal".
   (4) If air is allowed to penetrate the weld _____ its cooling period, it can greatly reduce the strength and quality of the weld due to pitting or high porosity.
   (5) The most common method of welding structural steel _____ arc welding. The two most basic types of arc welding _____ the shielded metal arc welding (SMAW) process and the submerged arc welding (SAW) process.
   (6) In the electrode _____, E70XX, the subscript symbols (XX) may reflect a variety of things such as coating, positions, and other characteristics.
   (7) The designation for submerged arc welding (SAW) is somewhat different than _____ for the SMAW method; a standard designation includes the combination _____ the flux and electrode.
   (8) There are many different ways to classify welds based on the type of weld, the welding position, and the type of end treatment _____ which a plate may be fabricated to better adapt to the welding procedure.

(9) Fillet welds also require less precise alignment of the members to be connected, _____ contrast to the stringent alignment required for groove-welded members.

(10) The throat dimension is critical because, _____ fillet welds have a generally rounded face, the throat distance is the probable line of failure through the weld.

2. Translate the following phrases into Chinese/English.

(1) the pool of molten weld　　　　　(6) 埋弧焊
(2) Structural Welding Code　　　　 (7) 角焊缝
(3) backup plate　　　　　　　　　　(8) 焊透的对接焊缝
(4) partial penetration groove weld　 (9) 电弧焊
(5) American Welding Society　　　　(10) 拼接板

3. Translate the following sentences into Chinese.

(1) In structural steel welding the heat source is most frequently generated through an electric arc that creates a confined temperature in excess of 6000°F.

(2) In gas welding the heat source is generated through the burning of gas (typically acetylene and oxygen) at the end of a welder's "torch".

(3) The weld must also be protected from coming in contact with the surrounding air during its cooling period. This is usually accomplished through some type of shielding mechanism.

(4) Flux can be either a loose, granular material through which the electrode is moved—or it can be contained on a coating that shrouds the electrode.

(5) Welding has a number of advantages, among which are a savings produced by the reduction of splicing plates, the ease of welding odd shapes, and the ease of implementing field changes.

(6) The shielded metal arc welding (SMAW) process is the traditional type of welding that is manually produced.

(7) This type of weld is very advantageous when welding long lengths and is considered to be superior because of the uniform quality characteristics, mechanical properties, and speed of production.

(8) The most common type of weld is the *fillet weld*, comprising probably 85% of all welds that are produced.

(9) The most important part of the fillet weld, as far as design is concerned, is the throat dimension.

(10) If a fillet weld should be asymmetrical (having unequal legs), the throat distance should be calculated as the perpendicular distance from the face of the weld to its root using trigonometric principles.

4. Fill in the blanks with the given words below.

　　　　　and, and, from, if, if, or, when, where

The other common type of weld is a groove _____ butt weld. This weld is used _____ connecting two plates that lie in the same plane _____ is meant to transfer the load in that plane from one member to the other. A groove weld is referred to as a full penetration groove weld _____ the weld extends the full thickness of the plate being joined _____ it is referred to as a partial penetration groove weld _____ the weld does not extend the full thickness. The partial penetration groove welds may occur in a situation _____ access to the welding area is restricted and can only be accomplished _____ one side.

5. Translate the following sentences into English.
　　(1) 主体金属就是要被连接的金属件。
　　(2) 焊剂是协防不良杂质侵入熔池的一种物质。
　　(3) 在焊条牌号 E70XX 中，70 表示焊条的极限抗拉强度(ksi)，后缀符号(XX)可以反映许多事情，诸如药皮类型、施焊位置和其他特性。
　　(4) 埋弧焊常被制造厂采用，并由自动焊接机实施。
　　(5) 最常见的角焊缝是等边角焊缝，此处焊脚的尺寸是相同的。

Reading Material

Welding Inspection

In the inspection phase, one is concerned primarily with the soundness and quality of a welded joint or weldment. Inspection should begin prior to the actual welding and should continue during welding as well as after the welding is completed. All personnel engaged in inspection operations should be familiar with their company inspection methods as well as all governing codes or standards. The service conditions to which the weldment might be subjected must be known and carefully evaluated before an inspection method can be specified.

　　The inspection process is only as good as the quality of the inspectors. Employment of competent(有能力的) inspectors is only one aspect of assuring weld quality. In addition, good welding procedures and the use of qualified and certified welders contribute to an acceptable weld. The weld testing methods generally used for structures may be categorized as nondestructive and include visual, magnetic particle, radiographic (X光照相的), liquid penetrant(渗透的), and ultrasonic methods.

　　Visual inspection(目测) is probably the most widely used of all inspection methods. It is simple and inexpensive, and the only equipment commonly used is a magnifying glass. Although many factors are beyond the scope of visual examination, it must be regarded as one of the most important methods for determining weld quality. Visual inspection should begin before the first arc is struck. The materials should be examined to see whether they meet specifications for quality, type, size, cleanliness(清洁度), and freedom from defects. Foreign matter, such as grease, paint, oil, oxide film, and heavy scale(锈片), which could be detrimental to the weld, should be removed. The pieces to be joined should be checked for straightness, flatness, and dimensions. Warped, bent, improperly cut, or damaged pieces should be repaired or rejected.

Alignment, fit-up(准备) of parts, and joint preparation should be checked. Inspection prior to welding also includes verification that the correct process and procedures are to be employed and that the electrode type and size are as specified.

Inspection during welding may detect errors and defects that can easily be remedied. It prevents minor defects from piling up into major defects and leading to ultimate rejection. When more than one layer of filler metal is to be deposited, it may be necessary to inspect each layer before a subsequent layer is deposited. The greater the degree of supervision and inspection during welding, the greater the probability of the joint being satisfactory and efficient in service.

Visual inspection after the weldment has been completed is also useful in evaluating quality even if ultrasonic, radiographic, or other methods are to be employed. The following quality factors can usually be determined by visual means: dimensional accuracy of the weldment, conformity to specification requirements, weld appearance, and surface flaws such as cracks and porosity. With only surface defects visible to the eye, however, additional nondestructive methods may be necessary and specified.

Magnetic particle inspection(磁粒检测法) is a nondestructive method used to detect the presence of cracks and seams(发裂，发纹) in magnetic materials. It is not applicable to nonmagnetic materials. This method will detect surface discontinuities that are too fine to be seen with the naked eye, those that lie slightly below the surface, and when special equipment is used, the more deeply seated discontinuities. The basic principle involved in magnetic particle inspection is that when a magnetic field is established in a piece of ferromagnetic material that contains one or more discontinuities in the path of the magnetic flux(磁力线), minute poles are set up at the discontinuities. These poles have a stronger attraction for the magnetic particles than the surrounding surface of the material. The particles form a pattern or indication on the surface that assumes the approximate shape of the discontinuity. Magnetic particle inspection is a relatively low-cost method of inspection and is considered outstanding for detecting surface cracks. It is also used to advantage on heavy weldments and assemblies.

Radiographic inspection is one of the most widely used techniques for showing the presence and nature of macroscopic defects and other discontinuities in the interior of welds. This test method is based on the ability of X-rays and gamma rays to penetrate metal and other opaque materials and produce an image on sensitized film or a fluorescent screen(荧光屏). It is a nondestructive test method and offers a permanent record when recorded on film. It is a relatively expensive type of inspection, and due to the radiation hazard, requires extensive safety precautions. Considerable skill is required in choosing angles of exposure, operating the equipment, and interpreting the results.

Liquid penetrant inspection is a nondestructive method for locating surface cracks and pinholes that are not visible to the naked eye. It is a favored technique for locating leaks in welds, and it can be applied where magnetic particle inspection cannot be used, such as with nonferrous metals. Fluorescent or dye penetrating substances may be used for liquid penetrant inspection.

Fluorescent penetrant inspection(荧光渗透检测法)makes use of a highly fluorescent liquid with unusual penetrating qualities. It is applied to the surface of the part to be inspected and is drawn into extremely small surface openings by capillary action. The excess liquid is then removed from the part, a "developer" is used to draw the penetrant to the surface, and the resulting indication is viewed by ultraviolet (black) light. The high contrast between the fluorescent material and the background makes possible the detection of minute traces of penetrant.

Dye penetrant inspection is similar to fluorescent penetrant inspection except that dyes visible under ordinary light are used. By eliminating the need for ultraviolet light, greater portability in equipment is achieved.

Ultrasonic inspection is a rapid and efficient nondestructive method of detecting, locating, and measuring both surface and subsurface defects in the weldment and/or base materials. Flaws that cannot be discovered by the other methods, and even cracks small enough to be termed microseparations(显微分离, 微裂纹), may be detected. Ultrasonic testing makes use of an electrically timed(同步的)wave of the same nature as a sound wave, but of a higher pitch(音调)or frequency. The frequencies used are far above those heard by the human ear, hence the name is ultrasonic. The sound waves or vibrations are propagated in the metal that is being inspected until a discontinuity or change of density is reached. At these points, some of the vibrational energy is reflected back and indicated on a cathode-ray tube(阴极射线管). The pattern on the face of the tube is thus a representation of the reflected signal and of the defect. The ultrasonic method requires special commercial equipment, and a high degree of skill is required in interpreting the cathode-ray tube patterns.

科技英语阅读与写作指南

科技英语写作——引言

引言又称为前言、序言、导言、绪论等，经常作为科技英语论文的开端，主要回答"为什么研究"这个问题。它简明介绍论文的背景、相关领域的前人研究历史与现状(有时亦称这部分为文献综述)，以及著者的意图与分析依据，包括论文的追求目标、研究范围和理论、技术方案的选取等。需要指出的是引言不应重述摘要中的内容，不对实验的理论、方法和结果作详尽说明，也不提前使用结论和建议。一般而言，科技英语论文的引言应包括以下三个内容：

1. 研究的范围

    常用句型

    The problem under discussion is within the scope of...

    In recent years, considerable effort has been directed towards investigating...

    ... has been widely applied to analyze...

    ... is involved in many industrial processes.

    ... is common among...

    ... is often used for...

    The use of... has been the universal choice to analyze...

... have attracted substantial attention lately due to their advantages over...

Many problems arose as a result of...

Various approaches such as... have been employed as...

Attention is being paid to...

Recently particular attention is given to...

Much attention has been directed toward...

2. 研究的历史与现状

常用句型

Much research has been published regarding...

Little work has been conducted on...

In most studies of..., ... has been emphasized with attention being given to...

The study of... has been the focus of interest of many recent studies...

The effect of... on... has been the subject of few studies.

... has been thoroughly investigated in recent years.

A study of... has been done theoretically and experimentally by...

However, little information has been published concerning...

Although much research has been devoted to..., little attention has been paid to...

While significant advances have been made in..., their application in ... is not widely reported.

So far there is not enough convincing evidence showing...

Much research has been done on..., yet few experimental studies have been conducted in...

3. 研究的目的与活动

常用句型

In this study, an experimental investigation was undertaken to...

This study aims to present...

The present work deals mainly with...

The purpose/objective of the present paper is to obtain the explicit results for...

The study is carried out in the context of...

This paper describes a preparatory investigation into the effect of... on...

In order to verify that..., the present study was initiated.

In this thesis, the results of theoretical and experimental analysis of... are presented and further steps towards... are discussed.

This paper will evaluate several approaches to improving...

LESSON 19

Eccentrically Loaded Bolted Connections

Bolts Subjected to Eccentric Shear

Eccentrically loaded bolt groups are subjected to shears and bending moments. You might think that such situations are rare, but they are much more common than most people suspect. For instance, in a truss it is desirable to have the center of gravity of a member lined up exactly with the center of gravity of the bolts at its end connections. This feat is not quite as easy to accomplish as it may seem, and connections are often subjected to moments.

Eccentricity is quite obvious in Fig. 19.1a, where a beam is connected to a column with a plate. In part b of the figure another beam is connected to a column with a pair of web angles. It is obvious that this connection must resist some moment because the center of gravity of the load from the beam does not coincide with the reaction from the column.

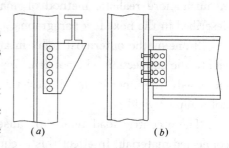

Fig. 19.1 Eccentrically loaded bolt groups.

In general, specifications for bolts and welds clearly state that the center of gravity of the connection should coincide with the center of gravity of the member unless the eccentricity is accounted for in the calculations. However, Section J1.8 of the LRFD Specification provides some exceptions to this rule. It states that the rule is not applicable to the end connections of statically loaded single angles, double angles, and similar members. In other words, the eccentricities between the centers of gravity of these members and the centers of gravity of the connections may be ignored unless fatigue loadings are involved. *Furthermore, the eccentricity between the gravity axes and the gage lines of bolted members may be neglected for statically loaded members.*

The LRFD Specification presents values for computing the design strengths of individual bolts, but does not specify a method for computing the forces on these fasteners when they are eccentrically loaded. As a result the method of analysis to be used is left up to the designer.

Three general approaches for the analysis of eccentrically loaded connections have been developed through the years. The first of the methods is the very conservative *elastic method* in which friction or slip resistance between the connected parts is neglected. In addition these connected parts are assumed to be perfectly rigid. This type of analysis has been commonly used since at least 1870.

Tests have shown that the elastic method usually provides very conservative results. As a consequence various *reduced* or *effective eccentricity methods* have been proposed. The analysis is handled just as it is in the elastic method except that smaller eccentricities and thus smaller moments are used in the calculations.

The third method, called the *ultimate strength method*, provides the most realistic values as compared with test results, but is extremely tedious to apply, at least with hand-held calculators. Tables 7.17 to 7.24 in Part 7 of the Manual for eccentrically loaded connections are based on the ultimate strength method and enable us to solve most of these types of problems quite easily, as long as the bolt patterns are symmetrical. The remainder of this section is devoted to the ultimate strength method.

Ultimate Strength Method

Both the elastic and reduced eccentricity methods for analyzing eccentrically loaded fastener groups are based on the assumption that the behavior of the fasteners is elastic. A much more realistic method of analysis is the *ultimate strength method*, which is described in the next few paragraphs.

If one of the outermost bolts in an eccentrically loaded connection begins to slip or yield, the connection will not fail. Instead, the magnitude of the eccentric load may be increased, the inner bolts will resist more load, and failure will not occur until all of the bolts slip or yield.

The eccentric load tends to cause both a relative rotation and translation of the connected material. In effect this is equivalent to pure rotation of the connection about a single point called the *instantaneous center of rotation*. An eccentrically loaded bolted connection is shown in Fig. 19.2, and the instantaneous center is represented by point O. It is located a distance e' from the center of gravity of the bolt group.

The deformations of these bolts are assumed to vary in proportion to their distances from the instantaneous center. The ultimate shear force that one of them can resist is not equal to the pure shear force that a bolt can resist. Rather, it is dependent upon the load-deformation relationship in the bolt. Studies by Crawford and Kulak have shown that this force may be closely estimated with the following expression:

$$R = R_{ult}(1 - e^{-10\Delta})^{0.55}$$

In this formula R_{ult} is the ultimate shear load for a single fastener, e is the base of the natural logarithm (2.718), and Δ is the total deformation of a bolt. Its maximum value is experimentally determined. [1] The Δ values for the other bolts are assumed to be in proportion to R as their d distances are to d for the bolt with the largest d. The coefficients 10.0 and 0.55 also were experimentally obtained. Fig. 19.3 illustrates this load-deformation relationship.

This expression clearly shows that the ultimate shear load taken by a particular bolt in an eccentrically loaded connection is affected by its deformation. Thus, the load applied to a particular bolt is dependent upon its position in the connection with respect to the instantaneous center of rotation.

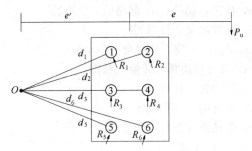

Fig. 19.2 Eccentrically loaded bolt groups.

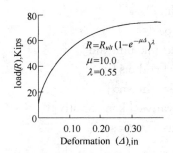

Fig. 19.3 Ultimate shear force R in a single bolt at any given deformation.

The resisting forces of the bolts of the connection of Fig. 19.2 are represented with the letters R_1, R_2, R_3, and so on. Each of these forces is assumed to act in a direction perpendicular to a line drawn from point O to the center of the bolt in question. For this symmetrical connection the instantaneous center of rotation will fall somewhere on a horizontal line through the center of gravity of the bolt group.[2] This is the case because the sum of the horizontal components of the R forces must be zero as also must be the sum of the moments of the horizontal components about point O. The position of point O on the horizontal line may be found by a tedious trial-and-error procedure to be described here.

With reference to Fig. 19.2, the moment of the eccentric load about point O must be equal to the summation of the moments of the R resisting forces about the same point. If we knew the location of the instantaneous center we could compute R values for the bolts with the Crawford-Kulak formula and determine P_u from the expression to follow in which e and e' are distances shown in Fig. 19.2.

$$P_u(e'+e)=\Sigma Rd$$
$$P_u=\frac{\Sigma Rd}{e'+e}$$

To determine the design strength of such a connection according to the LRFD Specification, we can replace R_{ult} in the Crawford-Kulak formula with the design shearing strength of one bolt in a connection where the load is not eccentric.

The location of the instantaneous center is not known, however. Its position is estimated, the R values determined, and P_u calculated as described. It will be noted that P_u must be equal to the summation of the vertical components of the R resisting forces (ΣR_v). If the value is computed and equals the P_u computed by the formula above we have the correct location for the instantaneous center. If not, we try another location, and so on.

New Words

1. eccentric [ik'sentrik]　　　　　　　　$a.$ 偏心的，异常的
2. bolt [bəult]　　　　　　　　　　　　$n.$ 螺钉，螺栓

3. outermost ['autəmoust]　　　　a. 最外面的，最远的
4. feat [fi:t]　　　　　　　　　　n. 技艺，功绩；a. 漂亮的，合适的
5. gage [geidʒ]　　　　　　　　　n. 标准度量，计量器
6. coincide [ˌkəuin'said]　　　　vi. 与…一致［相符合］（with）
7. reduce [ri'dju:s]　　　　　　　vt. 折合，换算，转换，对比
8. fastener ['fɑ:snə]　　　　　　 n. 紧固件，扣件
9. conservative [kən'sə:vətiv]　　a. 保守的，守旧的
10. tedious ['ti:diəs]　　　　　　 a. 单调乏味的，冗长乏味的

Phrases and Expressions

1. bending moment　弯矩
2. line up　对齐，排成一线
3. reduced eccentricity method　折算偏心距法
4. effective eccentricity method　有效偏心距法
5. ultimate strength method　极限强度法
6. relative rotation and translation　相对转动和移动
7. eccentrically loaded bolted connection　偏心受荷的螺栓连接
8. the center of gravity of the bolt group　螺栓群的重心
9. trial-and-error procedure　试算法
10. design strength　设计强度

Notes

［1］The Δ values for the other bolts are assumed to be in proportion to R as their d distances are to d for the bolt with the largest d. as 引导原因状语从句，句中省去了 in proportion。全句可译为：因为其他螺栓的距离 d 与具有最大距离 d 的螺栓的 d 成比例，所以可假定他们的 Δ 值与 R 成比例。

［2］This is the case because the sum of... the R forces must be zero as also must be the sum of the moments of the horizontal components about point O. as 引导方式状语从句，采用了倒装语序并省略了 zero。全句可译为：这是因为诸 R 力水平分量之和必须为零，同样诸力水平分量对 O 点的力矩之和也必须为零。

Exercises

1. Fill in the blanks with proper words.

   (1) This feat is not quite as easy ＿＿＿＿ accomplish as it may seem, and connections are often subjected to moments.

   (2) It is obvious that this connection must resist some moment ＿＿＿＿ the center of gravity of the load from the beam does not coincide with the reaction from the column.

   (3) In other words, the eccentricities ＿＿＿＿ the centers of gravity of these

LESSON 19

members _____ the centers of gravity of the connections may be ignored unless fatigue loadings are involved.

(4) The LRFD Specification presents values for computing the design strengths of individual bolts, but does not specify a method for computing the forces on these fasteners _____ they are eccentrically loaded.

(5) Tests have shown that the elastic method usually provides very conservative results. _____ a consequence various *reduced* or *effective eccentricity methods* have been proposed.

(6) This expression clearly shows that the ultimate shear load taken by a particular bolt in an eccentrically loaded connection is affected _____ its deformation.

(7) Each of these forces is assumed _____ act in a direction perpendicular to a line drawn from point O to the center of the bolt in question.

(8) With reference to Fig. 19.2, the moment of the eccentric load about point O must be equal to the summation of the moments of the R resisting forces _____ the same point.

2. Translate the following phrases into Chinese/English.
    (1) reduced eccentricity method   (6) 设计强度
    (2) ultimate strength method   (7) 有效偏心距法
    (3) eccentrically loaded bolted connection   (8) 相对转动和移动
    (4) friction or slip resistance   (9) 螺栓群的重心
    (5) statically loaded members   (10) 试算法

3. Translate the following sentences into Chinese.

(1) You might think that such situations are rare, but they are much more common than most people suspect.

(2) In general, specifications for bolts and welds clearly state that the center of gravity of the connection should coincide with the center of gravity of the member unless the eccentricity is accounted for in the calculations.

(3) Furthermore, the eccentricity between the gravity axes and the gage lines of bolted members may be neglected for statically loaded members.

(4) The *ultimate strength method* provides the most realistic values as compared with test results, but is extremely tedious to apply, at least with hand-held calculators.

(5) Instead, the magnitude of the eccentric load may be increased, the inner bolts will resist more load, and failure will not occur until all of the bolts slip or yield.

(6) The ultimate shear force that one of them can resist is not equal to the pure shear force that a bolt can resist.

(7) In this formula R_{ult} is the ultimate shear load for a single fastener, e is the base of the natural logarithm (2.718), and Δ is the total deformation of a bolt.

(8) Thus, the load applied to a particular bolt is dependent upon its position in the connection with respect to the instantaneous center of rotation.

(9) This is the case because the sum of the horizontal components of the R forces must be zero as also must be the sum of the moments of the horizontal components about

point O.

(10) If the value is computed and equals the P_u computed by the formula above we have the correct location for the instantaneous center.

4. Translate the following sentences into English.
   (1) 偏心受荷的螺栓群承受剪力和弯矩的作用。
   (2) 第一种方法是非常保守的弹性法，这个方法忽略了连接件间的摩擦阻力或滑移阻力。
   (3) 弹性法和折算偏心距法都基于紧固件的性能是弹性的假定。
   (4) 这实际上等同于连接关于瞬时转动中心点的纯转动。
   (5) 螺栓的变形假定与它们到瞬时转动中心的距离成正比。

Reading Material

Behaviour of Connections

Force Connections

A force connection is one in which there is no moment acting on a group of connectors and which is only required to transmit a force. In a force connection using shear and bearing bolts in clearance (间隙) holes, there is an initial slip when any force is applied to the connection as some of the clearances are taken up, and the connection becomes increasingly stiffer as more of the bolts come into play (Fig. 19.4). At higher forces, the more highly loaded bolts start to yield, and the connection becomes less stiff. Later, a state may be reached in which each bolt is loaded to its maximum capacity.

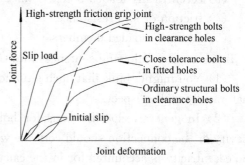

Fig. 19.4　Behaviour of bolted connections.

It is not usual to analyze this complex behavior, and instead it is commonly assumed that equal size bolts share equally in transferring the force, even in the working load range. This is the case if there are no clearances and all the bolts fit perfectly, and if the member and connection plates act rigidly and the bolts elastically. If, however, the flexibilities (柔性) of the members and plates are taken into account, it is found that the forces transferred are highest in the end bolts of any line of bolts parallel to the connection force, and lowest in the center bolts. In long bolted connections, the end bolt forces may be so high as to lead to premature (过早的) failure (before these forces can be redistributed by plastic action) and the subsequent 'unbuttoning'(解扣现象) of the connection.

When designing a shear and bearing bolted connection, it is necessary to check the shear and bearing capacities of the bolts as well as the load capacities of the members and connection plates, including their shear and bearing capacities at the holes.

Connections using close tolerance bolts in fitted (配合的) holes behave in a similar manner to connections with clearance holes, except that the bolt slips are greatly reduced. On the other hand, slip is not reduced in high-strength, friction-grip, bolted connections, but is postponed until the frictional resistance is overcome at the slip load as shown in Fig. 19.4. Such connections are designed on the basis of the slip load, which depends on the tensile bolt forces achieved and on the coefficient of friction of the contact surfaces.

Welded connections do not slip, but behave as if almost rigid. Welds are often designed as if uniformly stressed, but, as in the case of long bolted joints, there may be significantly higher stresses at the ends of long welds parallel to the connection force. Often the maximum design stresses permitted are based on comparatively high load factors, and so these high-end stresses are not usually important.

Because of the great differences in the stiffness of connections using different types of connectors, it is not usual to allow the connection force to be shared between two or more types of connectors, and instead, the stiffest connectors are required to transfer all the force. For example, when field bolting is used to hold two members in place at a joint which is subsequently field welded, the bolts are designed for the erection conditions only, while the welds are designed for the total force. This practice is not universal, and in some cases when welds are used to augment (加强) high strength friction grip bolts, the connection force may be shared.

The total flexibility of a connection can be determined from the sum of the flexibilities of the components used at each link in the chain of force transfer through the connection. Thus the flexibilities of any plates or cleats used must be included with those of the connectors. Plates are comparatively stiff (and often assumed to be rigid) when loaded in their planes, but are comparatively flexible when bent out of their planes. In general, the overall behavior of a connection can be assessed by determining the path by which force is transferred through the connection, and by synthesizing the responses of all the elements to their individual loads.

Moment Connections

A moment connection is one which is only required to transmit a moment, as shown in Fig. 19.5, where the connectors joining the two plates transfer a moment M acting in the plane of one plate to the other.

If all the connectors fit perfectly, and if each plate acts as if rigid, so that the relative rotation between them is θ, each connector transfers a shear force P from one plate to the other. This shear force acts perpendicular to the radius r_i to axis of rotation and is

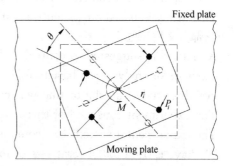

Fig. 19.5 Connector forces in moment connection.

proportional to the relative displacement $r_i\theta$ of the two plates at the connector, whence

$$P_{si}=kA_ir_i\theta \tag{19.1}$$

where A_i is the shear area of the connector, and the constant k depends on the shear stiffness of that type of connector. It can be shown by considering the equilibrium of the connector forces P_{si} that the axis of rotation lies at the centroid of the connectors. The moment exerted by the connector force is $P_{si}r_i$, and so the total moment M is given by

$$M=k\theta\sum A_ir_i^2 \tag{19.2}$$

If this is substituted into Eq. 19.2, the connector force can be evaluated as

$$P_{si}=\frac{MA_ir_i}{\sum A_ir_i^2} \tag{19.3}$$

This equation is often used to analyze moment connections.

However, the real behaviour of moment connections is likely to be somewhat different, just as it is for the force connections discussed in the previous sub-section. This difference is due to the flexibility of the plates, the inelastic behaviour of the connections at higher moments, and the slip due to the clearances between any bolts and their holes.

科技英语阅读与写作指南

科技英语写作——正文

正文是科技英语论文的核心组成部分，主要回答"怎么研究"这个问题。正文的内容必须将科研工作的目的、实验方法、实验结果、数据分析、科研成果的研究过程及结论等内容完整、精确地用英语表达出来。根据需要，论文可以分层深入，逐层剖析，按层设分层标题。科技英语论文的正文的具体陈述方式往往因不同学科、不同文章类型而有很大差别，但一般应包括材料、方法、结果、讨论等几个部分。

1. 材料部分常用句型

   In this study, two kinds of ... were used.

   The material to be used is ...

   For experiments under conditions similar to ... , ... was developed.

   In order to measure... , ... was chosen in this experiment.

   The apparatus fundamentally consisted of...

   This study is based on... and the data are available from...

2. 方法部分常用句型

   A method is suggested to control and evaluate ...

   Methods of analysis are based on ...

   For this study, all the testing was conducted individually by ...

   The experiment consisted of three steps, ...

   The experimental system was composed of four parts, ...

   We have carried out several sets of experiments to test the validity of ...

   It was designed for the application of ...

   The factors involved in ... can be difficult to measure directly, but we can ...

The experiments were performed using the following procedure.

We can compare the theoretical and experimental models by using plotting both on the same graph.

3. 结果部分常用句型

The research we have done suggests an increase in ...

Our experimental data are briefly summarized as follows ...

Table 5 presents the data provided by the experiments on ...

The results of all measurements of ... are given in Table 4.

Figure 6 shows a sketch of ...

The effect of ... on ... is shown in Figure 5

As shown in Figure 6, ...

The readings for ... are graphed in Figure 1 below.

The graph clearly shows that there is good agreement between the two curves, except for the point at ..., where there is a difference of ...

This gives an overall error of ... % between these two curves, compared to the total range of the data.

4. 讨论部分常用句型

Such results could be of benefit for ...

The measured ... were all highly consistent with the predictions of the theoretical model.

These results agree with ...

It is clear from the data that ...

A possible explanation for this is that ...

These results can be explained by assuming that ...

This finding seems to show that ...

This inconsistency may be caused by an error in ...

The rapid increase/decrease can be attributed to ...

These results contradict the original hypothesis.

In general the models agreed well, except for a single ...

The error was relatively small, only being ... % of the entire data range.

This error was most likely caused by a single measurement error.

Lesson 20

Traditional Construction Procedures

As mentioned before, construction under the traditional construction procedure is performed by contractors. While they would like to satisfy the owner and the building designers, contractors have the main objective of making a profit. Hence, their initial task is to prepare a bid price based on an accurate estimate of construction costs. This requires development of a concept for performance of the work and a construction time schedule. After a contract has been awarded, contractors must furnish and pay for all materials, equipment, power, labor, and supervision required for construction. The owner compensates the contractors for construction costs and services.

A *general contractor* assumes overall responsibility for construction of a building. The contractor engages *subcontractors* who take responsibility for the work of the various trades required for construction. For example, a plumbing contractor installs the plumbing, an electrical contractor installs the electrical system, and an elevator contractor installs elevators. Their contracts are with the general contractor, and they are paid by the general contractor.

Sometimes, in addition to a general contractor, the owners contracts separately with specialty contractors, such as electrical and mechanical contractors, who perform a substantial amount of the work required for a building. Such contractors are called *prime contractors*. Their work is scheduled and coordinated by the general contractor, but they are paid directly by the owner.

Sometimes also, the owner may use the design-build method and award a contract to an organization for both the design and construction of a building. Such organizations are called *design-build contractors*. One variation of this type of contract is employed by developers of groups of one-family homes or low-rise apartment buildings. The *homebuilder* designs and constructs the dwellings, but the design is substantially completed before owners purchase the homes.

Administration of the construction procedure often is difficult. Consequently, some owners seek assistance from an expert, called a *professional construction manager*, with extensive construction experience, who receives a fee. The construction manager negotiates with general contractors and helps select one to construct the building. Managers usually also supervise selection of subcontractors. During construction, they help control costs, expedite equipment and material deliveries, and keep the work on schedule. In some cases, instead, the owner may prefer to engage a *construction program manager*, to assist in administrating both design and construction.

Construction contractors employ labor that may or may not be unionized. Unionized

LESSON 20

craftspeople are members of unions that are organized by construction trades, such as carpenter, plumber, and electrician unions. Union members will perform only the work assigned to their trade.

During construction, all work should be inspected. For this purpose, the owner, often through the architect and consultants, engages inspectors. The field inspectors may be placed under the control of an owner's representative, who may be titled *clerk of the works*, *architect's superintendent*, *engineer's superintendent*, or *resident engineer*. The inspectors have the responsibility of ensuring that construction meets the requirements of the contract documents and is performed under safe conditions. Such inspections may be made at frequent intervals.

In addition, inspections also are made by representatives of one or more governmental agencies. They have the responsibility of ensuring that construction meets legal requirements and have little or no concern with detailed conformance with the contract documents. Such legal inspections are made periodically or at the end of certain stages of construction. One agency that will make frequent inspections is the local or state building department, whichever has jurisdiction. The purpose of these inspections is to ensure conformance with the local or state building code.

Following is a description of the basic traditional construction procedure for a multistorey building:

After the award of a construction contract to a general contractor, the owner may ask the contractor to start a portion of the work before signing of the contract by giving the contractor a letter of intent or after signing of the contract by issuing a written notice to proceed. [1] The contractor then obtains construction permits, as required, from governmental agencies, such as the local building, water, sewer, and highway departments.

The general contractor plans and schedules construction operations in detail and mobilizes equipment and personnel for the project. Subcontractors are notified of the contract award and issued letters of intent or awarded subcontracts, then are given, at appropriate times, notices to proceed.

Before construction starts, the general contractor orders a survey to be made of adjacent structures and terrain, both for the record and to become knowledgeable of local conditions. A survey is then made to lay out construction.

Field offices for the contractor are erected on or near the site. If desirable for safety reasons to protect passersby, the contractor erects a fence around the site and an overhead protective cover. Structures required to be removed from the site are demolished and the debris is carted away.

Next, the site is prepared to receive the building. This work may involve grading the top surface to bring it to the proper elevations, excavating to required depths for basement and foundations, and shifting of utility piping. For deep excavations, earth sides are braced and the bottom is drained.

Major construction starts with the placement of foundations, on which the building rests. This is followed by the erection of load-bearing walls and structural framing. Depending on the height of the building, ladders, stairs, or elevators may be installed to enable construction personnel to travel from floor to floor and eventually to the roof. Also, hoists may be installed to lift materials to upper levels. If needed, temporary flooring may be placed for use of personnel.

As the building rises, pipes, ducts, and electric conduit and wiring are installed. Then, permanent floors, exterior walls, and windows are constructed. At the appropriate time, permanent elevators are installed. If required, fireproofing is placed for steel framing. Next, fixed partitions are built and the roof and its covering are put in place.

Finishing operations follow. These include installation of the following: ceilings; tile; wallboard; wall paneling; plumbing fixtures; heating furnaces; air-conditioning equipment; heating and cooling devices for rooms; escalators; floor coverings; window glass; movable partitions; doors; finishing hardware; electrical equipment and apparatus, including lighting fixtures, switches, transformers, and controls; and other items called for in the drawings and specifications. Field offices, fences, bridges, and other temporary construction must be removed from the site. Utilities, such as gas, electricity, and water, are hooked up to the building. The site is landscaped and paved. Finally, the building interior is painted and cleaned.

The owner's representatives then give the building a final inspection. If they find that the structure conforms with the contract documents, the owner accepts the project and gives the general contractor final payment on issuance by the building department of a certificate of occupancy, which indicates that the completed building meets building-code requirements.

New Words

1. furnish ['fə:niʃ]　　　　　　　　　　　　　　　vt. 供应，提供
2. supervision [ˌsju:pə'viʒən]　　　　　　　　　n. 监督，管理
3. subcontractor [ˌsʌbkən'træktə(r)]　　　　　　n. 分包商
4. plumbing ['plʌmiŋ]　　　　　　　　　　　　　n. 卫生管道工程
5. homebuilder ['həumˌbildə]　　　　　　　　　n. 房屋营造商
6. superintendent [ˌsju:pərin'tendənt]　　　　　n. 主管，负责人
7. consultant [kən'sʌltənt]　　　　　　　　　　n. 顾问，咨询者
8. jurisdiction [ˌdʒuəris'dikʃən]　　　　　　　　n. 权限，权力
9. terrain ['terein]　　　　　　　　　　　　　　n. 地形，地层
10. tile [tail]　　　　　　　　　　　　　　　　　n. 瓦片，瓷砖
11. administration [ədminis'treiʃən]　　　　　　n. 管理，经营
12. expedite ['ekspidait]　　　　　　　　　　　　v. 加速；a. 畅通的
13. unionize ['ju:njənaiz]　　　　　　　　　　　v. 成立工会
14. superintendent [ˌsju:pərin'tendənt]　　　　n. 主管，负责人

15. conformance [kɔn'fɔːməns]　　　　　　n. 顺应，一致
16. demolish [di'mɔliʃ]　　　　　　　　vt. 毁坏，破坏
17. cart [kɑːt]　　　　　　　　　　　　vt. 用车装载
18. hoist [hɔist]　　　　　　　　　　　n. 提升间，升起
19. escalator ['eskəleitə]　　　　　　 n. 自动扶梯
20. transformer [træns'fɔːmə]　　　　 n. 变压器

Phrases and Expressions

1. bid price　出价，标价
2. general contractor　总承包商（人）
3. prime contractor　专业承包商
4. professional construction manager　专业施工经理
5. architects' superintendent　建筑师主管
6. engineers' superintendent　工程师主管
7. clerk of the works　现场监工员，工程管理员
8. resident engineer　工地工程师，驻工地工程师
9. letter of intent　合同之草约，意向书
10. for the record　正式的，有案可查的
11. utility piping　公用管线
12. plumbing fixtures　卫生设备
13. design-build contractors　设计-建造承包商
14. construction program manager　项目咨询经理

Notes

[1] The contractor then obtains construction permits, as required, from governmental agencies, such as the local building, water, sewer, and highway departments. as 引起定语从句修饰全句，从句中省去了 is。全句可译为：然后，根据需要，承包商要获得政府机构的施工许可，如地方建筑、供水、排水和公路主管部门。

Exercises

1. Fill in the blanks with proper words.

（1）While they would like to satisfy the owner and the building designers, contractors have the main objective of _____ a profit.

（2）The owner compensates the _____ for construction costs and services.

（3）A general contractor assumes overall _____ for construction of a building.

（4）The subcontractors' contracts are with the _____ contractor, and they are paid by the general contractor.

（5）Sometimes, in addition to a general contractor, the owners contracts separately with _____ contractors.

(6) The prime contractors' work is scheduled and coordinated by the general contractor, but they are paid directly by the _____.

(7) The construction manager negotiates with general contractors and helps _____ one to construct the building.

(8) Construction contractors employ labor that may or may _____ be unionized.

(9) Union members will perform only the work assigned to their _____.

(10) The inspectors have the responsibility of ensuring that construction meets the _____ of the contract documents and is performed under safe conditions.

2. Translate the following phrases into Chinese/English.
    (1) field office   (6) 工地工程师
    (2) professional construction manager   (7) 合同文件
    (3) plumbing fixtures   (8) 总承包者
    (4) bid price   (9) 意向书
    (5) deep excavations   (10) 空调系统

3. Translate the following sentences into Chinese.

(1) While they would like to satisfy the owner and the building designers, contractors have the main objective of making a profit.

(2) After a contract has been awarded, contractors must furnish and pay for all materials, equipment, power, labor, and supervision required for construction. The owner compensates the contractors for construction costs and services.

(3) A general contractor assumes overall responsibility for construction of a building.

(4) The inspectors have the responsibility of ensuring that construction meets the requirements of the contract documents and is performed under safe conditions.

(5) After the award of a construction contract to a general contractor, the owner may ask the contractor to start a portion of the work before signing of the contract by giving the contractor a letter of intent or after signing of the contract by issuing a written notice to proceed.

(6) Before construction starts, the general contractor orders a survey to be made of adjacent structures and terrain, both for the record and to become knowledgeable of local conditions.

(7) Major construction starts with the placement of foundations, on which the building rests. This is followed by the erection of load-bearing walls and structural framing.

(8) As the building rises, pipes, ducts, and electric conduit and wiring are installed. Then, permanent floors, exterior walls, and windows are constructed.

(9) During construction, they help control costs, expedite equipment and material deliveries, and keep the work on schedule.

4. Fill in the blanks with the given words below.

also, by, for, from, if, on, on, to, with

Major construction starts _____ the placement of foundations, _____ which the building rests. This is followed _____ the erection of load-bearing walls and structural framing. Depending _____ the height of the building, ladders, stairs, or elevators may be installed _____ enable construction personnel to travel _____ floor to floor and eventually to the roof. _____, hoists may be installed to lift materials to upper levels. _____ needed, temporary flooring may be placed _____ use of personnel.

5. Translate the following sentences into English.

(1) 在某些情况下，业主更愿意聘用施工管理项目经理，帮助其进行设计与施工的管理。

(2) 检验员负责确保工程满足合同文件的要求，并在安全的情况下进行施工。

(3) 此外，一个或多个政府机构的代表也要对其进行检查。

(4) 因此，一些业主会寻求被称为专业项目经理的专家的帮助，他们具有丰富的施工经验，且要获取报酬的。

(5) 然后，根据需要，承包商要获得政府机构的施工许可，如地方建筑、供水、排水、以及公路主管部门。

Reading Material

Movement in Natural and Artificial Slopes

Soil or rock masses with sloping surfaces may be the result of natural agencies or they may be man-made. In all slopes there exists an inherent tendency to degrade to a more stable form—ultimately towards horizontal and in this context instability is construed(解释) as the tendency to move, and failure as an actual mass movement. The forces which cause instability are mainly those associated with gravity and seepage, while resistance to failure is derived mainly from a combination of slope geometry and the shear strength of the rock or soil mass itself.

Mass movement may take place as the result of a shear failure along an internal surface or when a general decrease in effective stress between particles causes full or partial liquefaction. A wide variety of types of movement (failure) have been observed; it is convenient here, however, to consider three classes.

Falls. These are characterized by movement away from existing discontinuities, such as joints(节理), fissures(裂缝), steeply-inclined bedding planes(陡斜岩层面), fault planes, etc. and within which the failure condition may be assisted or precipitated(促成) by the effects of water or ice pressure.

Slides. In this form of movement the mass remains essentially intact while sliding along a definite failure surface. Two structural sub-divisions are apparent: (*a*) Translational slides(平移滑坡) which may involve linear movement of rock blocks along bedding planes or of a soil layer lying near to the (sloping) surface. Such movements are normally fairly shallow and parallel to the surface; (b) Rotational slips(转动滑坡) occur characteristically in homogeneous soft rocks or cohesive soils; the movement taking place along a curved shear surface in such a way that the slipping mass slumps down near the top of the slope and bulges up near the toe.

Flows. Here the slipping mass is internally disrupted and moves partially or wholly as a fluid. Flows often occur in weak saturated soils when the pore pressure has increased sufficiently to produce a general loss of shear strength; true shear surface development may be intermittent or mostly absent.

Slope failures are usually precipitated by a variation in conditions, such as a change in rainfall, drainage, loading or surface stability (e.g. removal of vegetation). Such changes may occur immediately after construction, or they may develop slowly over a number of years, or they may be imposed suddenly at any time. In the analysis of both cut and built slopes it is necessary to consider both immediate and long-term stability conditions. It is also necessary to consider whether failure is likely along a newly created slip surface, or along a pre-existing one, since the difference between the peak and residual shear strength in some soils may be considerable.

Some slopes may exist for years in a state of incipient failure(早期破裂), i.e. on the brink of further movement. This is particularly evident in natural slopes and the slopes of spoil tips, and it should be borne in mind that many hill slopes have been naturally degraded by weathering and may also be close to a failure state. In these situations, man-made interference, such as the removal of trees or other vegetation, or cutting into the toe of the slope, may precipitate movement.

Choice of Shear Strength Parameters for Slope Design

As discussed before, the parameters used to quantify shear strength depend fundamentally on both the stress history of the soil and the operational drainage conditions. In the case of slope stability problems, a further consideration is whether the failure movement will take place on a newly created slip surface or on an existing surface where slipping has occurred previously.

The following recommendations are made for general purpose design, but it should be remembered that many soil engineering problems are individualistic. Guidelines for design are helpful, but general rules can often lead the unwary into difficulties.

Slides along Pre-Existing Slip Surfaces

These failure states occur only where large displacements have already occurred; perhaps of several metres. Residual strength parameters should be used:

Undrained: $\tau_r = c_w$; Drained: $\tau_r' = \sigma_n' \tan \phi_r'$

Slides Creating New Slip Surfaces

A new slip surface will occur either when the critical strength or the peak strength of the soil is reached consistently within the soil mass. The choice of parameter should be made only after careful examination of the stress history and the predicted drainage state(s).

For undrained conditions, the peak strength will be lower than the critical strength, so use: $\tau_f = c_u$

Slope Failure Mechanisms in Cohesive Soils

The most usual methods of providing an analysis of stability in slopes in cohesive soils are based on a consideration of limiting plastic equilibrium. Fundamentally, a condition of limiting plastic equilibrium exists from the moment that a shear slip movement commences and strain continues at constant stress. It is first necessary to define the geometry of the slip surface; the mass of soil about to move over this surface is then considered as a free body in equilibrium. The forces or moments acting on this free body are evaluated and those shear forces acting along the slip surface compared with the available shear resistance offered by the soil.

Several forms of slip surface may be considered for cohesive soils. The simplest of these, suggested by Cullmann in 1866, consists of an infinitely long plane passing through the toe of the slope. Although the analysis of the free body equilibrium is simple in this case, the method yields factors of safety which grossly overestimate the true stability conditions. On the other hand, while the choice of a more complex surface, such as a log-spiral or an irregular shape, may produce results near to the actual value, the analysis tends to be long and tedious. For most purposes, a cylindrical surface, i.e. circular in cross-section, will yield satisfactorily accurate results without involving analytical routines of any great complexity.

The stability of a cut or built slope depends very largely on changes in the pore pressure regime(状态). During the construction of embankments(堤防，堤坝) pore pressures will rise and, after construction, they will gradually fall. In cuttings, however, excavation causes an initial fall in pore pressures, but as seepage develops they gradually rise. Effective stresses and therefore shear strengths are generally inversely related to pore pressures. The most critical (lowest) factor of safety may therefore be expected to occur immediately after or during the construction of an embankment; after this the soil will gradually get stronger. In contrast, the shear strength in a cutting diminishes with time and so does the factor of safety.

Thus, it is necessary to consider both short-term (end-of-construction) and long-term stability. In this context it is convenient to think of short-term conditions as being completely undrained, in which the shear strength is given by $\tau_f = c_u$ (i.e. $\phi_u = 0$). In the next section, the first case to be considered will be that of undrained stability of a slope in a saturated clay; this type of analysis is often referred to as a total stress, or $\phi_u = 0$, method.

For long-term problems, and problems where changes in conditions may occur long after the end of construction (such as the sudden draw-down of level in a reservoir), a form of effective stress analysis is required. These methods may take the form of either a force-or moment-equilibrium analysis, involving plane circular or irregular slip surfaces.

For complex problems, stress path and slip line field methods are used. The shear strength parameters must be chosen with care.

Location of the Most Critical Circle

The most critical circle is the one for which the calculated factor of safety has the lowest value. The minimum factor of safety is clearly the criterion required for design. The problem of locating the most critical circle may be approached in one of two ways:

(a) By a process of trial and error, using a reasonable number of 'trial' circles and a thoughtful search pattern.

(b) By employing an empirical rule to prescribe an assumed critical circle and setting the factor of safety.

In the trial and error approach, the method has to allow for variation in three of the geometric parameters: the position of the centre, the radius and the intercept distance in front of the toe. For acceptable reliability, a very large number of trials may have to be made. The use of computers has made this method much more feasible and also more reliable.

Even when a large number of trials are to be the method employed, it is still useful to produce a good estimate for the first or 'seed' value. Slip circle behavior is not completely random; on the contrary, some definite patterns may be observed. For example, when the angle of friction is greater than 3°, the critical circle will almost always pass through the toe of the slope. This is also the case when, irrespective of the value of the slope angle exceeds 53°.

科技英语阅读与写作指南

科技英语写作——结论

科技英语论文的结论是整篇文章的最后总结,位于论文的最后。多数科技论文的著者都采用结论的方式作为结束,并通过它传达自己欲向读者表述的主要意向。结论是文章逻辑发展的必然和自然结果。结论不应是正文中各段小结的简单重复,主要回答"研究出什么"。它应该以正文中的试验或考察中得到的现象、数据和阐述分析作为依据,由此形成的总的观念。科技英语论文的结论部分通常应包含以下内容:

1. 概述主要的研究工作、研究目的;

   常用句型:

   The primary objective of our study was to examine …

   The goal of this study was to select … and to see whether …

   This paper describes an experiment done to test the effects of … on …

   This research investigated the differences between …

   This study attempted to investigate whether …

   This paper has proposed a detailed assessment of …

   This study has presented a unique method for …

   In this paper, we have reported the significant effect of …

2. 研究对象进行研究或实验得到的结果所揭示的原理;

常用句型：
Our analysis indicates that ...
These findings confirm that ...
These finding seems to show that ...
The data reported here suggest that ...
The evidence led us to infer that ...
These findings support the hypothesis that ...
These results provide substantial evidence for ...
Based on the analytical and experimental investigations presented in this paper, the following conclusions may be made.

3. 研究方法的限制及这些限制对研究结果可能产生的影响；

常用句型：
The analysis neglects several potentially important conditions.
An experiment using different ... might produce different results.
One drawback is that the process is only suitable for ...
The method presented here is accurate, but cannot be implemented in real time applications.
We recognize that the method adopted in this paper doesn't ...
We readily admit that a single test may not fully reflect ...

4. 与先前已经发表过的(包括他人或著者自己)研究工作的异同；

常用句型：
These results agree well with the findings of ...
These data are consistent with earlier findings showing that ...
The present results are consistent with those reported in our earlier work.
These results appear to refute the original assumptions.
Our findings are in substantial agreement with those of ...

5. 本研究结果在理论上与实用上的意义与价值以及进一步深入的研究方向。

常用句型：
These results are higher than would be expected.
The experimental values are all lower than the theoretical predictions.
The results of this study may lead to the development of effective methods for ...
The methods presented in this paper should be useful in ...
The results of this research may be useful for various ...
A further experiment should be conducted with a more ...
Future research should focus on ...
... merits further study.
Further research is needed to quantify the effect of ... on ...
... is an interesting problem requiring further research.
However, there are still some ... and more study is needed to solve the issues.

LESSON 21

Plate Girders

A plate girder is usually thought of as a flexural member whose cross section is composed of plate elements. A plate girder is basically a large beam, both in span and cross section, the large cross section usually being a consequence of the long span. If the largest available hot-rolled steel shape is inadequate for a given span and loading, the first alternative would normally be a rolled shape with cover plates added to one or both flanges. If this could not provide enough moment strength, a cross section with exactly the properties needed could be fabricated from plate elements. If the span is long enough, however, the depth and weight of a built-up girder may be excessive, and other alternatives, such as a truss, may be necessary.

A plate girder cross section can take several forms. Fig. 21.1 shows some of the possibilities. The usual configuration is a single web with two equal flanges, with all parts connected by welding. The box section, which has two webs as well as two flanges, is a torsionally superior shape and can be used when large unbraced lengths are necessary. Hybrid girders, in which the steel in the flanges is of a higher strength than that in the web or webs, are sometimes used.

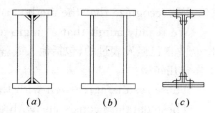

Fig. 21.1 Plate girder cross sections.

Before the widespread use of welding, connecting the components of the cross section was a major consideration in the design of plate girders. Since all of the connections were made by riveting, there was no way to attach the flange directly to the web, and additional cross-sectional elements were introduced for the specific purpose of transmitting the load from one component to the other. The usual technique was to use a pair of angles, placed back-to-back, to attach the flange to the web; one pair of legs was attached to the web, and the other pair attached to the flange (Fig. 21.1c). If web stiffeners were needed, pairs of angles were used for that purpose also. To avoid a conflict between the stiffener angles and the flange angles, filler plates were added to the web so that the stiffeners could clear the flange angles. If a variable cross section was desired, one or more cover plates of different lengths were riveted to the flanges. (Although cover plates can also be used with welded plate girders, a simpler approach is to use different thicknesses of flange plate, welded end-to-end, at different locations along the length of the girder.) It should be evident that the welded plate girder is far superior to the riveted or bolted girder in terms of simplicity and efficiency.

Structural steel design is largely a matter of providing for stability, either locally or

LESSON 21

in an overall sense. Many standard hot-rolled structural shapes are proportioned so that local stability problems have been eliminated or minimized. When a plate girder is used, however, the designer must account for factors that in many cases would not be a problem with a rolled shape. Deep, thin webs account for many of the special problems associated with plate girders, including local instability. A thorough understanding of the basis of the AISC provisions for plate girders requires a background in stability theory, particularly plate stability. Such a treatment is beyond the scope of this text, however, and the emphasis will be on the qualitative basis of the Specification requirements and their application. For those interested in delving deeper, the *Guide to Stability Design Criteria for Metal Structures* is a good starting point, and *Buckling Strength of Metal Structures and Theory of Elastic Stability* will provide the fundamentals of stability theory.

Plate girders rely on the strength available after the web has buckled, so most of the flexural strength will come from the flanges. The limit states considered are yielding of the tension flange and buckling of the compression flange. The compression flange buckling can take the form of vertical buckling into the web or flange local buckling, or it can be caused by lateral-torsional buckling.

At a location of high shear in a girder web, usually near the support and at or near the neutral axis, the principal planes will be inclined with respect to the longitudinal axis of the member, and the principal stresses will be diagonal tension and diagonal compression. The diagonal tension poses no particular problem, but the diagonal compression can cause buckling of the web. This problem can be addressed in one of three ways: (1) the depth-to-thickness ratio of the web can be made small enough so that the problem is eliminated, (2) web stiffeners can be used to form panels with increased shear strength, or (3) web stiffeners can be used to form panels that resist the diagonal compression through *tension-field action*. Fig. 21.2 illustrates the concept of tension-field action. At the point of impending buckling, the web loses its ability to support the diagonal compression, and this stress is shifted to the transverse stiffeners and the flanges. The stiffeners resist the vertical component of the diagonal compression, and the flanges resist the horizontal component. The web will need to resist only the diagonal tension, hence the term *tension-field action*. This behavior can be likened to that of a Pratt truss, in which the vertical web members carry compression and the diagonals carry tension (Fig. 21.2b). Since the tension field does not actually exist until the web begins to buckle, its contribution to the web shear strength will not exist until the web buckles. The total strength will consist of the strength prior to buckling plus the post-buckling strength deriving from tension-field action.

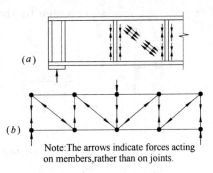

Fig. 21.2 The concept of tension-field action.

If an unstiffened web is incapable of resisting the applied shear, appropriately spaced stiffeners are used to develop tension-field action. Cross-section requirements for these stiffeners, called *intermediate stiffeners*, are minimal, since their primary purpose is to provide stiffness rather than resist directly applied loads.

Additional stiffeners may be required at points of concentrated loads for the purpose of protecting the web from the direct compressive load. These are called *bearing stiffeners*, and they must be proportioned to resist the applied loads. They can also simultaneously serve as intermediate stiffeners. Fig. 21.3 shows a bearing stiffener consisting of two rectangular plates, one on each side of the girder web. The plates are notched at the inside top and bottom corners so as to avoid the flange-to-web welds. If the stiffeners are conservatively assumed to resist the total applied load P (this neglects any contribution by the web), the bearing stress on the contact surfaces may be written as

$$f_p = \frac{P}{A_{pb}}$$

where A_{pb} = projected bearing area = $2at$ (see Fig. 21.3) or, expressing the bearing load in terms of the stress,

$$P = f_p A_{pb}$$

In addition, the pair of stiffeners together with a short length of web, is treated as a column with an effective length less than the web depth and is investigated for compliance with the same Specification provisions as any other compression member. This cross section is illustrated in Fig. 21.4. The compressive strength should always be based on the radius of gyration about an axis in the plane of the web, since instability about the other principal axis is prevented by the web itself.

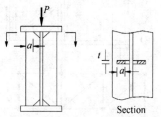

Fig. 21.3 Bearing stiffeners consisting of two rectangular plates.

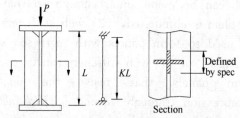

Fig. 21.4 Analysis model of stiffeners.

Other limit states resulting from the application of concentrated loads to the top flange are web yielding, web crippling (buckling), and sidesway web buckling. Sidesway web buckling occurs when the compression in the web causes the tension flange to buckle laterally.[1] This phenomenon can occur if the flanges are not adequately restrained against movement relative to one another by stiffeners or lateral bracing.

The welds for connecting the components of a plate girder are designed in much the same way as for other welded connections. The flange-to-web welds must resist the horizontal shear at the interface between the two components.[2] This applied shear, called the *shear flow*, is usually expressed as a force per unit length of girder to be resisted by the weld. The shear flow, based on elastic behavior, is given by

$$f = \frac{VQ}{I_x}$$

where Q is the moment about the neutral axis, of the area between the horizontal shear plane and the outside face of the section. This is the equation for shearing stress multiplied by the width of the shear plane. [3] Since the applied shear force V will usually be variable, the spacing of intermittent welds, if used, can also vary.

New Words

1. girder ['gə:də] n. (大)梁，纵梁
2. flexural ['flekʃərəl] a. 弯曲的，曲折的
3. riveting ['rivitiŋ] n. 铆接(法)
4. attach [ə'tætʃ] vt. 附上，贴上；连接；参加(to)
5. provide [prə'vaid] v. 保持，预防，规定；供应
6. stability [stə'biliti] n. 稳定(性)，稳度；刚[强]度
7. provision [prə'viʒən] n. 规定，条款，供给[应]
8. qualitative ['kwɔlitətiv] a. 性质上的，定性的
9. delve [delv] v. 探究，钻研
10. panel ['pænl] n. 区格，面，板；嵌板
11. impending [im'pendiŋ] a. 逼近的，即将发生的
12. deriving [di'raiv] v. 起源于，出自，获得
13. notched [nɔtʃt] a. 有凹口的，有锯齿状的
14. compliance [kəm'plaiəns] n. 符合，一致；依从
15. crippling ['kripliŋ] n. 局部压屈，局部失稳破坏
16. intermittent [ˌintə(:)'mitənt] a. 间断的；断续的

Phrases and Expressions

1. hot-rolled steel shape 热轧型钢
2. built-up girder 组合梁
3. hybrid girder 异种钢组合梁，杂交梁
4. web stiffener 腹板加劲肋
5. filler plate 填板
6. account for… 是…的原因；计及，对…负责
7. lateral-torsional buckling 弯扭屈曲
8. web member 腹杆
9. tension-field action 拉力场效应
10. intermediate stiffener 中间加劲肋
11. bearing stiffener 支承加劲肋
12. sidesway web buckling 腹板侧倾压曲
13. shear flow 剪力流

Notes

[1] This phenomenon can occur if the flanges are not adequately restrained ... by stiffeners or lateral bracing. 全句可译为：如果加劲肋或侧向支撑不能充分约束上下翼缘间的相对运动，这种现象就会发生。

[2] This applied shear, called the *shear flow*, is usually expressed as a force per unit length of girder to be resisted by the weld. 全句可译为：这一施加的剪力称作剪力流，通常表示为焊缝抵抗的梁单位长度的剪力。

[3] Since..., the spacing of intermittent welds, if used, can also vary. if used 为 if the intermittent welds is used 的省略。全句可译为：由于施加的剪力 V 通常是变化的，如果采用间断焊缝的话其间距也可以变化。

Exercises

1. Fill in the blanks with proper words.

    (1) A plate girder is basically a large beam, both in span and cross section, the large cross section usually _____ a consequence of the long span.

    (2) The box section, which has two webs _____ two flanges, is a torsionally superior shape and can be used when large unbraced lengths are necessary.

    (3) To avoid a conflict _____ the stiffener angles _____ the flange angles, filler plates were added to the web so that the stiffeners could clear the flange angles.

    (4) Plate girders rely on the strength available _____ the web has buckled, so most of the flexural strength will come from the flanges.

    (5) The compression flange buckling can take the form of vertical buckling _____ the web or flange local buckling, _____ it can be caused by lateral-torsional buckling.

    (6) Web stiffeners can be used to form panels that resist the diagonal compression _____ tension-field action.

    (7) The stiffeners resist the vertical component of the diagonal compression, _____ the flanges resist the horizontal component. The web will need to resist only the diagonal tension, hence the term tension-field action.

    (8) This behavior can be likened _____ that of a Pratt truss, in which the vertical web members carry compression and the diagonals carry tension.

2. Translate the following phrases into Chinese/English.

    (1) plate girder　　　　　　　　　(6) 组合梁
    (2) web stiffener　　　　　　　　 (7) 弯扭屈曲
    (3) filler plate　　　　　　　　　　(8) 支承加劲肋
    (4) diagonal web member　　　　(9) 拉力场效应
    (5) flange-to-web welds　　　　　(10) 热轧型钢

3. Translate the following sentences into Chinese.

    (1) If the largest available hot-rolled steel shape is inadequate for a given span and

loading, the first alternative would normally be a rolled shape with cover plates added to one or both flanges.

(2) Since all of the connections were made by riveting, there was no way to attach the flange directly to the web, and additional cross-sectional elements were introduced for the specific purpose of transmitting the load from one component to the other.

(3) Although cover plates can also be used with welded plate girders, a simpler approach is to use different thicknesses of flange plate, welded end-to-end, at different locations along the length of the girder.

(4) A thorough understanding of the basis of the AISC provisions for plate girders requires a background in stability theory, particularly plate stability.

(5) The diagonal tension poses no particular problem, but the diagonal compression can cause buckling of the web.

(6) At the point of impending buckling, the web loses its ability to support the diagonal compression, and this stress is shifted to the transverse stiffeners and the flanges.

(7) Cross-section requirements for the intermediate stiffeners are minimal, since their primary purpose is to provide stiffness rather than resist directly applied loads.

(8) Bearing stiffeners may be required at points of concentrated loads for the purpose of protecting the web from the direct compressive load.

4. Fill in the blanks with the given words below.

against, and, if, or, resulting, to, to, when

Other limit states _____ from the application of concentrated loads _____ the top flange are web yielding, web crippling (buckling), _____ sidesway web buckling. Sidesway web buckling occurs _____ the compression in the web causes the tension flange _____ buckle laterally. This phenomenon can occur _____ the flanges are not adequately restrained _____ movement relative to one another by stiffeners _____ lateral bracing.

5. Translate the following sentences into English.
   (1) 通常认为板梁是横截面由板件组成的受弯构件。
   (2) 采用板梁时,设计人员必须考虑许多情况下对热轧型钢不是问题的问题。
   (3) 高而薄的腹板是引起包括局部稳定在内的许多板梁特殊问题的原因。
   (4) 如果腹板不能抵抗施加的剪力,就设置适当间距的加劲肋以产生拉力场效应。
   (5) 在焊接广泛使用之前,截面的板件间的连接是板梁设计需要考虑的一个主要事项。

Reading Material

Concrete Strength Tests and Test Evaluation

Strength Tests

Generally, concrete quality is measured by the specified compressive strength f'_c of 6-×

12-in cylinders after 28 days of laboratory curing.

Conventional Tests. The strength tests performed after various periods of field curing are typically specified to determine curing adequacy. For lightweight-aggregate concretes only, the same type of laboratory-cured test specimen is tested for tensile splitting strength f_{ct} to establish design values for deflection, development of reinforcing steel, and shear. Applicable ASTM specifications for these tests are

C31, "Making and Curing Concrete Test Specimens in the Field."

C39, "Test for Compressive Strength of Cylindrical Concrete Specimens."

C496, "Test for Splitting Tensile Strength of Cylindrical Concrete Specimens."

The specifications for standard methods and procedures of testing give general directions within which the field procedures can be adjusted to jobsite conditions. One difficulty arises when the specimens are made in the field from samples taken at the jobsite. During the first 48h after molding, the specimens are very sensitive to damage and variations from standard laboratory curing conditions, which can significantly reduce the strength-test results. Yet, jobsite conditions may preclude(使不可能) sampling, molding, and field storage on the same spot.

If the fresh-concrete sample must be transported more than about 100 ft to the point of molding cylinders, some segregation occurs. Consequently, the concrete sample should be remixed to restore its original condition. After the molds for test cylinders have been filled, if the specimens are moved, high-slump specimens segregate in the molds; low-slump specimens in the usual paper or plastic mold are often squeezed out of shape or separated into starting cracks. Such accidental damage varies with slump, temperature, time of set and molding, and degree of carelessness.

If the specimen cylinders are left on the jobsite, they must be protected against drying and accidental impact from construction traffic. If a worker stumbles(绊倒)over a specimen less than 3 days old, it should be inspected for damage. The best practice is to provide a small, insulated, dampproofed, locked box on the site in which specimens can be cast, covered, and provided with 60 to 80°F temperature and 100% humidity for 24 to 72h. Then, they can be transported and subjected to standard laboratory curing conditions at the testing laboratory. When transported, the cylinders should be packed and handled like fresh eggs, since loose rattling(振动)will have about an equivalent effect in starting incipient(初始的)cracks.

Similarly, conditions for field-cured cylinders must be created as nearly like those of the concrete in place as possible. Also, absolute protection against impact or other damage must be provided. Because most concrete in place will be in much larger elements than a test cylinder, most of the in-place concrete will benefit more from retained heat of hydration. This effect decreases rapidly, because the rate of heat development is greatest initially. To ensure similar curing conditions, field-cured test cylinders should be stored for the first 24h in the field curing box with the companion cylinders for laboratory curing. After this initial curing, the field-cured cylinders should be stored near the concrete they represent and cured under the same conditions.

Exceptions to this initial curing practice arise when the elements cast are of dimensions comparable to those of the cylinders, or the elements cast are not protected from drying or low temperatures, including freezing, or test cylinders are cured *inside* the elements they represent.

These simple, seemingly over-meticulous(过度小心翼翼的) precautions will eliminate most of the unnecessary, expensive, project-delaying controversies over low tests. Both contractor and owner are justifiably annoyed when costly later tests on hardened concrete, after an even more costly project delay, indicate that the original fresh-concrete test specimens were defective and not the building concrete.

Special Tests. Many other strength tests or tests for special qualities are occasionally employed for special purposes. Those most often encountered in concrete building construction are strength tests on drilled cores and sawed beams; impact tests; pullout tests; penetration tests; determination of modulus of elasticity during the standard compression test; and deflection measurements on a finished building element under load.

Newer methods for evaluating in-situ strength of concrete include the following: Methods, such as the one in which test cylinders are field-cured inside the in-situ concrete, measure compressive strength directly, refined even to measuring it in a desired direction. Others actually measure other properties, such as penetration, impact, or pullout, which are indirect measures of compressive strength, but may be employed because the property they measure is itself important. For example, in cantilevered form construction where forms for each new lift are bolted into the previous lift, pullout results may be more meaningful than standard compression tests. Most of the in-situ tests may also be classified as accelerated tests, although not all accelerated tests are performed in situ.

Because construction time is continually becoming a more important factor in overall construction economy, the standard 28-day strength becomes less significant. For example, the final strength at completion of a high-rise project requiring high-strength concrete in lower-story columns is often specified 90-days. At the other extreme, a floor system may be loaded by the forms and concrete for the floor above in as little as 2 days. These conditions demand accelerated testing.

Test Evaluation

On small projects, the results of tests on concrete after the conventional 28 days of curing may be valuable only as a record. In these cases, the evaluation is limited to three options: (1) accept results, (2) remove and replace faulty concrete, or (3) conduct further tests to confirm option (1) or (2) or for limited acceptance at a lower-quality rating. The same comment can be applied to a specific element of a large project. If the element supports 28 days' additional construction above, the consequences of these decisions are expensive.

Samples sufficient for at least five strength tests of each class of concrete should be taken at least once each day, or once for each 150 yd³ of concrete or each 5000 ft² of surface area placed. Each strength test should be the average for two cylinders from the same sample. The strength level of the concrete can be considered satisfactory if the averages of all sets of three consecutive(连续的) strength-test results equal or exceed the specified strength and no individual strength-test result falls below f'_c by more than 500 psi.

If individual tests of laboratory-cured specimens produce strengths more than 500 psi below f'_c, steps should be taken to assure that the load-carrying capacity of the structure is not jeopardized(危害). Three cores should be taken for each case of a cylinder test more than 500 psi below f'_c. If the concrete in the structure will be dry under service conditions, the cores should be air-dried (temperature 60 to 80°F, relative humidity less than 60%) for 7 days before the tests and should be tested dry. If the concrete in the structure will be more than superficially(表面上) wet under service conditions, the cores should be immersed in water for at least 48h and tested wet.

Regardless of the age on which specified design strength f'_c is based, large projects of the long duration offer the opportunity for adjustment of mix proportions during the project. If a running average of test results and deviations from the average is maintained, then, with good control, the standard deviation achieved may be reduced significantly below the usually conservative, initially assumed standard deviation. In that case, a saving in cement may be realized from an adjustment corresponding to the improved standard deviation. If control is poor, the owner must be protected by an increase in cement. Project specifications that rule out either adjustment are likely to result in less attention to quality control.

LESSON 22

Alignment Design

The alignment of a road is shown on the plan view and is a series of straight lines called tangents connected by circular curves. In modern practice it is common to interpose transition or spiral curves between tangents and circular curves.

Alignment must be consistent. Sudden changes from flat to sharp curves and long tangents followed by sharp curves are to be avoided; otherwise accident hazards are created. Likewise, placing circular curves of different radii end to end (compound curves) or having a short tangent between two curves is poor practice unless suitable transitions between them are provided. Long, flat curves are preferable at all times, as they are pleasing in appearance and decrease the possibility of future obsolescence. However, alignment without tangents is undesirable on two-lane roads because some drivers hesitate to pass on curves. Long, flat curves should be used for small changes in direction, as short curves appear as "kinks." Also, as indicated above, horizontal and vertical alignment must be considered together, not separately. For example, a sharp horizontal curve beginning near a crest can create a serious accident hazard.

A vehicle traveling in a curved path is subject to centrifugal force. This is balanced by an equal and opposite force developed through superelevation and side friction. [1]From a highway design standpoint, neither superelevation nor side friction can exceed certain maximums and these controls place limits on the sharpness of curves that can be used with a prescribed design speed. Usually the sharpness of a given circular curve is indicated by its radius. However, for alignment design, sharpness is commonly expressed in terms of degree of curve, which is the central angle subtended by a 100-ft (30m) length of curve. Degree of curve is inversely proportional to the radius.

Tangent sections of highways carry normal cross slope; curved sections are superelevated. Provision must be made for gradual change from one to the other. A common method is to maintain the centerline of each individual roadway at profile grade while raising the outer edge and lowering the inner edge to produce the desired superelevation. This involves first raising the outside edge of the pavement with relation to the centerline until the outer half of the cross section is flat, next the outer edge is raised further until the cross section is straight, then the entire cross section is rotated as a unit until full superelevation is reached. [2]For smoother riding, A Policy on Geometric Design recommends that short vertical curves having a length in feet equal to the design speed in miles per hour be introduced into the edge profiles at their break points.

Where the alignment consists of tangents connected by circular curves, introduction of superelevation usually is begun on tangent before the curve is reached and full superelevation is attained some distance beyond the point of curve. It is recommended that 60 to 80% of the runoff be on tangent.

Where the alignment includes easement curve (see below), superelevation is applied entirely on the easement curve, except for bringing the outer pavement edge to a level position. It follows that, at times, the superelevation application rate sets the minimum length of the easement curve.

If a vehicle travels at high speed on a carefully restricted path made up of tangents connected by sharp circular curves, riding is extremely uncomfortable. As the car approaches a curve, superelevation begins and the vehicle is tilted inward, but the passengers must remain vertical since there is no centrifugal force requiring compensation. When the vehicle reaches the curve, full centrifugal force develops at once, and pulls the riders outward from their vertical positions. To achieve a position of equilibrium, the riders must force their bodies far inward. As the remaining superelevation takes effect, further adjustments in position are required. This process is repeated in reverse order as the vehicle leaves the curve. When easement curves are employed, the change in radius from infinity on the tangent to that of the circular curve is effected gradually so that centrifugal force also develops gradually. [3]By introducing superelevation along the spiral, a smooth and gradual application of centrifugal force can be had and the roughness avoided.

Easement curves have been used by the railroads for many years, but their adoption by highway agencies came much later. Many agencies do not use them even today. This is understandable. Railroad trains must follow the precise alignment of the tracks, and the discomfort described above can be avoided only by adopting easement curves. On the other hand, motorvehicle operators are free to alter their lateral positions on the road and can provide their own easement curves by steering into circular curves gradually. However, this weaving within a traffic lane (sometimes into other lanes) is dangerous. Properly designed easement curves make weaving unnecessary and make driving safer. Another is that they give alignments a smoother, more flowing appearance.

The point of beginning of an ordinary circular curve is usually labeled the PC (point of curve) or BC (beginning of curve). Its end is marked the PT (point of tangency) or EC (end of curve). For curves that include easements, the common notation is, as stationing increases, TS (tangent to spiral), SC (spiral to circular curve), CS (circular curve to spiral), and ST (spiral to tangent).

The sharpness of the commonly used easement curves, measured in terms of degree of curvature, increases uniformly from their beginnings. If, for instance, easement curves 400 ft (20m) long are selected to connect each end of a 4° circular curve to its tangents, the sharpness of the easement curves will increase by 1° each 100 ft (30m). At the TS or ST, where the curve begins, the degree of curve is zero and the radius infinite. At 100 ft along the curve, the spiral has the same radius as a 1° curve; at 200 ft, its radius equals that of a 2° curve; at 400 ft, where the easement curve ends (SC or CS) both easement and circular curves have the sharpness of a 4° curve and a common radius point. If length is added to this identical spiral, it will also fit sharper circular curves. Thus, if it is extended to 1000 ft, it will fit a 10° curve. A particular sharpness of easement curve, then, may be designated by its increase in degree of curve per 100 ft station, which is denoted by some writers with the letter k. For the curve described here, k equals 1°.

As a vehicle travels around a horizontal curve, obstructions such as buildings, signs, or cut banks located inside the curve can block the driver's view ahead. Any specific combinations of sharpness of curve with position of obstruction establish a horizontal sight distance, which is the greatest distance at which a driver can see an object lying in the roadway ahead. If the design is to provide for safe operation, this horizontal sight distance measured along the curve must equal or exceed the stopping distance for each design speed.

On two-lane pavements provision of a wider roadway is advisable on sharp curves. This will allow for such factors as (1) the tendency for drivers to shy away from the pavement edge, (2) increased effective transverse vehicle width because the front and rear wheels do not track, and (3) added width because of the slanted position of the front of the vehicle to the roadway centerline. For 24-ft (7.2m) roadways on open highways, an added width of 1 ft (0.3m) is recommended for, for example, a 5° curve and 50-mph (80km/h) design speed or 1° curve and 30-mph speed. For narrower pavement and sharp curves, widening assumes importance; with a 20-ft pavement, 250-ft radius, and 30-mph design speed, widening is 5 ft.

[4] Where vehicles must make sharp turns as is common at intersections or on turning roadways, both pavement widening and inside curve radii become important design features.

New Words

1. tangent ['tændʒənt]   n. 直线，切线
2. interpose [ˌintə(:)'pəuz]   v. 插入，干预
3. transition [træn'ziʒən]   n. 过渡，缓和
4. spiral ['spaiərəl]   a. 螺旋线；n. 螺旋线，回旋线
5. obsolescence [ˌɔbsə'lesns]   n. 废弃，过时
6. kink [kiŋk]   n. 纽结，纠缠
7. crest [krest]   n. 凸形竖曲线
8. centrifugal [sen'trifjugəl]   a. 离心的
9. superelevation ['sjuːpəreli'veiʃən] n. 超高
10. sharpness ['ʃɑːpnis]   n. 曲度，锐度
11. subtend [səb'tend]   v. 对应
12. runoff ['rʌnɔːf]   n. 超高缓和段，径流，流量
13. tilt [tilt]   v. 使倾斜
14. roughness ['rʌfnis]   n. 粗糙度，颠簸

15. weave [wiːv]　　　　　　　　　　　v. 交织，编(织)
16. notation [nəuˈteiʃən]　　　　　　 n. 记法，标志
17. stationing [ˈsteiʃəniŋ]　　　　　　n. 测站
18. slant [slɑːnt]　　　　　　　　　　v. 倾斜

Phrases and Expressions

1. plan view　　平面图
2. sharp curve　　锐曲线，小半径曲线，急弯
3. horizontal alignment　　平面线形，水平线形
4. side friction　　横向摩擦(力)
5. profile grade　　纵(断面)坡度
6. easement curve　　缓和曲线
7. stopping (sight) distance　　停车视距
8. flat curve　　平缓曲线，大半径曲线
9. compound curve　　复曲线
10. vertical alignment　　纵断面线形
11. be inversely proportional to　　与…成反比
12. break point　　转折点，断点
13. flowing appearance　　流畅(平顺)的外观
14. turning roadway　　转弯车道

Notes

[1] From..., neither superelevation nor side friction can exceed certain maximums and these controls place limits on...speed. controls 指 maximums。全句可译为：从公路设计的观点看，超高或横向摩擦力都不能超过一定的最大值，这些控制值对于每一设计车速可采用的曲线曲度做出了限制。

[2] For...Design recommends that...at their break points. having 引导的分词短语修饰 curves，recommends 的宾语从句中动词用原形或 should＋动词原形。全句可译为：为行车平稳，"线形设计原则"建议，在边缘纵断面转折点处插入短的竖曲线，其长度(英尺)等于设计车速(英里/小时)。

[3] By..., a smooth and gradual application of...can be had and the roughness avoided. roughness 后省略了 can be。全句可译为：通过沿缓和曲线设置的超高，离心力能够平稳地、逐渐地增加，避免了颠簸。

[4] Where vehicles must make sharp turns as is common at intersections or on turning roadways...become important design features. as 作关系代词，引导定语从句，修饰 vehicles must make sharp turns。全句可译为：在汽车必须做急转弯处(这在交叉路口或弯道上很常见)，路面加宽和内侧曲线半径成为重要的设计要点。

Exercises

1. Fill in the blanks with proper words.

   (1) The alignment of a road is shown _____ the plan view and is a series _____ straight lines called tangents connected by circular curves.

   (2) Likewise, placing circular curves of different radii end _____ end (compound curves) or having a short tangent _____ two curves is poor practice unless suitable transitions between them are provided.

   (3) However, _____ alignment design, sharpness is commonly expressed _____ terms of degree of curve.

   (4) A common method is to maintain the centerline of each individual roadway at profile grade _____ raising the outer edge and lowering the inner edge to produce the desired superelevation.

   (5) Introduction of superelevation usually is begun on tangent _____ the curve is reached and full superelevation is attained some distance _____ the point of curve.

   (6) Superelevation is applied entirely _____ the easement curve, except _____ bringing the outer pavement edge to a level position.

   (7) However, this weaving _____ a traffic lane (sometimes into other lanes) is dangerous.

   (8) The sharpness _____ the commonly used easement curves, measured _____ terms of degree of curvature, increases uniformly from their beginnings.

   (9) If the design is _____ provide for safe operation, this horizontal sight distance measured along the curve must equal _____ exceed the stopping distance for each design speed.

   (10) _____ a vehicle travels around a horizontal curve, obstructions such as buildings, signs, or cut banks located _____ the curve can block the driver's view ahead.

2. Translate the following phrases into Chinese/English.

   (1) compound curve
   (2) be inversely proportional to
   (3) flowing appearance
   (4) profile grade
   (5) horizontal alignment
   (6) 大半径曲线
   (7) 平面图
   (8) 停车视距
   (9) 横向摩擦(力)
   (10) 缓和曲线

3. Translate the following sentences into Chinese.

   (1) Sudden changes from flat to sharp curves and long tangents followed by sharp curves are to be avoided; otherwise accident hazards are created.

   (2) A common method is to maintain the centerline of each individual roadway at profile grade while raising the outer edge and lowering the inner edge to produce the desired superelevation.

   (3) By introducing superelevation along the spiral, a smooth and gradual application of centrifugal force can be had and the roughness avoided.

   (4) Likewise, placing circular curves of different radii end to end (compound curves)

or having a short tangent between two curves is poor practice unless suitable transitions between them are provided.

(5) A Policy on Geometric Design recommends that short vertical curves having a length in feet equal to the design speed in miles per hour be introduced into the edge profiles at their break points.

(6) Motorvehicle operators are free to alter their lateral positions on the road and can provide their own easement curves by steering into circular curves gradually.

(7) The sharpness of the commonly used easement curves, measured in terms of degree of curvature, increases uniformly from their beginnings.

(8) Long, flat curves are preferable at all times, as they are pleasing in appearance and decrease the possibility of future obsolescence.

(9) As the car approaches a curve, superelevation begins and the vehicle is tilted inward, but the passengers must remain vertical since there is no centrifugal force requiring compensation.

(10) Where vehicles must make sharp turns as is common at intersections or on turning roadways, both pavement widening and inside curve radii become important design features.

4. Fill in the blanks with the given words below.

and, as, because, because of, for, for, for, for, on, on

_____ two-lane pavements provision of a wider roadway is advisable _____ sharp curves. This will allow _____ such factors _____ (1) the tendency _____ drivers to shy away from the pavement edge, (2) increased effective transverse vehicle width _____ the front and rear wheels do not track, and (3) added width _____ the slanted position of the front of the vehicle to the roadway centerline. For 24-ft (7.2m) roadways on open highways, an added width of 1 ft (0.3m) is recommended _____, _____ example, a 5° curve and 50-mph (80km/h) design speed or 1° curve and 30-mph speed. For narrower pavement _____ sharp curves, widening assumes importance; with a 20-ft pavement, 250-ft radius, and 30-mph design speed, widening is 5 ft.

5. Translate the following sentences into English.

(1) 线形必须是连续的。

(2) 不同半径的圆曲线首尾相接的作法是不好的。

(3) 平面线形和纵断面线形必须一起考虑。

(4) 离心力由超高和横向摩擦力产生的一个与其大小相等、方向相反的力所平衡。

(5) 曲度是100英尺长的曲线所对应的圆心角,且与半径成反比。

Reading Material

Surface Drainage

The portions of the highway structure that provide for surface drainage in rural locations include the roadway crown(路拱), shoulders(路肩) and side slopes, longitudinal ditches (channels), culverts(涵洞), and bridges. Divided highways in rural areas also have inlets and storm drains (underground pipes) in the median strip to handle a portion of the surface flow.

Pavement and Shoulder Cross Slopes

Consistent with other design objectives, highway designers should ensure that precipitation is removed from the pavement as expeditiously as possible. Roadway surfaces are normally crowned (or sloped as in the case of a superelevated section) to facilitate the removal of surface water from the wearing surface. The recommended crown or cross slope tends to be a compromise between the needs of vehicular traffic and those for drainage. Pavement cross slopes should be so steep enough to ensure expeditious drainage, but not so steep as to cause driver annoyance, discomfort, or hazard. Recommended ranges of pavement cross slopes are given in Table 22-1. The amount of cross slope varies with the type of surface, being generally small for relatively impervious surfaces such as portland cement concrete and large for previous surfaces such as gravel or earth. Shoulders are normally sloped to drain away from the pavement surfaces. Precipitation that occurs on the shoulder area largely flows to the side ditches or the median swale, as does that which falls on the roadway proper. As Table 22-1 indicates, recommended shoulder cross slopes vary from about 2 to 6 percent depending on the type of surface and whether or not curbs are provided.

Side Slopes and Side Ditches

Open side ditches(边沟)are generally provided in cut sections in highway locations in rural areas to provide for surface drainage. Side ditches may also be constructed along embankment sections when needed to supplement natural drainage channels. Both flat-bottomed and V-section ditches are used, with preference being given to the former type, with slope changes in the ditch section being rounded to improve appearance and prevent erosion. In either case, side slopes are made as flat as possible consistent with drainage requirements and limiting width of right-of-ways. Deep, narrow side ditches are to be avoided whenever possible because of the increased hazards presented by such construction. Where they must be used, adequate provision should be made for safeguarding traffic through use of traffic barriers.

Water flows in side ditches in a direction that is generally parallel to the roadway centerline. Grades used in open ditches may also be roughly the same as those used on the highway centerline; on the other hand, flat roadway grades and steeper ditch grades in the same location are very frequently used. In very flat country, ditch grades as low as 0.1 or 0.2 percent may be used while in rolling or mountainous terrain the maximum grade may be dictated only by the necessity for preventing erosion.

Side ditches provide open channels for the removal of surface water from within the limits of the highway right-of-way. In certain circumstances, areas adjacent to the right-of-way may also contribute to the flow. The water must be carried to an outlet, in the form of either a natural or an artificial drainage channel. The ditch must be hydraulically capable of handling the anticipated flow of surface water in such fashion that the roadway structure is not endangered or the safety of the motorist threatened.

Recommended Ranges of Cross Slopes for Pavements and Shoulders   Table 22-1

Roadway Element	Range in rate of cross slope(%)
High-type surface	
Two lanes	1.5~2.0
Three or more lanes in each direction	1.5 minimum; increase 0.5%~1.0% per lane; 4.0 maximum
Intermediate surface	1.5~3.0
Low-type surface	2.0~6.0
Urban arterials	1.5~3.0; increase 1.0% per lane
Shoulders	
Bituminous or concrete	2.0~6.0
With curbs	≥4.0

Culverts, Bridges, and Storm Drains

Culverts and bridges constitute the "cross-drainage" system of a highway in a rural location through which water flowing in natural streams or collected on the high side of the right-of-way is transmitted from one side of the highway to the other.

Where space is restricted, in median swales, in urban areas, or where the natural slope of the ground is unsuited for drainage by open channels, storm drains are provided for the disposal of surface water. Storm drains and appurtenant structures are discussed when consideration is given to the drainage of city streets.

LESSON 23

Construction Contracts (1)

Fixed-Price Contract

One of the most important types of construction contracts is the fixed-price or lump-sum contract. [1] Under such a contract the contractor agrees to perform the entire work specified in the contract at a price agreed to and fixed at the time the contract is entered into. Frequently the price is determined by competitive bidding. As noted in a preceding section, public works contracts are, with few exceptions, required by law to be let on the basis of competitive bidding and must be for a fixed price. Of course, where competitive bidding is not required by law, it is also possible to arrive at a fixed price by negotiation between the parties to the contract without resort to competitive bidding.

A fixed-price contract is normally contrasted with cost-plus contracts, in which the price is determined by actual costs as they are incurred plus whatever additional payment in the way of a fee for profit the parties have agreed to. The cost-plus type of contract will be discussed more fully later in this unit.

A variant of the fixed-price contract is the unit-price contract. Some contractors consider unit-price contracts as something different from lump-sum or fixed-price contracts and they therefore treat such contracts as a separate species. The significant characteristics of a unit-price contract is that, although quantities may vary (which means the total compensation paid to the contractor will vary), the price *per unit* is fixed at the time the contract is entered into and is intended to remain unchanged throughout performance of the work.

[2] For example, a highway construction contract typically contains some items for which a lump-sum or fixed price for the entire item is required, but there are many items which are contracted for on a unit-price basis, such as roadway excavation per units of volume, aggregate base materials by weight or volume, concrete for pavement by volume, fencing or pipe by units of length, etc. Such a contract normally contains estimated or approximate quantities and a bidder is required to quote his unit price and is also asked to extend the price based upon the estimated quantity for each such item. The total price for such items are added to the total of those items quoted on a lump-sum basis to arrive at a total bid price. This total bid price is then used as a basis for bid comparison and the invitation for bid and contract documents so specify.

The actual final contract price, i.e., the total amount ultimately paid to the successful bidder who enters into the contract, is not his total bid price but is determined by multiplying actual quantities, determined in the manner specified in the contract, with the agreed applicable unit price. In other words, payment is not based on the approximate or estimated quantities but instead on actual results, and the unit price remains fixed.

A problem peculiar to unit prices sometimes arises if there is a substantial overrun or underrun of quantities. A contractor makes his determination of the unit price, anticipating that the actual quantities will be reasonably close to the quantities listed in the invitation for bids. His price might well have varied if the quantities had been substantially different. If, then, the actual quantities do differ substantially, the contractor or the owner may feel he is entitled to a price adjustment.

A carefully drafted contract will contain a clause specifying what percentage increase or decrease shall trigger a price adjustment and will spell out the cutoff point for applying unit prices and the basis for pricing the balance. In the absence of such a clause it has been held that the contractor will be paid on the agreed unit-price basis for actual quantities even when the contractor had a high profit on each unit, there being no other basis for a price adjustment. It is true, as noted below, that a contractor may have cause to adjust or modify the unit price on the same kind of grounds or by applying the same principles which apply to adjusting or modifying the price of fixed-price or lump-sum controls.

Some fixed-price contracts contain a bonus provision which typically allows the contractor to receive stated bonus payments for completion of the work before the specified contract completion date. In most, if not all, such contracts there is a liquidated damages provision requiring the contractor to pay the owner stipulated amounts (usually at least equal to the amount of the bonus payments) if the work is completed after the contract completion date. However, many contracts contain a liquidated damages clause for failure to complete the work within the time stated in the contract, and the enforceability of such a clause does not depend on there being a provision for payment of a bonus for early completion.

A major characteristic of the fixed-price type of contract is the principle that a contractor agrees to perform the work at the agreed price no matter what it may actually cost him to do the work, and conversely the owner agrees to pay the price whether the contractor enjoys an unusually large profit or suffers a huge loss.

Another way to express it is to say that the contractor assumes the risk of all unforeseen conditions, such as increases in labor, and material costs, unanticipated subsurface soil conditions, adverse weather, and the like. The owner, on the other hand, is able to anticipate that his building will be built or his project completed at a known price, determined before commencement of any work, regardless of the actual cost to the contractor.

There are circumstances where a contractor may be entitled to an adjustment in the price under a fixed-price contract. [3] We shall consider some of these circumstances as illustrative, but not exhaustively so, of the kinds of problems that can arise and the effect that contract clauses covering those situations might have.

LESSON 23

We shall use as examples construction contracts with the United States and specific contract clauses found in such contracts. These contract forms and contract clauses are in the public record, and there is a history of their use over the years to which we can refer. It must be emphasized that every contract is governed first by its own terms and second by the law of the appropriate jurisdiction, whether it be federal or state. [4] Hence, although basic principles of contract law apply generally, the specifics of each contract, of each set of facts, and of the law applicable to each situation, govern most and, control the result.

Perhaps the most commonly recurring problem under fixed-price contracts arises in connection with changes or extra work. The underlying rule is that a contractor is entitled to perform the contract in accordance with the original plans and specifications without interference from the owner. Without a changes clause, an owner has no legal right unilaterally to change the work. Since it usually happens that owners, for a variety of reasons, wish or are required to make changes in the work as it progresses, a well-drafted changes clause is an important part of any construction contract. However, only changes within the scope of the changes clause will be governed by it.

A common pitfall to contractors who have claims based on asserted changes is the failure of the contractor to give the notice in the time or manner required by the changes clause of the contract; another is to fail to get a written change order or to get the order issued prior to doing the work. If for any reason no change order is forthcoming where one is required, the contractor is faced with the alternative either of not doing the changed work or proceeding with the work and notifying the contracting officer in writing that the work is being done under protest, and reserving the right to claim additional compensation and time.

A problem can also arise if the changes clause fails to spell out a precise pricing method applicable to changed work. In a recent California case, it was ruled that when the contract (in this case a detailed purchase order) provided that the owner could require changes at a price to be agreed upon by the parties in the future, the validity of the contract depended on future events. If no agreement on price could be reached, the contractor would be required nonetheless to perform minor changes for a "reasonable" price, to be determined subsequently. If, however, the change requested was a major one, the contractor could not be compelled to perform the changed work if no price had been agreed upon following a good faith attempt to do so. In the latter situation, the court held that the contractor could walk off the job and rescind the contract if the owner insisted on a major change being performed without having reached an agreement as to price after a good faith attempt to do so.

Extra work as distinguished from changed work is work completely outside the basic contract and therefore not governed by its terms. Instead, it is governed by a separate, independent contract, unless the parties agree otherwise, or unless the basic contract expressly provides that extra work, as such, is subject to the original contract.

One potential problem, applicable to public works contracts, is the possible application of competitive bidding requirements to extra work. Generally speaking, the more obviously that the work is an "extra" and not merely a change, the more likely it is that courts will hold that the parties should have resorted to competitive bidding, with the result that compensation for any extra work actually performed may be denied to the contractor unless competitive bidding requirements were complied with.

New Words

1. resort [ri'zɔːt]   vi. 诉诸，采取（某种手段等）
2. anticipate [æn'tisipeit]   vt. 预期，期望
3. bonus ['bəunəs]   n. 奖金，额外的津贴
4. liquidate ['likwideit]   v. 清算，结清债务
5. enforceability [in'fɔːsə'biliti] n. 强制性，可执行性
6. exhaustively [ig'zɔːstivli]   ad. 用尽一切地
7. pitfall ['pitfɔːl]   n. 缺陷，陷阱
8. recur [ri'kəː]   vi. 复发，重现
9. unilateral ['juːnilætərəl]   a. 单方面，单边的
10. rescind [ri'sind]   v. 废除
11. overrun [ˌəuvə'rʌn]   n. 超出限度；v. 超过
12. underrun ['ʌndə'rʌn]   n. 低于估计的产量
13. entitle [in'taitl]   vt. 有资格，有权利
14. trigger ['trigə]   vt. 引发，引起，触发
15. cutoff ['kʌtɔːf]   n. 近路，中止，切掉

Phrases and Expressions

1. construction contract   工程合同，施工合同
2. fixed-price contract   固定价格合同
3. lump-sum contract   价合同
4. competitive bidding   竞标，竞争出价
5. bid price   递价，投标价格
6. bonus payment   奖金支出
7. liquidated damages   规定的违约偿金，延期违约偿金
8. contract clause   合同条款
9. walk off   离开，退出
10. change order   变更通告单
11. spell out   讲清楚，清楚地说明

Notes

[1] Under such a contract the contractor agrees … the contract is entered into.   全

LESSON 23

句可译为：在这种合同中，承包商同意按合同中规定的价格和合同约定的时间完成所有工作。

［2］For example, a highway construction contract typically contains …, concrete for pavement by volume, fencing or pipe by units of length, etc. 全句可译为：比如，公路施工合同中一般要包含总价或固定价所涉及的所有单项，而同时要约定许多基本单价，如公路土方工程的单位土方价，基层骨料的单位重量或体积价，混凝土路面单位方量价，围墙或管道的每延米价等。

［3］We shall consider some of these circumstances as illustrative, …, of the kinds of problems that can arise and the effect that contract clauses covering those situations might have. 全句可译为：在此，我们将列举其中几种情形（而不是所有情形），来说明它们所带来的问题以及相关这些情形对合同条款可能产生的影响。

［4］Hence, …, the specifics of each contract, of each set of facts, and of the law applicable to each situation, govern most and, control the result. 句中后两个 of 前省略了 the specifics；applicable to each situation 为后置定语修饰 the law。全句可译为：因此，虽然合同的基本原则普遍适用，但每一合同各自的特殊性、各自的实际情况、以及适用各自情形的法律才决定其大部分内容并控制其结果。

Exercises

1. Fill in the blanks with proper words.

（1）Under such a contract the contractor agrees to perform the entire work specified in the _____ at a price agreed to and fixed at the time the contract is entered into.

（2）Of course, where competitive bidding is not required by law, it is also possible to arrive at a fixed price by _____ between the parties to the contract without resort to competitive bidding.

（3）A fixed-price contract is normally contrasted with cost-plus contracts, in which the price is determined by actual _____ as they are incurred plus whatever additional payment in the way of a fee for profile the parties have agreed to.

（4）The actual final contract price, i.e., the total amount ultimately paid to the successful _____ who enters into the contract, is not his total bid price but is determined by multiplying actual quantities, determined in the manner specified in the contract, with the agreed applicable unit price.

（5）A major characteristic of the fixed-price type of contract is the principle that a contractor agrees to perform the work at the _____ price no matter what it may actually cost him to do the work.

（6）Perhaps the most commonly recurring problem under fixed-price contracts arises in connection with changes or _____ work.

（7）Extra work as distinguished from changed work is work completely outside the basic _____ and therefore not governed by its terms.

（8）It must be emphasized that every contract is governed first by its own _____ and second by the law of the appropriate jurisdiction, whether it be federal or state.

(9) Some fixed-price contracts contain a bonus provision which typically allows the contractor to receive stated _____ payments for completion of the work before the specified contract completion date.

2. Translate the following phrases into Chinese/English.

(1) bonus payment 　　　　(5) 合同条款
(2) competitive bidding　　　(6) 投标价格
(3) lump-sum contract　　　 (7) 固定价格合同
(4) liquidated damages　　　 (8) 施工合同

3. Translate the following sentences into Chinese.

(1) A fixed-price contract is normally contrasted with cost-plus contracts, in which the price is determined by actual costs as they are incurred plus whatever additional payment in the way of a fee for profile the parties have agreed to.

(2) The total price for such items are added to the total of those items quoted on a lump-sum basis to arrive at a total bid price.

(3) In summary, a lump-sum contract is intended to place the risk of all unanticipated or unforeseen additional costs on the contractor so that the owner can expect the project to be constructed at the fixed price agreed to by the parties at the time the contract is entered into.

(4) A contractor makes his determination of the unit price, anticipating that the actual quantities will be reasonably close to the quantities listed in the invitation for bids.

(5) The advantage of a changed conditions clause to the contractor is dual.

(6) However, many contracts contain a liquidated damages clause for failure to complete the work within the time stated in the contract, and the enforceability of such a clause does not depend on there being a provision for payment of a bonus for early completion.

(7) When a contractor encounters unforeseen difficulties, such as unexpected adverse soil conditions, a high-water level, extremely bad weather, or the like, the general rule is that any additional construction costs incurred by the contractor must be borne by him, because this is the very risk he assumed in a fixed-price contract.

(8) We shall consider some of these circumstances as illustrative, but not exhaustively so, of the kinds of problems that can arise and the effect that contract clauses covering those situations might have.

(9) Without a changes clause, an owner has no legal right unilaterally to change the work.

(10) Generally speaking, the more obviously that the work is an "extra" and not merely a change, the more likely it is that courts will hold that the parties should have resorted to competitive bidding, with the result that compensation for any extra work actually performed may be denied to the contractor unless competitive bidding requirements were complied with.

4. Fill in the blanks with the given words below.

　　　for, likely, merely, obviously, to, to, to, unless, with, with

One potential problem, applicable _____ public works contracts, is the possible application of competitive bidding requirements _____ extra work. Generally speaking, the more _____ that the work is an "extra" and not a change, the more _____ it is that courts will hold that the parties should have resorted _____ competitive bidding, _____ the result that compensation _____ any extra work actually performed may be denied to the contractor _____ competitive bidding requirements were complied _____.

5. Translate the following sentences into English.

(1) 在固定价合同中，承包商同意按合同中规定的价格和约定的时间完成所有工作。

(2) 单价合同的显著特点在于，虽然其量可能改变(指给承包商的总的酬金会改变)，但合同约定期内的单价是固定的，它在整个工期内是不能改变的。

(3) 换句话说，不是依据概算或估算的工程量，而是依据实际发生的工程量以固定单价来付款。

(4) 另一方面，不管承包商的实际成本是多少，业主能在开工前预估到他的建筑以某一价格建造或项目以某一价格完成。

(5) 固定价合同中最常出现的问题可能都与变更或额外工作有关。

Reading Material

Construction Contracts (2)

Cost-Plus Contracts

Frequently contrasted with fined-price or lump-sum contracts are the cost-price type of contracts. Under cost-plus contracts, the contractor agrees to perform the specified work at his cost, plus an additional amount, known as the fee, to cover the contractor's profit.

There are many variations of cost-plus contracts and we shall enumerate and describe a few:

(a) *Cost-Plus-a-Fixed-Fee* This contract contemplates reimbursement to the contractor of his actual costs, but his compensation by way of profit is fixed at an agreed amount at the time of contracting. The fee is frequently determined by a percentage of the originally estimated cost, but it will not vary if actual costs subsequently do vary.

(b) *Cost-Plus-a-Percentage-of-Cost* Here the contractor will be reimbursed for his actual costs and he will receive additional compensation measured by an agreed percentage of the actual costs. His fee, in these circumstances, will vary in proportion to the amount of the actual costs.

(c) *Cost-Plus-an-Incentive-Fee* Here the contractor receives reimbursement for actual costs plus compensation based on a special formula for sharing in actual costs over or under target costs.

Additional variations cover special situations, many of which are not common to the construction industry, such as *cost contracts* (with no fee, used for example when the contractor is a nonprofit corporation, or when the contractor is producing a pilot or model, anticipating award of a subsequent contract if the model turns out to be successful), *costs - with - guaranteed - maximums* (with provisions for sharing or not sharing of overruns, with maximums based on dollars, or on man-hours), etc.

A variation of both fixed-price and cost-plus type contracts are the so-called "*target*" contracts. There are many types of target contracts, but common to all is an agreement between the parties on estimated target cost, target profit or fee, ceiling price, or some combination of these or other targets.

In a *fixed - price target contract* it is common for the parties to negotiate a target cost, a target profit, and a ceiling price as well as a formula for determining the final profit and price. Upon completion of the work required under the contract, the final cost is determined and, if less than the target cost, the final profit will be increased according to the formula to an amount which is greater than the target profit. On the other hand, if the final cost exceeds the target cost, the contract's final profit will be less than the target profit. If the final cost exceeds the ceiling price, the contractor will incur any out of pocket loss sine he must pay all costs in excess of the ceiling price.

In a *cost-plus type target contract*, the parties negotiate a target cost and a target fee. Upon completion of the work, the contractor's fee is increased above the target fee if the actual cost is less than the target cost and the fee is decreased if the actual cost exceeds the target costs, but the contractor will not incur a loss since he will be reimbursed by the owner for all costs incurred.

When the owner desires to start work before complete plans and estimates have been prepared, the contract may provide for initial work, to be done on a cost-plus type basis with a target estimate of cost, to be followed by a subsequent agreement on a detailed estimate based on complete plans at which time the basis of payment may either continue on some form of cost-plus basis or the parties may enter into a fixed price contract based on the detailed estimate.

A *letter of intent or letter contract* is a preliminary contract under which the contractor may commence work and in which the owner and the contractor agree to negotiate a definitive contract of a specified type. Such letter contracts with the federal government specify the maximum costs and fee for which the government will be liable prior to the execution of the definitive contract. They also provide for the payments to be made to the contractor in the event the letter contract is terminated because a definitive contract cannot be agreed upon or for other reasons, such as the contractor's default or the convenience of the government.

Descriptive terms, such as *turnkey* or *gross roots*, are sometimes applied to construction or design and construction contracts. These terms are used when the contractor undertakes to design and build or to build a project from its very "grass roots" to final, ultimate completion as a completed plant or facility ready to be put into operation immediately and the contractor turns over a key to the entire, completed facility

LESSON 23

to the owner. Such terms would more accurately apply to the job or project rather than to the contract, since a turnkey project may be constructed or designed and constructed under the provisions of any of the types of contracts discussed in this chapter.

Similarly, there are terms used to describe other types of construction contracts by function. These include *Construction Management*, *Design and Build*, and *Phased Design and Construction* or *Fast Tracking*.

The Construction Management contract requires the contractor to participate in both the design and the construction phases of the project. Ordinarily, an outside designer is employed by the owner, and the management contractor performs none of the construction itself. This method of constructing, when used by a public agency, has been held to be subject to competitive bidding requirements. The Design and Build contract like a turnkey contract requires the contractor to furnish both design and construction services, but ordinarily not land acquisition or financing which are sometimes required for a turnkey project. Such contracts have been competitively bid Phased Design and Construction or Fast Tracking contracts call for construction to proceed in stages or phases by two or more contracts, let separately as the design of each such phase is sufficiently completed.

LESSON 24

Earthquake Effects

The effect of earthquakes on civil engineering structures is primarily a question of the dynamic response of the structure excited by motion of the ground; in general, it is the horizontal components of ground acceleration that govern, although increasing attention is being paid to the effect of the vertical component of ground motion on such cases as large-span sheds having only small live load effects from other causes. The ground motion is normally assumed to be the same at all points on the foundation of the structure; it is not within the practical power of the engineer to deal with the possibility of major relative movement on some fault-line passing within the foundation, apart from site investigation to minimize the risk of building over an existing or incipient fault where movement can be expected.

[1] The equations of motion of the masses of a structure excited by ground motion can be manipulated to give exactly the same differential equations for the displacements *relative to the ground* (and thus the strains in the structure) as for the case of the structure on a fixed base, subjected to horizontal loads applied to every mass equal to the product of the mass and the ground acceleration. A simple basis for design is thus to express an acceleration as a fraction of the acceleration of gravity (g) and to design for this fraction of the weight of the system, treated as a horizontal loading. Due to the dynamic nature of the problem, however, this equivalent acceleration is not simply equal to the maximum ground acceleration but will depend on the natural frequency (or natural period) of the structure and on the history of the ground motion extending over some time prior to the instant when maximum relative displacement is found to occur. For a given ground motion it is a straightforward matter to solve the equations of motion numerically and record the maximum response; repeating this process for single-degree of freedom structures of varying natural frequency (or period) leads to the *spectrum* of the earthquake. The so-called velocity spectrum, S_v, is the most commonly given form; the equivalent acceleration for design is ωS_v, where ω is the 'circular' natural frequency, rad/s. The spectrum is also dependent on the natural damping of the structure. The maximum of ωS_v, typically occurs at a frequency of the order of 3Hz; the structures of fundamental natural frequency below 3Hz are progressively relatively less sensitive to earthquakes, although the effect of higher modes may become significant.

Unfortunately, the prediction of a ground motion to form a reasonable design basis for any specific structure is subject to many uncertainties. An earthquake occurs when strain energy gradually built up in the Earth's crust is suddenly released by movement on some fault plane. The energy released is measured by the *magnitude* of the earthquake, whereas its effect at some point on the ground is the *intensity* at that point. A rather crude single-parameter measure of intensity is given by scales such as the Modified Mercalli or Rossi-Forel ratings, which are based mainly on an only roughly quantified description of the human sensation or structural damage experienced (or expected). The intensity experienced at a given distance from an earthquake of given magnitude depends greatly on the subsoil or shallow-rock conditions and considerably worse ground motion can be experienced where a thick layer of low-density low-stiffness material overlies heavier, stiffer, material. The duration and frequency content (and thus the shape of the spectrum) can also vary greatly even for cases where the overall intensity rating would be similar; a motion of given intensity recorded close to a low-magnitude shock would be shorter and have higher predominant frequencies by comparison with motion of the same intensity recorded distant from a high-magnitude shock. In the case of energy release from long faults the movements may be progressive along the fault, again leading to considerable differences in duration and frequency content from point to point.

The final factor to be introduced before describing the most useful approaches to design is that experience has shown that for most structures and in most regions where earthquake is a major design consideration, it would be highly uneconomic to base design on an 'elastic' or 'no significant damage' criterion. [2] For most structures the aim must be to prevent major failures causing collapse and loss of life, while making use to the full of the possibility of inelastic structural behaviour resulting in dissipation of energy that is to a substantial degree analogous to increased structural damping. The obvious exceptions to the application of this principle are cases where even moderate damage must be prevented, such as nuclear reactor containment vessels, or buildings housing vital post-disaster services.

The most widely used format for a design code incorporating the factors described above is exemplified by the Unified Building Code of the US. The total horizontal load (base shear) V is given by:

$$V = ZISKAW \qquad (24.1)$$

in which W is the weight of the structure. Z, the zoning factor, reflects the basic seismicity of the region, modified where necessary by the soil effect factor, S. Factor I permits allowance to be made for the significance of possible failure of the structure, whether as a result of the importance of the structure to post-earthquake services, or the severity of consequential risks in the event of failure. Factor K expresses the capacity of the structure for inelastic energy dissipation, varying from 0.67 to 1.33 (1.5 for exceptional cases), with low values for 'brittle' structural forms. Factor A represents the spectrum ($2\pi n S_v$), a simple, perhaps crude, approximation is generally specified, allowing a reduction as a function of predicted fundamental frequency where this is less than about 0.5 Hz. The UBC currently suggests $A = 0.07 n^{1/2}$ (but not more than 0.12) for the US.

The total force (V) is then distributed over the structure in proportion to the product of the mass and the mode shape function for the first mode (the latter is often approximated by direct proportionality to the height above the ground). It has been noted above that slender tall structures may also show significant higher-mode response, and this is most liable to increase stresses near the top (a so-called 'whiplash' effect); an added proportion of the total load, perhaps 15%, may thus be required to be applied at the highest point.

When it is desired to give more detailed consideration to the behaviour of the structure in the inelastic range, the 'reserve energy' technique is simple to apply and can quickly give very useful guidance and economy in design. To proceed to greater detail requires ad hoc computer step-by-step solution of the response to a given ground motion; this is increasingly commonly done in both US and Japan, and is general practice in the latter country for buildings exceeding fifteen storeys. Two important points must be noted. Firstly, that most of the available ground motion records to input to this procedure were obtained at a substantial distance from a large shock, so that special consideration is necessary for sites in a region where more localized energy release is typical (producing a higher characteristic frequency in ground motion) as well as sites on soft subsoil (possibility of lower frequencies as well as overall magnification). Secondly, any one record is but one chance example of the superposition of ground-wave motions of considerable complexity. Although the broad statistical properties of the ground motion are thus generally representative, the actual net peak response of one specific structure will vary greatly owing to the random factors in this superposition. One technique is to generate artificial ground motion sequences, all having the same broad statistical properties, so that the calculated maximum responses can be averaged (or the value for any given probability of occurrence selected). A somewhat more crude method to make use of a single record is to repeat analysis with a scale factor applied to the mass of the structure to modify the natural frequency. Averaging the responses obtained over a range of (say) ±30% of frequency greatly reduces the probable error due to the random factors.

Finally, it is worth repeating that design to ensure ductility can give much more benefit for a given cost than directly increasing strength. Good design keeps to simple shapes and simple structural forms to reduce the risk of large-scale 'stress concentrations' which would arise, for example, between two wings of a building having different natural frequencies.

New Words

1. shed [ʃed]   n. 小屋，工棚
2. manipulate [mə'nipjuleit]   vt. (熟练地)操作，利用，巧妙地处理
3. incipient [in'sipiənt]   a. 初始的
4. damping ['dæmpiŋ]   n. 阻尼，减幅，衰减
5. release [ri'li:s]   n. 释放；vt. 释放
6. dissipation [,disi'peiʃən]   n. 消散，分散

7. seismicity [saiz'misiti]　　　　　　　　　　n. 地震活动性，地震活动度
8. ad hoc ['æd'hɔk]　　　　　　　　　　　　ad. 特别地，尤其
9. magnification [ˌmægnifi'keiʃən]　　　　　n. 扩大，放大

Phrases and Expressions

1. ground acceleration　　地面加速度
2. natural frequency (or natural period) of the structure　　结构自振频率(或自振周期)
3. single-degree of freedom structures　　单自由度结构
4. intensity of the earthquake　　地震烈度
5. magnitude of the earthquake　　地震震级
6. frequency content　　频谱，频率成分
7. Modified Mercalli or Rossi-Forel ratings　　修正默卡尼或罗西·福雷尔烈度等级
8. predominant frequency　　卓越周期
9. zoning factor　　分区系数
10. 'whiplash' effect　　"鞭梢"效应

Notes

[1] The equations... can be manipulated to give exactly the same differential equations... acceleration. the same (...) as... 意为"像…一样的(…)"；subjected to 修饰 the structure on a fixed base。全句可译为：巧妙处理地面运动引起的结构质量的运动方程，可给出与该结构处于固定基础上、每个质量受到数值等于该质量和地面加速度乘积的水平荷载作用时完全相同的相对地面的位移微分方程(因而结构中的应变也相同)。

[2] For most structures the aim must be to prevent... that is to a substantial degree analogous to increased structural damping. to the full of the possibility 和 to a substantial degree 为插入语，意思分别为："最大可能地" 和 "在很大程度上"。全句可译为：对大多数结构来说，设计的目的是在充分利用引起能量耗散(能量耗散在很大程度上类似于增大了结构的阻尼)的非弹性性能的同时还必须防止造成倒塌和伤亡的重大破坏。

Exercises

1. Fill in the blanks with proper words.

(1) The ground motion is normally assumed to be the _____ at all points on the foundation of the structure.

(2) An earthquake occurs when strain energy gradually built up in the Earth's crust is suddenly _____ by movement on some fault plane.

(3) The intensity experienced at a given distance from an earthquake of given magnitude depends greatly on the subsoil or shallow-rock conditions and considerably _____ ground motion can be experienced where a thick layer of low-density low-stiffness material overlies heavier, stiffer, material.

(4) The energy released is measured by the _____ of the earthquake, whereas its effect at some point on the ground is the intensity at that point.

(5) In the case of energy release from long faults the movements may be progressive along the fault, again leading to considerable _____ in duration and frequency content from point to point.

(6) The total force (V) is then distributed over the structure in proportion to the _____ of the mass and the mode shape function for the first mode (the latter is often approximated by direct proportionality to the height above the ground).

(7) It has been noted above that slender tall structures may also show significant higher-mode response, and this is most liable to _____ stresses near the top.

(8) For most structures the aim must be to _____ major failures causing collapse and loss of life.

(9) Finally, it is worth repeating that design to ensure ductility can give much more benefit for a given cost than directly _____ strength.

2. Translate the following phrases into Chinese/English.

(1) differential equation   (5) 地面加速度
(2) natural frequency of the structure   (6) 单自由度结构
(3) fault plane   (7) 地震烈度
(4) magnitude of the earthquake   (8) 鞭梢效应

3. Translate the following sentences into Chinese.

(1) A simple basis for design is thus to express an acceleration as a fraction of the acceleration of gravity (g) and to design for this fraction of the weight of the system, treated as a horizontal loading.

(2) It is not within the practical power of the engineer to deal with the possibility of major relative movement on some fault-line passing within the foundation, apart from site investigation to minimize the risk of building over an existing or incipient fault where movement can be expected.

(3) For a given ground motion it is a straightforward matter to solve the equations of motion numerically and record the maximum response.

(4) The maximum of ωS_v, typically occurs at a frequency of the order of 3Hz; the structures of fundamental natural frequency below 3Hz are progressively relatively less sensitive to earthquakes, although the effect of higher modes may become significant.

(5) The duration and frequency content (and thus the shape of the spectrum) can also vary greatly even for cases where the overall intensity rating would be similar; a motion of given intensity recorded close to a low-magnitude shock would be shorter and have higher predominant frequencies by comparison with motion of the same intensity recorded distant from a high-magnitude shock.

(6) The most widely used format for a design code incorporating the factors described above is exemplified by the Unified Building Code of the US.

(7) When it is desired to give more detailed consideration to the behaviour of the structure in the inelastic range, the 'reserve energy' technique is simple to apply and can

quickly give very useful guidance and economy in design.

(8) The obvious exceptions to the application of this principle are cases where even moderate damage must be prevented, such as nuclear reactor containment vessels, or buildings housing vital post-disaster services.

(9) Although the broad statistical properties of the ground motion are thus generally representative, the actual net peak response of one specific structure will vary greatly owing to the random factors in this superposition.

4. Fill in the blanks with the given words below.

as, by, from, of, on, or, that, to, with, within,

The effect _____ earthquakes _____ civil engineering structures is primarily a question of the dynamic response of the structure excited _____ motion of the ground; in general, it is the horizontal components of ground acceleration _____ govern, although increasing attention is being paid _____ the effect of the vertical component of ground motion on such cases _____ large-span sheds having only small live load effects _____ other causes. The ground motion is normally assumed to be the same at all points on the foundation of the structure; it is not _____ the practical power of the engineer to deal _____ the possibility of major relative movement on some fault-line passing within the foundation, apart from site investigation to minimize the risk of building over an existing _____ incipient fault where movement can be expected.

5. Translate the following sentences into English.

(1) 地震频谱还依赖于结构自身的阻尼特性。

(2) 对任一具体结构来说,地面运动的预估是形成合理设计的依据,这种预估受许多不确定因素的制约。

(3) 系数 K 表示结构耗散非弹性能的能力,其值在 0.67 到 1.33 之间变化(例外情况取 1.5),脆性结构形式取低值。

(4) 一种方法是使用具有相同宽广统计特性的人工地面运动序列,从而使计算的最大响应能有平均水平。

(5) 好的设计应具有简单外形和简单结构形式,以减少可能产生大面积"应力集中"的危险。

Reading Material

Earthquake Structural Damage

Introduction

As discussed before, the actual rupture of the ground due to fault movement could damage a structure. Secondary effects, such as the liquefaction of loose granular soil, slope movement or failure, and inundation(洪水)from a tsunami(海啸), could also cause structural damage. This article discusses some of the other earthquake-induced effects or structural conditions that can result in damage.

Earthquakes throughout the world cause a considerable amount of death and destruction. Earthquake damage can be classified as being either structural or non-structural. For example, the Federal Emergency Management Agency (联邦应急管理局) (1994) states:

Damage to buildings is commonly classified as either structural or non-structural. Structural damage means the building's structural support has been impaired. Structural support includes any vertical and lateral force resisting systems, such as the building frames, walls, and columns. Non-structural damage does not affect the integrity of the structural support system. Examples of non-structural damage include broken windows, collapsed or rotated chimneys, and fallen ceilings. During an earthquake, buildings get thrown from side to side, and up and down. Heavier buildings are subjected to higher forces than lightweight buildings, given the same acceleration. Damage occurs when structural members are overloaded, or differential movements between different parts of the structure strain the structural components. Larger earthquakes and longer shaking durations tend to damage structures more. The level of damage resulting from a major earthquake can be predicted only in general terms, since no two buildings undergo the exact same motions during a seismic event. Past earthquakes have shown us, however, that some buildings are likely to perform more poorly than others.

There are four main factors that cause structural damage during an earthquake:

1. *Strength of shaking*: For small earthquakes (magnitude less than 6), the strength of shaking decreases rapidly with distance from the epicenter (震中) of the earthquake. According to the USGS (United States Geological Survey 美国地质勘探局), the strong shaking along the fault segment that slips during an earthquake becomes about one-half as strong at a distance of 8mi, one-quarter as strong at a distance of 17mi, one-eighth as strong at a distance of 30mi, and one-sixteenth as strong at a distance of 50mi.

In the case of a small earthquake, the center of energy release and the point where slip begins are not far apart. But in the case of large earthquakes, which have a significant length of fault rupture, these two points may be hundreds of miles apart. Thus for large earthquakes, the strength of shaking decreases in a direction away from the fault rupture.

2. *Length of shaking*: The length of shaking depends on how the fault breaks during the earthquake. For example, the maximum shaking during the Loma Prieta earthquake lasted only 10 to 15s. But during other magnitude earthquakes in the San Francisco Bay area, the shaking may last 30 to 40s. The longer the ground shakes, the greater the potential for structural damage. In general, the higher the magnitude of an earthquake, the longer the duration of the shaking ground.

3. *Type of subsurface conditions*: Ground shaking can be increased if the site has a thick deposit of soil that is soft and submerged. Many other subsurface conditions can cause or contribute to structural damage. For example, as discussed in Sec. 3.4, there could be structural damage due to liquefaction of loose submerged sands.

4. *Type of building*: Certain types of buildings and other structures are especially susceptible to the side-to-side shaking common during earthquakes. For example, sites located within approximately 10mi (16km) of the epicenter or location of fault rupture are generally subjected to rough, jerky(急动的), high-frequency seismic waves that are often more capable of causing short buildings to vibrate vigorously. For sites located at greater distance, the seismic waves often develop into longer-period waves that are more capable of causing high-rise buildings and buildings with large floor areas to vibrate vigorously.

Much as diseases will attack the weak and infirm, earthquakes damage those structures that have inherent weaknesses or age-related deterioration. Those buildings that are not reinforced, poorly constructed, weakened from age or rot, or underlain by soft or unstable soil are most susceptible to damage. The following discusses some of these susceptible structures.

Torsion

Torsional problems develop when the center of mass of the structure is not located at the center of its lateral resistance, which is also known as the center of rigidity. A common example is a tall building that has a first-floor area consisting of a space that is open and supports the upper floors by the use of isolated columns, while the remainder of the firstfloor area contains solid load-bearing walls that are interconnected. The open area having isolated columns will typically have much less lateral resistance than that part of the floor containing the interconnected load-bearing walls. While the center of mass of the building may be located at the midpoint of the first-floor area, the center of rigidity is offset toward the area containing the interconnected load-bearing walls. During the earthquake, the center of mass will twist about the center of rigidity, causing torsional forces to be induced into the building frame.

Soft story

A *soft story*, also known as a *weak story*, is defined as a story in a building that has substantially less resistance, or stiffness, than the stories above or below it. In essence, a soft story has inadequate shear resistance or inadequate ductility (energy absorption capacity) to resist the earthquake-induced building stresses. Although not always the case, the usual location of the soft story is at the ground floor of the building. This is because many buildings are designed to have an open first-floor area that is easily accessible to the public. Thus the first floor may contain large open areas between columns, without adequate shear resistance. The earthquake-induced building movement also causes the first floor to be subjected to the greatest stress, which compounds the problem of a soft story on the ground floor.

Concerning soft stories, the National Information Service for Earthquake Engineering (2000) states:

In shaking a building, an earthquake ground motion will search for every structural weakness. These weaknesses are usually created by sharp changes in stiffness, strength and/or ductility, and the effects of these weaknesses are accentuated by poor distribution of reactive masses. Severe structural damage suffered by several modern buildings during recent earthquakes illustrates the importance of avoiding sudden changes in lateral stiffness and strength. A typical example of the detrimental effects that these discontinuities can induce is seen in the case of buildings with a "soft story."Inspection of earthquake damage as well as the results of analytical studies have shown that structural systems with a soft story can lead to serious problems during severe earthquake ground shaking. Numerous examples illustrate such damage and therefore emphasize the need for avoiding the soft story by using an even distribution of flexibility, strength, and mass.

The following are four examples of buildings having a soft story on the ground floor:

1. *Chi-chi earthquake in Taiwan on September 21, 1999:* In Taiwan, it is common practice to have an open first-floor area by using columns to support the upper floors. In some cases, the spaces between the columns are filled in with plate-glass windows in order to create ground-floor shops.

2. *Northridge earthquake in California on January 17, 1994:* Many apartment buildings in southern California contain a parking garage on the ground floor. To provide an open area for the ground-floor parking area, isolated columns are used to support the upper floors. These isolated columns often do not have adequate shear resistance and are susceptible to collapse during an earthquake.

3. *Loma Prieta earthquake in California on October 19, 1989:* Another example of a soft story is due to a first-floor garage area. The four-story apartment building was located on Beach Street, in the Marina District, San Francisco. The first-floor garage area, with its large open areas, had inadequate shear resistance and was unable to resist the earthquake-induced building movements.

4. *Izmit earthquake in Turkey on August 17, 1999:* Details concerning this earthquake have been presented in Sec. 3.3. In terms of building conditions, it has been stated:

A typical reinforced concrete frame building in Turkey consists of a regular, symmetric floor plan, with square or rectangular columns and connecting beams. The exterior enclosure as well as interior partitioning are of non-bearing unreinforced brick masonry infill walls. These walls contributed significantly to the lateral stiffness of buildings during the earthquake and, in many instances, controlled the lateral drift and resisted seismic forces elastically. This was especially true in low-rise buildings, older buildings where the ratio of wall to floor area was very high, and buildings located on firm soil. Once the brick infills failed, the lateral strength and stiffness had to be provided by the frames alone, which then experienced significant inelasticity in the critical regions. At this stage, the ability of reinforced concrete columns, beams, and beam-column joints to sustain deformation demands depended on how well the seismic design and detailing requirements were followed both in design and in construction. A large number of residential and commercial buildings were built with soft stories at the first-floor level. First stories are often used as stores and commercial areas, especially in the central part of cities. These areas are enclosed with glass windows, and sometimes with a single masonry infill at the back. Heavy masonry infills start immediately above the commercial floor. During the earthquake, the presence of a soft story increased deformation demands very significantly, and put the burden of energy dissipation on the first-story columns. Many failures and collapses can be attributed to the increased deformation demands caused by soft stories, coupled with lack of deformability of poorly designed columns. This was particularly evident on a commercial street where nearly all buildings collapsed towards the street.

LESSON 25

High-Rise Buildings

It is difficult to define a high-rise building. A mid-rise building generally less than 10 stories (28m). Thus a high-rise building is one that has at least 10 stories or more.

Although the basic principles of vertical and horizontal subsystem design remain the same for mid-, or high-rise buildings, when a building gets high the vertical subsystems become a controlling problem for two reasons. Higher vertical loads will require larger columns, walls, and shafts. But, more significantly, the overturning moment and the shear deflections produced by lateral forces are much larger and must be carefully provided for.

The vertical subsystems in a high-rise building transmit accumulated gravity load from story to story, thus requiring larger column or wall sections to support such loading. In addition, these same vertical subsystems must transmit lateral loads, such as wind or seismic actions, to the foundations. However, in contrast to vertical load, lateral load effects on buildings are not linear and increase rapidly with increase in height. [1]For example, under wind load, the overturning moment at the base of a building varies approximately as the square of the height of the building, and the lateral deflection at the top of a building may vary as the fourth power of building height, other things being equal. Earthquake produces an even more pronounced effect.

When the structure for a mid-rise building is designed for dead and live load, it is almost an inherent property that the columns, walls, and stair or elevator shafts can carry most of the horizontal forces. The problem is primarily one of shear resistance. Moderate additional bracing for rigid frames in "short" buildings can easily be provided by filling certain panels (or even all panels) without increasing the sizes of the columns and girders otherwise required for vertical loads.

Unfortunately, this is not so for high-rise buildings because the problem is primarily resistance to moment and deflection rather than shear alone. Special structural arrangements will often have to be made and additional structural material is always required for the columns, girders, walls, and slabs in order to make a high-rise building sufficiently resistant to much higher lateral loads and deformations.

As previously mentioned, the quantity of structural material required per square foot of floor of a high-rise building is in excess of that required for a low-rise building. The vertical components carrying the gravity load, such as walls, columns, and shafts, will need to be strengthened over the full height of the building. But quantity of materials required for resisting lateral forces is even more significant. The graph shown in Fig. 25.1 illustrates how the weight of structural steel in pounds per square foot of floor increases as the number of stories increases from 1 up to 100. Note that by using optimum structural systems with suitable width and arrangement, the additional material required for lateral force resistance can be controlled such that, even for buildings of 100 stories, the total structural weight of steel may be only about 34 pounds per square foot, whereas it is noted previously, some buildings quite a bit shorter require much more structural steel. Curve A in Fig. 25.1 represents the average unit weight of a

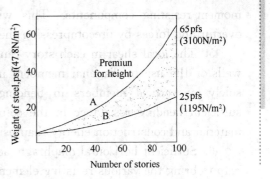

Fig. 25.1 The curve of weight of steel and number stories.

conventional frame with increasing numbers of stories. Curve B represents the average steel weight if the frame is protected from all lateral loads. The gap between the upper boundary and the lower boundary represents the premium for height for the traditional column-and-beam frame. Structural engineers have developed structural systems with a view to eliminating this premium.

With reinforced concrete, the quantity of material also increases as the number of stories increases. But here it should be noted that the increase in the weight of material added for gravity load is much more sizable than for steel, whereas for wind load the increase for lateral force resistance is not that much more since the weight of a concrete building helps to resist overturn. On the other hand, the inherently greater mass of a concrete building can aggravate the problem of design for earthquake actions. Additional mass in the upper floors will give rise to a greater overall lateral force under the action of seismic effects.

In the case of either concrete or steel design, there are certain basic principles for providing additional resistance to lateral forces and deflections in high-rise buildings without too much sacrifice in economy:

1. Increase the effective width of the moment-resisting subsystems. This is very useful because increasing the width will cut down the overturn force directly and will reduce deflection by the third power of the width increase, other things remaining constant. However, this does require that the vertical components of the widened subsystem be suitably connected to actually gain this benefit.

2. Design subsystems such that the components are made to interact in the most efficient manner. For example, use truss systems with chords and diagonals efficiently stressed, place reinforcing for walls at critical locations, and optimize stiffness ratios for rigid frames.

3. Increase the material in the most effective resisting components. For example, materials added in the lower floors to the flanges of columns and connecting girders will directly decrease the overall deflection and increase the moment resistance without contributing mass in the upper floors where the earthquake problem is aggravated.

4. Arrange to have the greater part of vertical loads be carried directly on the primary

moment-resisting components. This will help stabilize the building against tensile overturning forces by precompressing the major overturn-resisting components.

5. The local shear in each story can be best resisted by strategic placement of solid walls or the use of diagonal members in a vertical subsystem. Resisting these shears solely by vertical members in bending is usually less economical, since achieving sufficient bending resistance in the columns and connecting girders will require more material and construction energy than using walls or diagonal members.

6. Sufficient horizontal diaphragm action should be provided at each floor. This will help to bring the various resisting elements to work together instead of separately.

7. Create mega-frames by joining large vertical and horizontal components such as two or more elevator shafts at multistory intervals with a heavy floor subsystem, or by use of very deep girder trusses.

Remember that all high-rise buildings are essentially vertical cantilevers which are supported at the ground. When the above principles are judiciously applied, structurally desirable schemes can be obtained by walls, cores, rigid frames, tubular construction, and other vertical subsystems to achieve horizontal strength and rigidity.

New words

1. shaft [ʃɑːft]   n. 电梯井
2. overturn [ˌəuvəˈtəːn]   n. 倾覆；v. 推翻，翻倒
3. pronounced [prəˈnaunst]   a. 显著的，明确的
4. boundary [ˈbaundəri]   n. 边界，分界线
5. optimize [ˈɔptimaiz]   vt. 使最优化
6. solely [ˈsəu(l)li]   adv. 独自地，单独地
7. cantilever [ˈkæntiliːvə]   n. 悬臂
8. premium [ˈprimjəm]   n. 奖赏[励]，额外的费用
9. aggravate [ˈægrəveit]   vt. 加重；加剧
10. sizable [ˈsaizəbl]   a. 相当大的，大的
11. diaphragm [ˈdaiəfræm]   n. 横隔板
12. judiciously [dʒuː(ː)ˈdiʃəsli]   ad. 明智地

Phrases and Expressions

1. high-rise building   高层建筑
2. the overturning moment   倾覆力矩
3. the shear deflection   剪切变形
4. the lateral deflection   横向变形
5. tubular construction   筒体结构
6. vertical component   竖向构件
7. girder trusses   桁梁

LESSON 25

8. horizontal diaphragm 水平隔板

Notes

[1] For example,..., the overturning moment... varies approximately as the square of the height of the building, and ..., other things being equal. other things being equal 为独立主格结构，意为"其他条件都相同时"。全句可译为：例如，其他条件相同时，在风荷载作用下，建筑物底部的倾覆力矩大致随建筑物高度的平方而变化，而建筑物顶部的横向位移会随建筑物高度的四次方而变化。

Exercises

1. Fill in the blanks with proper words.

（1）A medium-rise building probably ranges between 3 or 4 stories up to 10 or 20 stories. Thus a high-rise building is probably one that has _____ least some 10 stories or more.

（2）In addition, these same vertical subsystems must transmit lateral loads, _____ as wind or seismic actions, to the foundations.

（3）However, in contrast to vertical load, lateral load effects _____ buildings are not linear and increase rapidly with increase in height.

（4）When the structure for a low-or medium-rise building is designed _____ dead and live load, it is almost an inherent property that the columns, walls, and stair or elevator shafts can carry most of the horizontal forces.

（5）Unfortunately, this is not so for high-rise buildings _____ the problem is primarily resistance to moment and deflection rather than shear alone.

（6）As previously mentioned, the quantity of structural material required per square foot of floor of a high-rise building is _____ excess of that required for a low-rise building.

（7）The graph shown in Fig. 25.1 illustrates _____ the weight of structural steel in pounds per square foot of floor increases as the number of stories increases from 1 up to 100.

（8）Note that by using optimum structural systems with suitable width and arrangement, the additional material required for lateral force resistance can be controlled such that, even for buildings of 100 stories, the total structural weight of steel may be only about 34 pounds per square foot, _____ it is noted previously, some buildings quite a bit shorter require much more structural steel.

（9）Curve A in Fig. 25.1 represents the average unit weight of a conventional frame _____ increasing numbers of stories.

（10）With reinforced concrete, the quantity of material also increases _____ the number of stories increases.

2. Translate the following phrases into Chinese/English.

(1) the overturning moment
(2) seismic actions
(3) the lateral deflection
(4) the local shear
(5) girder trusses
(6) 高层建筑
(7) 刚架
(8) 局部剪力
(9) 剪切变形
(10) 筒体结构

3. Translate the following sentences into Chinese.

(1) It is difficult to define a high-rise building. One may say that a low-rise building ranges from 1 to 2 or 3 stories. A medium-rise building probably ranges between 3 or 4 stories up to 10 or 20 stories. Thus a high-rise building is probably one that has at least some 10 stories or more.

(2) Higher vertical loads will require larger columns, walls, and shafts. But, more significantly, the overturning moment and the shear deflections produced by lateral forces are much larger and must be carefully provided for.

(3) The vertical subsystems in a high-rise building transmit accumulated gravity load from story to story, thus requiring larger column or wall sections to support such loading.

(4) For example, under wind load, the overturning moment at the base of a building varies approximately as the square of the height of the building, and the lateral deflection at the top of a building may vary as the fourth power of building height, other things being equal. Earthquake produces an even more pronounced effect.

(5) When the structure for a low-or medium-rise building is designed for dead and live load, it is almost an inherent property that the columns, walls, and stair or elevator shafts can carry most of the horizontal forces.

(6) Special structural arrangements will often have to be made and additional structural material is always required for the columns, girders, walls, and slabs in order to make a high-rise building sufficiently resistant to much higher lateral loads and deformations.

(7) The vertical components carrying the gravity load, such as walls, columns, and shafts, will need to be strengthened over the full height of the building.

(8) The graph shown in Fig. 25.1 illustrates how the weight of structural steel in pounds per square foot of floor increases as the number of stories increases from 1 up to 100.

(9) The gap between the upper boundary and the lower boundary represents the premium for height for the traditional column-and-beam frame.

(10) Increase the effective width of the moment-resisting subsystems. This is very useful because increasing the width will cut down the overturn force directly and will reduce deflection by the third power of the width increase, other things remaining constant.

4. Fill in the blanks with the given words below.

as, as, for, hand, more, since, to, up, whereas, with

As previously mentioned, the quantity of structural material required per square foot of floor of a high-rise building is in excess of that required _____ a low-rise building. The vertical components carrying the gravity load, such _____ walls, columns, and shafts, will need to be strengthened over the full height of the building. But quantity of materials required for resisting lateral forces is even _____ significant. The graph shown in Fig. 25.1 illustrates how the weight of structural steel in pounds per square foot of floor increases as the number of stories increases from 1 _____ to 100. Note that by using optimum structural systems _____ suitable width and arrangement, the additional material required for lateral force resistance can be controlled such that, even for buildings of 100 stories, the total structural weight of steel may be only about 34 pounds per square foot, _____ it is noted previously, some buildings quite a bit shorter require much more structural steel.

With reinforced concrete, the quantity of material also increases _____ the number of stories increases. But here it should be noted that the increase in the weight of material added for gravity load is much more sizable than for steel, whereas for wind load the increase for lateral force resistance is not that much more _____ the weight of a concrete building helps to resist overturn. On the other _____, the inherently greater mass of a concrete building can aggravate the problem of design for earthquake forces. Additional mass in the upper floors will give rise _____ a greater overall lateral force under the action of seismic effects.

5. Translate the following sentences into English.

(1) 虽然中、高层建筑竖向和水平体系设计的基本原理是相同的，但当建筑很高时，其顶端的侧移控制是很重要的。

(2) 对钢筋混凝土而言，随着楼层的增加材料的用量也增加；但这里应注意的是其材料重量对重力荷载的增加量远大于钢材的增加量。

(3) 增大抗弯体系的有效宽度是非常有用的，因为增大宽度将直接削减倾覆力并会减少变形。

(4) 安排大部分的竖向荷载直接由主要抗弯构件承担，通过预压抗倾覆构件，将有助于稳定建筑抵抗受拉倾覆力。

(5) 策略地布置实体墙或在竖向体系中使用斜向构件可很好地抵抗每一楼层中的局部剪力。

Reading Material

Structural Type of high-rise Buildings

Shear-Wall Systems

When shear walls are compatible with other functional requirements, they can be economically utilized to resist lateral forces in high-rise buildings. For example, apartment buildings naturally require many separation walls. When some of these are designed to be solid, they can act as shear walls to resist lateral forces and to carry the vertical load as well. For buildings up to some 20 stories, the use of shear walls is common. If given sufficient length, such walls can economically resist lateral forces up to 30 to 40 stories or more.

However, shear walls can resist lateral load only in the plane of the walls. Therefore, it is always necessary to provide shear walls in two perpendicular directions, or at least in sufficient orientation so that lateral force in any direction can be resisted. In addition, the wall layout should reflect consideration of any torsional effect.

Two or more shear walls can be connected to form L-shaped or channel-shaped subsystems. Indeed, four internal shear walls can be connected to form a rectangular shaft that will then resist lateral forces very efficiently. If all external shear walls are continuously connected, then the whole building acts as a tube, and is excellent in resisting lateral loads and torsion.

Whereas concrete shear walls are generally of solid type with openings when necessary, steel shear walls are usually made of trusses. These trusses can have single diagonals, "X" diagonals, or "K" arrangements. A trussed wall will have its members act essentially in direct tension or compression under the action of lateral forces. They are effective from a strength and deflection-limitation point of view, and they offer some opportunity for penetration between members. Of course, the inclined members of trusses must be suitably placed so as not to interfere with requirements for windows and for circulation and service penetrations through these walls.

As stated above, the walls of elevator, staircase, and utility shafts form natural tubes and are commonly employed to resist both vertical and lateral forces. Since these shafts are normally rectangular or circular in cross-section, they can offer an efficient means for resisting moments and shear in all directions due to tube structural action. But a problem in the design of these shafts is to provide sufficient strength around door openings and other penetrations through these elements. For reinforced concrete construction, special steel reinforcements are placed around such openings. In steel construction, heavier and more rigid connections are required to resist racking(抵压) at the openings.

In many high-rise buildings, a combination of walls and shafts can offer excellent resistance to lateral forces when they are suitably located and connected to one another. It is also desirable that the stiffness offered by these subsystems be more-or-less symmetrical in all directions.

Rigid-Frame Systems

Rigid-frame systems for resisting vertical and lateral loads have long been accepted as an important and standard means for designing buildings. They are employed for low-and medium-rise buildings up to high-rise buildings perhaps 70 or 100 stories high. When compared to shear-wall systems, these rigid frames provide excellent opportunity for rectangular penetration of wall surfaces both within and at the outside of a building. They also make use of the stiffness in beams and columns that are required for the building in any case, but the columns are made stronger when rigidly connected to resist the lateral as well as vertical forces through frame bending.

Frequently, rigid frames will not be as stiff as shear-wall construction, and therefore may produce excessive deflections for the more slender high-rise building designs. But because of this flexibility, they are often considered as being more ductile and thus less susceptible to catastrophic earthquake failure when compared with (some) shear-wall designs. For example, if over stressing occurs at certain portions of a steel rigid frame (i. e., near the joints), ductility will allow the structure as a whole to deflect a little more, but it will by no means collapse even under a much larger force than expected on the structure. For this reason, rigid-frame construction is considered by some to be a "best" seismic-resisting type for high-rise steel buildings. On the other hand, it is also unlikely that a well-designed shear-wall system would collapse.

In the case of concrete rigid frames, there is a divergence(分歧) of opinion. It is true that if a concrete rigid frame is designed in the conventional manner, without special care to produce higher ductility, it will not be able to withstand a catastrophic earthquake that can produce forces several times larger than the code design forces. Therefore, some believe that it may not have the additional reserve capacity possessed by steel rigid frames. But modern research and experience has indicated that concrete frames can be designed to be ductile, when sufficient stirrups and joinery reinforcement are designed into the frame. Modern building codes have specifications for the so-called ductile concrete frames. However, at present, these codes often require excessive reinforcement at certain points in the frame so as to cause congestion(拥挤) and result in construction difficulties. Even so, concrete frame design can be both effective and economical.

Of course, it is also possible to combine rigid-frame construction with shear-wall systems in one building. For example, the building geometry may be such that rigid frames can be used in one direction while shear walls may be used in the other direction.

Tubular Systems

High-rise buildings in excess of 30 or 40 stories may be best designed using tubular systems to resist lateral forces. This will give the building greater strength and rigidity compared to either the shear-wall or the rigid-frame system. By effective use of the enveloping material, maximum lever arm between the resisting forces is achieved.

A natural way to build a tubular system would be to connect the exterior walls to form an overall tube structure. The tube can be rectangular, circular, or some other fairly regular shape. The exterior walls may be penetrated with holes which form round or rectangular windows. An example is the newly completed Hong Kong high-rise of 50 or 60 stories and round windows.

If it is desired to have rectangular window frames on the outside of the high-rise building, these frames can be integrated into a frame-tube design using rather heavy spandrel(上下层窗间空间) beams, to connect the closely spaced columns or heavy window mullions(窗棂). However, it should be noted that when a frame-tube bends, as a vertical cantilever supported at the base, the frame racking effect may result in a significant shear lag(剪切滞后) between the supporting columns. As a result, the stress distribution would not be linear and those columns away from the neutral axis will be stressed quite a bit higher than would be expected for a linear assumption. Shear lag in tube design can be fairly well analyzed using modern computer programs. But, for schematic purposes, the figure suggests that the effect on corner columns can be approximated at 1.5 times greater than indicated by the linear assumption. The objection to these frame tubes is the necessity for fairly heavy spandrel girders. Of course, when the girders are so deep and the columns so wide that the openings are very small, the frame tube will degenerate into a perforated wall tube.

Although wall tubes with small windows are generally of concrete construction, the frame tubes can be either of concrete or steel. For steel, the trussed tube is often used. By trussing the exterior columns and forming them into a tube, they are very efficient in resisting lateral forces because they utilize overall dimensions for overturn resistance and efficient truss members in direct stress (rather than in bending) for shear resistance. The shape and size of windows are influenced by the location of diagonals, but a larger percentage of opening is possible in comparison to a concrete wall tube.

It is also possible to develop a concrete trussed tube design. This is accomplished by blocking certain panels at different levels so that these blocked panels along an inclined line form an inclined member of the truss. This apparently can be an economical solution for concrete high-rise buildings.

The tube-in-tube(筒中筒) concept offers another excellent approach. The exterior tube with its larger width can resist overturn forces very efficiently. But, the openings required in this tube may reduce its capacity to resist shear, particularly at the lower floors. On the other hand, an inner tube can better resist the story shear, being more solid than the exterior tube. But inner tubes will not be as effective in resisting the overturning moment since they will be quite slender in comparison to the outer tube. This tube-in-tube combination can be applied to either a steel building or a concrete building, or even used to combine steel and concrete design. For example, a concrete shaft as an inner tube in combination with a steel rigid-frame exterior tube can be very efficient in resisting the bending moment and in giving sufficient shear rigidity to the structure as a whole.

The bundled-tube(束筒) concept is a new one. Thus far, it has been applied only to the Sears Building in Chicago. The 110-story Sears Tower in Chicago, 1450ft high, is now the taller building in the world. The design calls for a steel frame of nine tubes, 75ft×75ft square, that make up the 225ft sq steel building. The nine tubes have common columns that link their faces to make up two exterior and two interior diaphragms in each direction. The building plan is thus trisected in two directions and the result is a greatly stiffened overall structure. This building has a steel weight of only 33lb per sq ft, whereas with a traditional rigid-frame system, the weight might have reached 60 to 70lb per sq ft.

Pavement

Background

Pavements serve structural, functional and safety purposes. They are necessary not only for roadways but also for parking lots, airports (i.e., runways, taxiways, aprons and service roads), industrial sites, ports and so forth. The structural performance of a pavement is aimed at distributing the loads under the wheels of vehicles over larger areas to prevent stressing, beyond the load-bearing capacity of the native soil (or subgrade) on which the pavement system is constructed. The load at the interface between the wheel and the pavement surface is applied over a relatively small area, causing high stresses at that point, but these stresses decrease with depth as the load is spread over large areas.

The functional performance of pavement is related to the users' requirement for smooth and comfortable riding conditions. The quality of riding comfort is typically measured by the Present Serviceability Index (PSI), which was developed in 1957 by the American Association of State Highway & Transportation Officials (AASHTO). The PSI is based primarily on measurements of pavement roughness. This is accomplished by a variety of available equipment that essentially measure the condition of the pavement along the traveled way. The PSI deteriorates with usage and pavement age and is one of several criteria employed to aid decisions relating to maintenance, rehabilitation, or reconstruction of the pavement. Typical symptoms of pavement distresses are longitudinal and transverse cracking, breaking, swelling and heaving. They affect the structural integrity of a pavement and the level of service to the users.

The safety performance of pavements is mainly related to the skid resistance developed at the pavement-tire interface. This friction or skid resistance can be enhanced by the choice of materials and the various treatments, such as texturing the pavement surface. Another characteristic that is related to safety is the light reflectance of the pavement surface.

Pavement Materials and Types

Throughout the ages compaction of the native soil by repetitive use was the common way in which roadbeds were maintained. Some exceptions were the heavy stone roadways constructed by some advanced ancient civilizations, including the Romans, whose famous Appian Way is extant to the present day. Any attempt to replicate the works of these ancient societies given today's material and labor costs would be prohibitively expensive.

A derivative of this method of road building, known as the French method, and the practice of overlaying a prepared roadbed with natural or artificial stones (e.g., cobblestones) continued until fairly recently. Other roadbed treatments include artificial compaction and stabilization of unpaved roads, which are typically found in rural areas, on farms, and at construction sites. There are also another two types of pavements: the asphalt pavements and the Portland-cement concrete pavements. The last two are the most common types of pavements in use today.

The Asphalt Institute describes asphalt as a "strong cement, readily adhesive, highly waterproof and durable. It is a plastic substance which imparts controllable flexibility to mixtures of mineral aggregates with which it is usually combined. Although a solid or semisolid at ordinary atmospheric temperatures, asphalt may be readily liquefied by the application of heat."

The combination of asphalt with graded mineral aggregates is known as asphalt concrete. It is in this manner that asphalt is usually applied to pavement design. Asphalt concrete mixtures are sometimes discussed in terms of the gradation of their component mineral aggregates and fillers into categories such as open-graded, coarse-graded or fine-graded. Open-graded aggregates contain little mineral filler material, and consequently it is characterized by relatively large void areas between aggregate particles in a compacted mix. Coarse-graded aggregates exhibit a continuous grading of sizes but show a predominance of coarse sizes, whereas fine-graded aggregates have a predominance of fine sizes. A coarse aggregate of uniform size, known as a macadam aggregate, received its name from the Scottish engineer John MacAdam, who first used it in an asphalt mix.

[1]When the asphalt concrete is placed, spread and compacted at atmospheric temperature, it is referred to as a cold-laid mixture, in contrast to hot-laid mixtures, which involve elevated temperatures. The combinations of material characteristics and proportions on one hand and mixing and placing conditions on the other can lead to asphalt concretes of differing characteristics in terms of their stability, durability and flexibility to suit a variety of application requirements.

It is worth to note that natural deposits of asphalt exist. For example, skeletons of prehistoric animals have been preserved in such deposits at the La Brea pit near Los Angeles, CA. Asphalt material was used in Mesopotamia for roadway construction and waterproofing purposes. According to the Asphalt Institute, imported rock asphalt was used in Philadelphia, PA in 1838, and the first asphalt pavement was built in Newark, NJ in 1870. Today asphalt is recovered from petroleum in the process of separation and refinement of constituents.

Portland cement is mainly a calcium aluminum silicate that is produced by fusing limestone and clay in a rotary kiln to form a clinker material, which is then ground into a fine powder. First used by an Englishman, Joseph Aspdin, who patented the substance in 1824, Portland cement derives its name from its ability to react with water and, through hydration, to produce an artificial stone that resembles the limestone deposits found on the Isle of Portland in England. It is a "nonbituminous" cement and is classified as a "hydraulic" cement because it solidifies under water. In various combinations with water, graded mineral aggregates and other admixtures, Portland cement is used to produce numerous construction materials, such as grout, plaster, mortar and Portland-cement concrete. By controlling the combinations of the constituents of the mix, a wide variety of desirable characteristics (e. g., strength, durability and workability) can be obtained to suit particular applications. The most notable characteristic of Portland-cement concrete is its compressive strength. It far exceeds its tensile strength, which is only about 10% of its compressive strength. For this reason Portland-cement concrete pavements are typically designed to resist compressive forces only. The first reported use of Portland-cement concrete for pavement construction in the United States occurred in 1891 in Bellefontaine, OH.

In case prominent tensile forces are present under particularly heavy loads continuous reinforcement with steel bars is applied to withstand the applied tension. Also, prestressing the structural element is another way for taking full advantage of the compressive strength. This involves the application, via tendons embedded in the concrete, of a compressive load on the structure prior to applying the service loads. The compressive prestress counterbalances tensile stress produced by the loads in such a way so that the concrete remains under compression. Continuously reinforced or prestressed concrete pavements are commonly used for airport runways and aprons.

A fundamental difference between asphalt and Portland-cement concrete pavements lies in the fact that the former is characterized by flexibility, whereas the latter provides rigidity. For this reason the two types of pavement are classified, respectively, as flexible and rigid pavements. The following are the corresponding AASHTO definitions.

Flexible pavement. A pavement structure which maintains intimate contact with and distributes loads to the subgrade and depends on aggregate interlock, particle friction and cohesion for stability.

Rigid pavement. A pavement structure which distributes loads to the subgrade, having as one course a Portland-cement concrete slab of relatively high bending resistance.

Rigid pavements are further subdivided according to the method of reinforcement into plain (unreinforced) with or without dowels, conventionally reinforced, continuously reinforced, and prestressed. Dowels are steel rods that connect individual pavement slabs to facilitate the transfer of loads between them. In the case of continuously reinforced Portland-cement concrete pavements the reinforcing steel serves this function.

Composite pavements consisting of an asphalt surface overlay on a Portland-cement concrete slab are common. Moreover, a recent practice of overlaying a Portland-cement concrete layer on old asphalt pavements, called "whitetopping" appears to be gaining in popularity.

New Words

1. pavement ['peivmənt]   *n.* 路面

2. apron ['eiprən] n. 停机坪
3. subgrade ['sʌbgreid] n. 路基
4. profile ['prəufail] n. 剖面
5. rehabilitation ['ri:(h)ə͵bili'teiʃən] n. 维修
6. swelling ['sweliŋ] n. 膨胀
7. heaving ['hi:viŋ] n. 鼓起，隆起
8. extant [eks'tænt] a. 现存的
9. overlay [͵əuvə'lei] n. 覆盖，上覆层
10. unpaved ['ʌn'peivd] a. 未铺路的，未铺装的
11. liquefy ['likwifai] v. (使)溶解，(使)液化
12. bituminous [bi'tju:minəs] a. 含沥青的
13. hydrocarbon ['haidrəu'kɑ:bən] n. 烃，碳氢化合物
14. macadam [mə'kædəm] n. 碎石，碎石路
15. silicate ['silikit] n. [化]硅酸盐
16. kiln [kiln, kil] n. (砖，石灰等的)窑，炉
17. clinker ['kliŋkə] n. 渣块
18. nonbituminous [͵nɔnbi'tju:minəs] a. 非沥青质的
19. solidify [sə'lidifai] v. (使)凝固
20. dowel ['dauəl] n. 传力杆，销子

Phrases and Expressions

1. traveled way 车行道
2. composite pavement 复合路面
3. flexible pavement 柔性路面
4. rigid pavement 刚性路面
5. open-graded 开级配(沥青混合料)
6. coarse-graded 粗级配(沥青混合料)
7. fine-graded 细级配(沥青混合料)
8. Asphalt Institute(A. I.) (美国)沥青协会
9. Present Serviceability Index(PSI) 现有(路况)性能指标
10. macadam aggregate (路面用)碎石骨料
11. cold-laid mixture 冷铺(沥青)混合料
12. hot-laid mixture 热铺(沥青)混合料
13. rock asphalt 岩沥青(一种天然沥青)
14. Appian Way 亚壁古道(古罗马时的一条道路)

Notes

[1] When the asphalt concrete is …, in contrast to hot-laid mixtures, which involve elevated temperatures. which 引导的非限定性定语从句在句中修饰 hot-laid

mixtures，译为：当沥青混合料在常温下摊铺和压实时，就被称作冷拌沥青混合料，它和需加热铺筑的热拌沥青混合料不同。

Exercises

1. Fill in the blanks with proper words.

（1）The structural performance of a pavement is aimed _____ distributing the loads under the wheels of vehicles _____ larger areas to prevent stressing, _____ its load-bearing capacity, the native soil (or subgrade) on which the pavement system is constructed.

（2）The quality of riding comfort is _____ measured _____ the Present Serviceability Index (PSI), which was developed in 1957 by the American Association of State Highway Officials.

（3）The safety performance of pavements is _____ related _____ the skid resistance developed at the pavement-tire interface.

（4）They are necessary not only _____ roadways but also for parking lots, airports (i.e., runways, taxiways, aprons, and service roads), industrial sites, ports and _____ forth.

（5）Other roadbed treatments include artificial compaction and stabilization of unpaved roads, typically found _____ rural areas, _____ farms and _____ construction sites.

（6）_____ a solid or semisolid _____ ordinary atmospheric temperatures, asphalt may be readily liquefied _____ the application of heat.

（7）It is _____ this manner that asphalt is usually applied _____ pavement design.

（8）Open-graded aggregates contain little mineral filler material, and consequently it is characterized _____ relatively large void areas _____ aggregate particles in a compacted mix.

（9）Coarse-graded aggregates exhibit a continuous grading of sizes _____ show a predominance of coarse sizes, _____ fine-graded aggregates have a predominance of fine sizes.

（10）When the asphalt concrete is placed, spread, and compacted at atmospheric temperature, it is referred to _____ a cold-laid mixture, in contrast to hot-laid mixtures, which involve elevated temperatures.

2. Translate the following phrases and expressions into Chinese/English.

（1）flexible pavement　　　　　　（6）荷载分布
（2）hot-laid mixture　　　　　　　（7）刚性路面
（3）A. I.　　　　　　　　　　　　（8）车行道
（4）Present Serviceability Index　　（9）复合路面
（5）fine-graded asphalt mixture　　（10）承载能力

3. Translate the following sentences into Chinese.

(1) Pavement are necessary not only for roadways but also for parking lots, airports (i.e., runways, taxiways, aprons, and service roads), industrial sites, ports and so forth.

(2) The load at the interface between the wheel and the pavement surface is applied over a relatively small area, causing high stresses at that point, but these stresses decrease with depth as the load is spread over large areas.

(3) The functional performance of pavement is related to the users' requirement for smooth and comfortable riding conditions.

(4) The PSI deteriorates with usage and pavement age and is one of several criteria employed to aid decisions relating to maintenance, rehabilitation or reconstruction of the pavement.

(5) Typical symptoms of pavement distresses are longitudinal and transverse cracking, breaking, swelling and heaving.

(6) The Asphalt Institute describes asphalt as a "strong cement, readily adhesive, highly waterproof and durable.

(7) Asphalt concrete mixtures are sometimes discussed in terms of the gradation of their component mineral aggregates and fillers into categories such as open-graded, coarse-graded, or fine-graded.

(8) The combinations of material characteristics and proportions on one hand and mixing and placing conditions on the other can lead to asphalt concretes of differing characteristics in terms of their stability, durability, and flexibility to suit a variety of application requirements.

(9) It is a "nonbituminous" cement and is classified as a "hydraulic" cement because it solidifies under water.

(10) Rigid pavement is a pavement structure which distributes loads to the subgrade, having as one course a Portland-cement concrete slab of relatively high bending resistance.

4. Fill in the blanks with the given words below.

by, in, into, throughout, of, including, as, to, with

_____ the ages compaction of the native soil _____ repetitive use was the common way _____ which roadbeds were maintained. Some exceptions were the heavy stone roadways constructed by some advanced ancient civilizations, _____ the Romans, whose famous Appian Way is extant to the present day. Any attempt _____ replicate the works of these ancient societies given today's material and labor costs would be prohibitively expensive. A derivative _____ this method of road building, known _____ the French method, was used _____ the nineteenth century, and the practice of overlaying a prepared roadbed _____ natural or artificial stones (e.g., cobblestones) continued until fairly recently.

5. Translate the following sentences into English.

(1) 值得指出的是在自然界存在着天然沥青矿。

(2) 根据集料和填料的级配, 沥青混合料经常被分为开级配、粗级配或细级配沥青混合料。

（3）根据配筋的方法，刚性路面可分为设置或未设置传力杆的素混凝土（无配筋的）路面、传统的加筋水泥混凝土路面、连续配筋水泥混凝土路面和预应力钢筋混凝土路面。

（4）在沥青路面上加铺一层波特兰水泥混凝土路面板的复合路面很常见。

（5）传力杆是连接每块混凝土路面板从而使得每块板之间可顺利传递荷载的钢杆。

Reading Material

New Advancement in Pavement Engineering in the U. S.

Pavement Management Systems

With nearly all of the interstate highway and roadway system completed in the United States, the emphasis is being switched from construction to maintenance. The development of a pavement management system that originated near the turn of the century has grown steadily due to the increased need for pavement maintenance.

A pavement management system incorporates the coordination of activities associated with the design, planning, construction, maintenance, research and evaluation of pavements. Most of these activities are focused on existing pavements. The system consists of three essential elements: (1) surveys related to pavement condition and serviceability and compilation (编辑) of a continuously updated data base; (2) prioritization of needs, alternative repair options, evaluation, and decision for action; and (3) implementation procedures.

The condition and serviceability of a pavement as perceived by the user is represented by its roughness, which is a measure of the irregularities in the pavement surface, causing discomfort to the users. Longitudinal, transverse and horizontal components of roughness affect the comfort and safety of users. Roughness is assessed with various mechanical devices called profilometers(表面光度仪). Advanced techniques utilize video imaging, radar, sonics and infrared technologies for assessing surface and structural pavement damage.

The FHWA as well as state agencies are largely responsible for the development of strategies for the prioritization of needs, evaluation and decision for action. Implementation involves the so-called 4R procedures (i. e., resurfacing, restoration, rehabilitation and reconstruction). Resurfacing is self-explanatory; both asphalt layer on a rigid pavement or Portland-cement layer on a flexible pavement are feasible resurfacing options, in addition to asphalt on asphalt and Portland cement on Portland cement. When resurfacing asphalt concrete pavements, a layer 1 to 3 in. thick is usually removed before the new surface layer is applied. Restoration includes the removal and replacement of Portland-cement slabs, the patching of potholes(坑槽), the sealing(封堵) of cracks, the retrofitting of edge support and various other localized repairs. Rehabilitation is large-scale restoration. It includes elements, such as replacement of bridge decks, resurfacing of a substantial segment of a roadway facility, recycling of materials and minor subgrade work incidental to other repairs. Reconstruction is the complete removal of the pavement structure to the base layer and the replacement with virgin or recycled materials. Recycling includes the removal and crushing of Portland-cement slabs and the use of the product as coarse aggregates or stockpile material for bases. In the case of flexible pavements, removed asphalt material is used as base material or it is recycled at a hot-mix plant. The overall network priorities and scheduling for 4R constitute a major part of pavement management systems (PMS). Most modern PMS are implemented as geographic information system (GIS) applications.

High Performance Concrete, Superpave（高性能沥青混凝土路面）**and LTPP**. Traditionally pavement design specifications have been based on empirical properties (such as "percent of air voids") which had been correlated to pavement performance. A recent trend has been the identification of performance based properties that can be used directly to predict pavement performance.

Performance-based specifications have been at the center of a major initiative of the Federal Highway Administration that was authorized by the Surface Transportation and Relocation Act of 1987. Known as the Strategic Highway Research Program (SHRP), this 5-year $150 million endeavor consisted of four major components: (1) Portland-cement concrete (PCC) and structures, (2) asphalt, (3) long-term pavement performance (LTPP), and (4) highway operations. Thus three of the four program elements were directly or indirectly associated with pavements. Upon completion of SHRP, FHWA proceeded with the implementation phase in cooperation with industrial partners, several lead states and university-based centers. The implementation phase continues to yield modifications and improvements in the earlier research-prescribed methods and practices.

High performance PCC. The pavement portion of the PCC component of SHRP emphasized high performance PCC. The term "high performance" in this context does not necessarily indicate "high strength". It is, instead, allowed to take a meaning that is applicable to the intended use. Examples of possible applicable criteria include durability, rapid setting for high early strength, low permeability and low life-cycle costs. Rapid setting is accomplished by the use of low water-cement ratios and various additives. In many applications rapid setting is considered highly desirable because it allows the opening of rehabilitated highway segments to the traffic soon after placement.

Superpave. The most important element of the asphalt component of SHRP was the development of a hot-mix superior performing asphalt pavement known as Superpave. Three mix design levels requiring increasingly more elaborate procedures have been developed. Level 1 applies to low traffic volumes (less than 10^6 ESALs—equivalent standard axle load 当量标准轴载) and is similar to traditional volumetric design methods based on empirical performance-related properties. Level 2 applies to intermediate traffic loads (between 10^6 and 10^7 ESALs) and builds upon the level 1 design by requiring additional performance-based tests and software analyses aimed at predicting pavement performance in terms of predicting fatigue cracking, low temperature cracking and permanent deformation versus time. Level 3 design applies to high traffic loads (more than 10^7 ESALs) and involves more comprehensive performance prediction models.

Long-term pavement performance. The LTPP component of SHRP is an extensive effort to extend the understanding of pavement performance and to support research by constructing a comprehensive database of field testing and monitoring more than 2400 asphalt and PCC test sections throughout the United States and Canada. Key features for each test location include pavement characteristics, construction methods, test results, maintenance practices and so forth. Updated versions of the database, along with data exploration and extraction utilities, are periodically issued on CDROM.